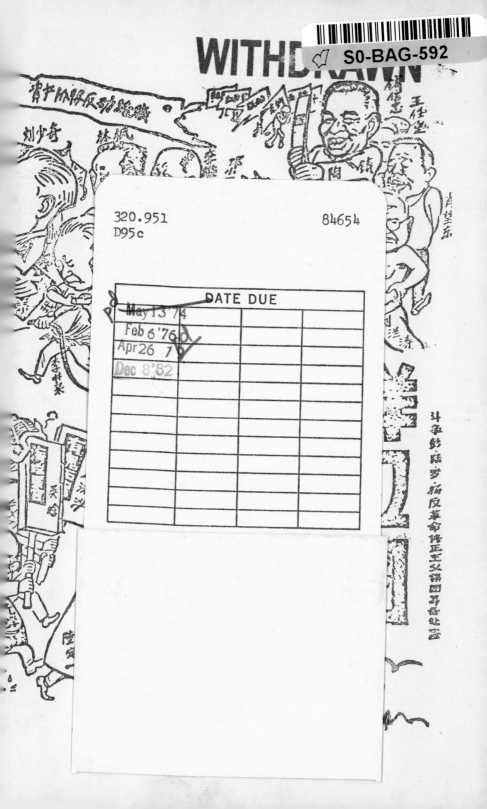

CHINA'S CULTURAL REVOLUTION

China's Cultural Revolution

GARGI DUTT
V.P. DUTT

ASIA PUBLISHING HOUSE

BOMBAY   CALCUTTA   MADRAS   NEW DELHI
LUCKNOW   BANGALORE   LONDON   NEW YORK

ISBN O. 210.98192. X

PRINTED IN INDIA

AT NATIONAL PRINTING WORKS, DARYAGANJ, DELHI-6, AND PUBLISHED BY P.S. JAYASINGHE, ASIA PUBLISHING HOUSE, BOMBAY-1

In the memory of
Ch. Krishna Gopal Dutt

PREFACE

CHINA'S "PROLETARIAN CULTURAL REVOLUTION" is admittedly one of the most convulsive events in recent history. It has few parallels. Its import both for the shape of things to come within China and for relations with the outside world is highly significant. It has been said with considerable justification that China will never be the same again. It is, therefore, obviously important to try to understand these portentious developments in China and to analyse the trends and the possible consequences.

The task is not easy. The difficulties are many. The drama is still unfolding and the curtain has not yet wrung down on the last act. Information is partial and necessarily laden with propaganda. What actually transpired in the highest councils of the Chinese Communist Party is not known and may not be fully revealed for many years. The media of information were from the beginning largely controlled by the Maoists and the so-called enemies or opponents did not make any direct public statements of where they stood and what they really wanted. How much of what is ascribed to them is propaganda and how much fact needs careful and cautious evaluation. Still, the task is not hopeless and its complexity is matched by the need and the urgency for a close study. A great deal of information has filtered through the official Maoist organs of publicity, and thousands of sheets of wall posters, both original photostats and many translations, are available from a variety of sources.

It is possible to construct an intelligent story by a careful and methodological use of these materials, applying the yardstick of internal consistency and comparison with independent knowledge of developments in China. The authors do not lay a claim to any finality in their analysis of the recent developments in China but feel confident that their basic premises and conclusions will stand the test of time.

The authors began their work on this study in the winter of 1966-67 and the first three chapters were written at that time. The next two chapters were written during the summer and autumn of 1967. Additional information has become available since then, but no attempt has been made to modify or rewrite the earlier chapters in the belief that the story as understood by the authors remains substantially sound. A final chapter, conclusions, takes note of developments since the autumn of 1967 up till the summer of this year, outlines the main trends, and records the over-all conclusions of the authors.

GARGI DUTT
June 1969   VIDYA PRAKASH DUTT

CONTENTS

CHAPTER ONE

PRELUDE TO THE CULTURAL REVOLUTION

THE RECENT UPHEAVAL in China has been described as a revolution which "touches people to the soul."[1] The "proletarian cultural revolution" has certainly shaken the nation and thrown it into turmoil and tension, confusion and conflict. It has led to uncertainty and discord. China, which had given the impression of solidity and unity to the world, has suddenly revealed deep fissures in its society and leadership. The struggle seems to be a presentiment of things to come, the winter of struggle and conflict that would inevitably follow the now past summer of harmony and unity.

COMPLEXITY OF THE STRUGGLE

What has happened in China is the interplay of complex factors, and, obviously, no simple and ready explanations can be offered. Emotions, personality clashes over policies, ambitions, rational calculations, and irrational impulses are all intertwined in the drama of the last one year. Students of the Chinese scene have often tried to look for a solitary, obvious answer, a single factor which would illuminate the secret and not-so-secret, but certainly confounding, goings-on in Peking. Developments in China are understood merely as a reflection of a struggle for power or exclusively as divergence among different schools of thought, or just a clash of personalities, or collision between different social categories: professionals, bureaucrats, technocrats, and ideologues. It is all these and much more. The complicated nature of the struggle in China calls for a somewhat complex explanation—one which will take due note of all the various factors that have gone into the creation of the crisis in Peking.

[1] *Jen-min Jih-pao*, editorial, 2 June 1967.

Peking has itself described the "revolution" in terms of a life-and-death struggle for power. The Maoists claim that the question is whether power will be held by those who are proletarian revolutionaries and are loyal to the thought of Mao Tse-tung, or by those who want to restore capitalism. Of course, the charge against the dissidents of trying to restore capitalism can be immediately discounted, but it does reveal serious differences over policies. Similarly, there is sufficient internal evidence to show that Mao's personality and, perhaps, an obsessive concern of a dying old man with the future of his name in history and of his country are equally important factors. Interwoven into all this are the demands of the ideologues against the caution and prudence of the bureaucrats and the professionals (whether in the Party or in the army) and of those entrusted with the task of implementing the goals, political and economic, set down by the ideologues.

It appears that the struggle in China was inevitable. Struggles of this kind have also taken place in other countries. When a country is faced with acute problems, the leadership often gets divided over the choice of alternatives. Differences over policies develop into sharp and often irreconcilable conflicts; they become identified with personalities and are overlaid with bids for power. If the leadership comprises hard-boiled, determined individuals, the struggle is all the more intense and fierce. Sometimes the megalomaniac visions or hallucinations of a leader or, at the very least, his egotism and egocentricity, his suspicions, and even his senility have been known to be significant reasons for divisions at the top and for the rolling of many heads in the dust. China has not proved to be immune to such processes.

What has surprised observers of the Chinese scene is the fact that the struggle began during Mao Tse-tung's lifetime and that Mao has himself initiated it and, also, perhaps, that Mao has run into so much opposition. The opposition, of course, is not, as we shall have occasion to note later, necessarily so much against Mao himself as against the kind of things that are being sought to be done. Students of the Chinese field had assumed much greater cohesion and solidarity among the top Chinese leaders than it seems realistic now from hindsight. The Chinese leaders had gone through thick and thin, through fire and hell together and at least since the thirties the unity and durability of the leadership had seemed impressive.

There were a few purges, like those of Kao Kang[2] and Jao Shu-shih[3] in 1954 but these did not result in a violent shake-up at the top. It was believed that the leaders had learnt to work together and the cohesion that they had displayed thus far would last until Mao lived, may be even for some time afterwards. The dominant figure of Mao was expected to still the undercurrents of factional or personal rivalries and prevent them from breaking out to the surface. The possibility of any real challenge to Mao's policies was also largely discounted. But, to the surprise and almost disbelief of everyone, Mao at the fag end of his life has launched a campaign which has triggered off violent turmoil and involved the entire leadership of the Communist Party. The facade of unity has been ripped open and the cohesion of the leadership is dead and gone.

The trouble in China is not of recent origin but dates back to about a decade and is intimately connected with the developments in 1957 and 1958, particularly the "big leap" and the people's communes. One of the first signs of this trouble showed itself over the question of a nuclear policy for China, the nature and role of the Chinese army and its quality of preparedness. The army leadership was concerned with the problem of the modernization of the Chinese army in the context of the latest technological developments. How could China's security be guaranteed in the age of atom and hydrogen bombs and intercontinental ballistic missiles? Some of the army leaders who have often been referred to as the professionals in the army, notably, Marshal P'eng Teh-huai,[4] were anxious to modernize the army with the help of the Soviet Union. They also wanted to model the Chinese army on the pattern of the Soviet army.

[2]Kao Kang was Chairman of the Northeast Administrative Committee and member of the Politbureau. He was accused of a conspiracy against the Party and reportedly committed suicide in 1955.

[3]Jao Shu-shih, First Secretary of the East China Bureau of the Communist Party and Director of the Organizational Department of the Central Committee, was accused in 1954 of being an accomplice of Kao Kang and purged in 1955.

[4]Marshal P'eng Teh-huai, member of the Politbureau of the Communist Party, was Defence Minister until his removal in 1959.

FIRST MANIFESTATIONS—TROUBLE IN THE ARMY

During 1957-58, the Soviet Union made a number of offers to assist in the modernization of the Chinese army. Reportedly, the Soviets also offered to help develop China's nuclear capability, though the precise nature of the Sino-Soviet agreement in this regard has not yet been made clear.[5] In October 1957, Mao Tse-tung went to Moscow to attend the fortieth anniversary of the Soviet Revolution and was accompanied by a military delegation headed by P'eng Teh-huai. The general theme in the Chinese press at that time was the important role played by Soviet assistance in the development of the Chinese armed forces and the Chinese aspiration to adopt the Soviet model for the organization of the Chinese army. Two of the important documents in this connection were articles written by Marshals P'eng Teh-huai and Ho Lung.[6] Both the articles stressed the need for Soviet help in achieving modernization at a fast rate as well as the invaluable role that this had played in the development of the Chinese army.

Soon, however, serious differences were to develop within the Party and the army regarding the fundamental strategy and the line to be adopted by China. It appears that Khrushchov offered to China, during 1958 and 1959, nuclear sharing arrangements by which Moscow would install nuclear weapons and bases in China under some kind of a joint control system in order to ensure Chinese security against an atomic attack by the United States. It seems reasonable to assume that P'eng Teh-huai was in favour of accepting the Soviet proposals as part of a package deal for the modernization of the Chinese army until Peking had developed its own nuclear armoury and a delivery system. But Mao would have none of it. He wanted Soviet assistance in developing an independent Chinese nuclear capability, but not the Soviet nuclear weapons and bases under joint control. Subsequently, the Chinese alleged that the Soviet Union made, in 1958, "unreasonable demands

---

[5]"The Origin and Development of the Differences Between the Leadership of the CPSU and Ourselves," *Jen-min Jih-pao* and *Hung-ch'i*, 6 September 1963. See also, V.P. Dutt, *China's Foreign Policy*, Asia Publishing House, Bombay, 1964, pp. 300-1.

[6]*New China News Agency*, Peking, 4 November 1957; *New China News Agency*, Peking, 5 November 1957.

designed to bring China under Soviet military control."[7] Mao totally rejected any arrangements which would not immediately lead to the manufacturing of an independent Chinese bomb. He wanted complete independence in this as in other matters. The Chinese, therefore, decided to spurn Soviet offers and, instead, started concentrating their efforts and energies on the development of a native nuclear capability. This formed part of the general effort, led by Mao, for a big leap to achieve rapid industrial expansion as the only means for providing an independent, modern military machine.

The differences between Mao and some of the army leaders involved not only the question of how best to modernize the Chinese army but also the role of the army and the general direction of the development, political and economic, of the country. Mao's prescription for the army was to put politics in command—in other words, to put the thought of Mao Tse-tung in command. With this "spiritualization" of the army through a fanatical indoctrination in Mao's ideology, it was possible to meet the challenge of an enemy army, howsoever heavily equipped with the latest and the most sophisticated weapons. (Not that the Chinese army would not be supplied with the latest weaponry, but this would take time to be produced nationally, and meanwhile the army should be politicized.) Mao still thought in terms of a highly mobile force, retaining some of its guerrilla characteristics, adept in the art of fighting partisan warfare according to the strategy evolved by him during the war against Japan and the civil war against the Kuomintang. It should also serve the ends of production and fulfil any economic tasks entrusted to it by the State. He wanted army officers to spend some time every year as ordinary soldiers. A logical corollary to this was the subsequent decision to abolish badges of ranks or distinction among army personnel.

There was undoubtedly resistance within the army to the Maoist policy. Marshal P'eng Teh-huai was the first prominent army leader to express dissatisfaction with Mao's line.[8] The Marshal's opposition ranged from relations with the Soviet Union to the big

[7] See fn. 5.

[8] As usual, direct evidence of all these differences is lacking but there is a good amount of inferential evidence available. See, for instance, *Jen-min Jih-pao*, editorials, 1 and 7 September 1959, and article by Liu Lan-t'ao on 28 September.

leap and the people's communes. He was concerned over the erosion of professionalism in the army and the subordination of its purely military functions to those of a political and economic character. The Marshal was equally unhappy over the extent of the attempted politicization and of the Party leadership's control over the army. He was also in favour of continuance of friendly relations with the Soviet Union and of its economic aid.[9] Moreover, he expressed strong misgivings about the formation of the rural communes and certain other aspects of the big leap.[10] It was obvious that he was not alone in his opposition to the Maoist line and had many adherents in the army, and perhaps elsewhere too. Along with P'eng, Huang K'o-ch'eng, Chief of Staff, was also denounced.

P'eng Teh-huai was dismissed in September 1959, condemned as a counter-revolutionary revisionist. In his place came Lin Piao who eventually became Mao's closest confidant. But Mao continued to have trouble with his line in the army, and during the next six years he made renewed and systematic efforts to indoctrinate the army with his ideas in order to weed out undesirable and unreliable elements. A series of measures inspired by Mao were carried out mainly through Lin Piao to strengthen control over the army and to fashion it in the image of Mao's ideology. Even as early as August 1958, Mao had pushed through the Politbureau a directive to the army to put into practice the policy of sending every officer to a company, the basic level unit of the Chinese army, to serve as a private for a certain period of time. This was done at the beginning of the high tension period of the big leap. The officers were required to eat, live, labour, work, and play with the common soldiers and to strictly abide by the various rules and regulations of the companies and the orders of the squad, platoon, and company leaders. It was stated in a report that, between August 1953 and the end of December, nearly 770,000 officers took to the companies to serve as privates, generally for a

[9]Since this chapter was written, Peking has finally released the resolution of the Central Committee in 1959 on Peng Teh-huai. The resolution substantially supports the analysis made here.

[10]See David A. Charles, "The Dismissal of Marshal P'eng Teh-huai," *China Quarterly*, October-December 1961.

period of one month, among them were over 250 generals.[11] It was feared, there was considerable anxiety over this directive even at that time, as many felt that this might result in the diminution of the officers' authority and constituted waste of their time—that it was like using steel for wood.[12]

Perhaps the opposition to Mao's line, of which this was only a minor part, became crystallized in the person of P'eng Teh-huai. After P'eng's dismissal, the drive towards Maoization of the army was intensified. At a conference of senior officers of the PLA in October 1960, Lin Piao gave the call for observing the principle of "four firsts" and the creation of "four good" companies. The first principle of the "four firsts" underlined the Maoist concept that man, and not weapon, was the decisive factor in war. Therefore, as between man and weapon, the first place had to be given to man. It followed logically that political work must be given the pride of place in relation to all other work in the army, and, further, that ideological work must be given precedence over all other political work. Finally, in ideological work, "living ideas" and "creative application" of theory should be preferred to ideas in books and abstract theory. A "four good" company was one which was "good" in political and ideological work, good in the "three-eight" working style,[13] good in military training, and good in making living arrangements for its inmates. All this had a direct relationship with the controversy over complete self-reliance, the rejection of the validity of the Soviet model, the prospect of the cessation of Soviet military assistance for the modernization of the Chinese army, and Mao's determination to go it alone.

POSITION OF LIU AND OTHERS BEFORE THE "BIG LEAP" FAILURE

Curiously enough, however, the "top person in authority taking the capitalist road," now in disgrace, Liu Shao-ch'i and his associates

[11]Kan Wei-han, "A Talk on the Practice of Army Cadres Going to Companies to Serve as Privates," *Jen-min Jih-pao*, 29 July 1963.

[12]*Ibid.*

[13]In the "three-eight" working style, the "three" refers to the three mottoes: keep firmly to the correct political orientation, maintain an industrious and simple style of work, and be flexible in strategy and tactics; the "eight" refers to the eight ideograms or characters (in the Chinese language) for unity, alertness, earnestness, and activity.

like P'eng Chen and Teng Hsiao-p'ing, seem to have sided with Mao over these issues at that time. In fact, what has baffled many observers is that this group was identified as the left-wing group within the Chinese Communist Party. It was more militantly nationalistic, at least apparently more stridently anti-Soviet, and more vociferous in its enthusiasm for a leftist line. It also stood foursquare for the Maoist concept of self-reliance in the mighty effort towards achieving parity of power with other big powers. There is no doubt that Liu Shao-ch'i, Teng Hsiao-p'ing, and P'eng Chen tended to give a more and more left-wing direction to the big leap movement.[14]   Liu Shao-ch'i spoke about the coming dawn of Communism, encouraged the adoption of the fanciful scheme of securing a higher yield from a smaller area of land and thus reducing the cultivated acreage, and lent his powerful support to the movement for taking children under the almost exclusive care of the State and for pushing the establishment of boarding schools and whole-time nurseries everywhere. These trends were encouraged by Teng Hsiao-p'ing also. Similarly, P'eng Chen enthusiastically campaigned for the propagation of the extreme features of the communes and the big leap, and a classic remark of his, during those days of mass production of backyard steel, may be noted: "Everybody who knew cooking knew how to temper steel." "This appeal to the masses," said P'eng, "is something very precious and indispensable so far as the speeding up of the industrialization process is concerned."[15]

Clearly, the group in the Party's top hierarchy which today stands condemned and dethroned, far from wishing to restore capitalism in China, showed considerable energy and enthusiasm in administering larger doses of Communism and fostering collectivization of both production and livelihood. They were active in pushing the movement towards extremes, and, with the blessings of Mao, were relatively behind the extremist policies of the great leap forward and the rural people's communes. Why then is the label of "counter-revolutionary revisionists" being pinned on them? A rational explanation is that these leaders were genuine supporters of the Maoist line on the big leap and the people's communes

---

[14]See for instance, Gargi Dutt, *Rural Communes of China: Organizational Problems*, Asia Publishing House, Bombay, 1967.
    [15]*Ibid.*

as well as the international posture of unrelenting struggle against both the Soviet Union and the United States, but that they were appalled by the catastrophic failure of this line, particularly at home. The failure on the domestic front was no doubt stunning. The whole economy went out of gear. Food production fell to just about 150 million tons[16] in 1960 as against the official figure of 250 million for 1958 (which includes sweet potatoes and soya bean). Industrial production slumped as a result of scarcity of raw materials and cutbacks in investment, and many plants worked on less than half their capacity.

The extent of the setback can be appreciated from the fact that Peking stopped releasing any production figures in 1960 and has not released them since then. The economic priorities had to be switched, with agriculture claiming the lion's share in investment. Heavy industry was relegated to the third place and, for the first time in Communist history, light industry got priority over heavy industry. Besides ploughing the State finances into the farms of China, many concessions were given to the peasant to induce him to produce more, including higher prices, the right to husband a tiny private plot and engage in side occupations, and the right to the income from the sale of these products. The role of material incentives in boosting production in the farms and factories was acknowledged. Willy-nilly, the leadership also had to make allowance for the consumption demands of the people and to bow to the fact that consumption could not be pushed below a certain level, and certainly to the fact that some proportion had to be maintained between rises in production and consumption. The subsequent period was marked by relatively liberal policies, relaxation of the tight controls, and material inducements. The recovery was slow and painful but it gradually pushed the level of consumption to well above that of 1959-60.

Thus, the Party had to make a substantial retreat in order to restore the sagging economy and regain the momentum of growth. This nightmarish experience appears to have chastened the erstwhile left-wing group and made it wary of any further adventurist experimentation. The lessons of the failure were apparent: the role

[16]This was the figure given to Lord Montgomery during his visit to China. See, *Sunday Times*, Magazine Section, 15 October 1961.

of material incentives could not be wished away by propaganda and ideological indoctrination; balanced and step-by-step development was inevitable and this could not be achieved by concentrating on one sector of the economy to the exclusion of others; a certain degree of professional competence was absolutely essential for sustained progress, and the intellectuals had to be let alone for some time at least to perform their tasks. In the period of the retreat, the intellectuals were left comparatively free to develop their talents and do their professional work. This was apparent not only in scientific and technical fields, but in the arts and literature also.

CRITICISM OF MAO

The convulsions caused by the failures were not limited to the economic policies and controls in the cultural field, but led to a questioning of the authority of the highest of the high. Almost for the first time, since Mao had gained complete control of the Party in 1935, was his own authority and judgement subjected to criticism. Even though acting indirectly and speaking through parables and fables, many high-ranking Party functionaries held Mao responsible for the mess that had been made of the economy and of the general situation in the country. The fiasco and the retreat shocked and emboldened many to pour scorn over "petty bourgeois" leftist fanaticism of the big leap and the people's communes and many an accusing finger was pointed at Mao himself. The Maoists themselves have published some material, for instance, *Evening Chats* of Teng T'o, formerly an editor of *Jen-min Jih-pao* and subsequently a member of the secretariat of the Peking Municipal Party Committee headed by P'eng Chen, which purports to criticize Mao for the mistakes of the big leap and for subjectivism and boastfulness. As the official comment puts it, "Teng T'o again and again attacks what he calls 'bragging' and 'boasting' and says that 'literary men are by no means the only persons' given to bragging and that 'great statesmen' have the same failing."[17]

Teng T'o particularly came down heavily upon the Maoist belief in the primacy of the subjective factor in remoulding man and his

[17]*The Great Socialist Cultural Revolution, No. 2*, Foreign Languages Press, Peking, 1966, p. 24. "Two Foreign Fables," in *Evening Chat* by Teng T'o, first appeared in *Peking Evening News*, 26 November 1961.

environment and in man's capacity to perform miracles through will power. For instance, he wrote[18]:

A titlark flying over the sea boasted that it would boil the sea dry....The rumour quickly spread and those easily taken in were the first to go to the seaside with spoons to join the feast of delicious fish soup.
   Followers of Ernst Mach exaggerated the role of what they called the psychological factor and talked boastfully to their hearts' content. Is this not the same as the titlark's nonsense about boiling the sea dry? Nevertheless, the Machians imagined that through reliance on the role of the psychological factor they could do whatever they liked, but the result was that they ran their heads against the brick wall of reality and went bankrupt in the end.

Again at another time Teng T'o writes: "As chance would have it, my neighbour's child has recently often imitated the style of some great poet (Mao?) and put into writing a lot of 'great empty talk....' " Not long ago, he wrote a poem entitled "Ode to Wild Grass" which is nothing but empty talk. The poem reads as follows:

> The Venerable Heaven is our father
> The Great Earth is our Mother
> And the Sun is our nanny
> The East Wind is our benefactor
> And the West Wind is our Enemy.

Although such words as heaven, earth, father, mother, sun, nanny, the East Wind, the West Wind, benefactor, and enemy catch our eye, they are used to no purpose here and have become mere cliches. Recourse to even the finest words and phrases is futile, or rather, the more such cliches are uttered, the worse the situation will become.[19]

[18]*The Great Socialist Cultural Revolution, No. 2,* Foreign Languages Press, Peking, 1966, p. 21.
[19]*Ibid.,* pp. 13-4. Originally published as "Great Empty Talk," *Frontline,* No. 21, 1961.

The reference here to Mao's thesis about the East Wind is too obvious to need any comment.

To take another instance, the powerful Politbureau member and Mayor of Peking P'eng Chen's deputy, Wu Han'[20] wrote a play in 1961 entitled, *Hai Jui Dismissed from Office*, and a number of other articles about Hai Jui.[21]   In 1965, the play came under heavy fire. Leaving aside the polemical question (for which Wu Han was also taken to task) whether Hai Jui was a loyal servant of the feudal system and whether the play was an attempt to "prettify" the officials, courts and laws of the landlord class, Wu Han was also accused of harbouring sly intentions in attacking "hypocritical" bureaucrats who flattered and deceived the Emperor and manoeuvred the dismissal of an upright official.   The inference drawn was that this was an allusion to Mao and his campaigns against the dissidents, and a call to the present-day administrators under Mao to show a similar spirit of fearlessness and uprightness.[22]

Maoist propaganda has alleged about many writers and functionaries that they used the past to satirize the present and to "slander" Party leadership.   While it is difficult to say whether a particular piece of writing about ancient happenings and sayings necessarily has a contemporary significance, and whether such allegations are not often used as a handy stick to beat the victims with, there seems sufficient evidence to justify the conclusion that the dark days of 1960 and 1961 emboldened many Party writers and functionaries to criticize, however obliquely, Mao himself for the economic and other domestic failures and to call for a more

[20]Wu Han was Deputy Mayor of Peking. He is a historian and playwright of distinction.

[21]Hai Jui was a high official of the sixteenth century and was believed to be an enlightened official, known for his uprightness and straightforwardness. He was also reputed to have stood against land alienation on a large scale by big landlords and bureaucrats.

[22]See a major criticism of Wu Han by Yao Wen-yuan, first published in Shanghai's *Wen-hui Pao* and subsequently reproduced by *Jen-min Jih-pao*, 30 November 1965 (English text in *Current Background*, Hong Kong, No. 783, 21 March 1966), and a bitter denunciation by the same author of Teng T'o, Wu Han, and others in "On Three-Family Village—The Reactionary Nature of 'Evening Talks at Yenshan' and 'Notes from Three-Family Village,' " first published in Shanghai's *Chieh-fang Jih-pao* and *Wen-hui Pao* (English text in *Peking Review*, No. 62, 27 May 1966).

rational and objective assessment of plans and policies, rather than be guided by subjective wishes.

It is noteworthy that unlike the Hundred Flowers Movement and the anti-rightist campaign, very few non-Communists were involved, and that the struggle was mainly confined to the Communists. It is even more significant that a large majority of the Party function-aries, particularly the Party intellectuals, purged during the last one year were mainly attacked for what they had said or written during the period—1960-1962—which underlines the importance of issues of economic policies and the motivating ideas of the big leap in the ensuing upheaval in China. The opposition to the big leap concepts and the manner in which it was sought to be carried out was minimal at the time these policies were first tried in 1958 and 1959. Most Party members had unreservedly, and even enthusias-tically, accepted Mao's line of thinking and plan of action but it was the tragic failure which aroused doubts and questioning. The failure bred disenchantment, and disenchantment led to criticism which reached right up to the top.

Undoubtedly, Mao was infuriated by this "revolt" within the Party and gradually got more and more worried about the direction of development. Material incentives, the private plot, the free market, the ideological respite, the partial "decontrol" of the intel-lectual class, and all the rest of it was for him a "freak" period. It could not be allowed to continue for a long time. The lesson, if there was one, was that ideological work was both insufficient and unsatisfactory and must be intensified: in case this was not done, the present state of affairs might be prolonged indefinitely, lead-ing to decline and degeneration. Not that those who differed from Mao on the question of the speed of development, the extent to which people could be driven to work, the need for professional competence, etc., were converts to capitalism; they were afraid of a repetition of the kind of setback that China had received from 1959 to 1961 and favoured a more pragmatic and cautious approach to meet China's problems.

It is significant that Mao stayed his hand for three to four years before punishing the critics. The crimes of the purged cadres, now recounted endlessly in Peking, generally refer back to their utterances and activity in the early sixties,[23] but retribution was not

23 This theme will be further substantiated in subsequent chapters.

immediate. Why then did Mao wait for years before settling scores with them? For various reasons, Mao did not feel the time was ripe for retaliation. For one thing, the economic decline had to be stopped and the country put back on the growth momentum. It was not before the end of 1964 that the worst could be believed to be over, and the pre-1958 levels of production, particularly in agriculture, regained, and only then were the wheels of industry set into full motion once again. Mao, therefore, had to bide his time and it is significant that the full fury of his latest political movement was let loose only when complete recovery had taken place in the economic field. Moreover, Mao must have realized that a sharp struggle lay ahead of him (although it became obvious later on that he had not fully foreseen the extent of the opposition) and he wanted to prepare carefully the ground and work out his strategy systematically. Thus, while Mao stayed his hand in so far as dealing with critics was concerned, he carefully laid the ground for the coming struggle and, it is clear now in retrospect that he took a number of steps to ensure his supremacy and his success. The cultural revolution was pre-planned by Mao, but it is doubtful if the last acts were foreseen by him.

CHAPTER TWO

THE HUNDRED DAYS OF STORM

STEP BY STEP Mao worked to launch the coming battle and to keep his grip over the situation. The first instrument of power on which Mao focused his attention was, inevitably, the army. The importance that Mao has always placed on the army is well known (his famous phrase that all power grows out of the barrel of a gun is oft quoted). Mao knew that the loyalty of the army would be a crucial factor in the kind of shake-up that he had in mind. Party members and many highly placed leaders were going to be the target of the forthcoming struggle and, even if Mao could not at that time surmise with certainty which leaders he would have to join issue with, he must have had a shrewd idea of who were going to be the main antagonists. In any case, there could have been no doubt in his mind that this struggle would be of a somewhat different kind than the previous campaigns launched after the assumption of power by the Chinese Communists, for this time it was going to be essentially an intra-Party conflict, involving a substantial, if not a major, part of the leadership.

In such a situation, the role of the army could be decisive; starting a campaign like this without first securing a tight grip over the army would be uncharacteristic of Mao. The cultural revolution first started with Mao's intensified efforts to get hold of the army and make it a reliable instrument of his policies. Mao's advantage was that he knew the moves he was making and could proceed step by step, but his victims could not foresee what was coming until it was almost too late. Mao's dominant position also ensured that he could make his moves with relative ease without showing his full hand.

INDOCTRINATION OF THE ARMY

So the first move was to secure full control over the army. Some of the measures taken even before the experience of the failure of the big leap and the divisions that it led to have already been noted. But it was in 1960, when the economic scene was bleak and grim, and when the Maoist experiments were being abandoned one after another, that the Military Affairs Committee of the CCP, at the instance of Lin Piao, decided upon a conscious and vigorous campaign of indoctrination of the army in the thought of Mao Tse-tung, so as to make it completely loyal to Mao. These efforts were greatly intensified during the subsequent period. It was stated by General Hsiao Hua, now the Chief of the Political Department of the PLA,* in an article in 1963 that "in the past few years, in accordance with the instructions of the Military Affairs Committee and Comrade Lin Piao, which urged us to hold high the red banner of the thought of Mao Tse-tung and to master the thought of Mao Tse-tung in the real sense, we inherited and developed the fine tradition of the past, and whipped up a new tide in the study of Mao Tse-tung's works among the officers and men."[1] The slogan was: "Let everybody read Chairman Mao's books, take heed of what Chairman Mao says, work as directed by Chairman Mao and be a good soldier of Chairman Mao."

This Maoization of the Chinese army was noticeably stepped up during 1962-63. A report in 1963 claimed that the "broad masses of young soldiers of the PLA have for the past year achieved splendid results in their dynamic study of Chairman Mao's works and creative application of the teachings, contained therein, all the while holding high the red banner of the thought of Mao Tse-tung." The first requirement of a "five good" soldier was to have "good political thinking," that is to "read Chairman Mao's books, listen to his words, follow his instructions in work and be a good soldier of his."[2] When new soldiers joined the army, they were organized to study Mao's articles with a view to raising their political conscious-

---

*Since the above was written, General Hsiao Hua also fell from grace and disappeared into obscurity.

[1]"Chairman Mao's Works Intensively Studied by Young PLA Soldiers," *Chung-kuo Ch'ing-nien Pao*, 22 January. 1963.

[2]*Ibid.*

ness. They were required to read such articles as "Serve the People" and "In Memory of Norman Bethune." In the course of combat training, they were required to study the relevant statements made by Mao. In the course of production, they were organized to study such articles as "On the Self-Sufficiency of the Army in Production," and "On the importance of the Two Big Movements, Rectification and Production." When an education campaign in rural collective economy was conducted, they were required to study the relevant chapters of "On the Question of Agricultural Cooperation" and documents about people's communes. The motto before the army men was: when you come across new words, consult the dictionary; when you come across problems, consult *Selected Works of Mao Tse-tung*.[3]

This indoctrination was intensified year after year and the pace for the campaign to create "four good" companies, which in effect meant indoctrination in the thought of Mao Tse-tung, was accelerated. General Hsiao Hua claimed in a report in 1964 that the year 1963 was a year of "bumper harvest" in the politicization of the army according to the precepts of Mao. Everybody at the company level was engaged in political and ideological work in 1963 and the unleashing of a large-scale movement of socialist education among the PLA troops was held to be an important work for "building ideology" among the troops. General Hsiao Hua underlined the continued necessity of organizing the cadres to "earnestly study Marxism-Leninism and Mao Tse-tung's thought." Mao's thought was the "contemporary Marxism-Leninism," and the "guideline for the socialist construction and the building of the armed forces in the country." The General advised the army men that Mao's writings were "extremely rich" and could not possibly be mastered after studying once or twice. "In order to comprehend their spirit one must study again and again. Repeated study is especially necessary when a genuine application is intended."[4]

Thus, year after year, the Mao-study campaigns were stepped up. Again and again the soldiers and officers were made to study the new scriptures until they had been thoroughly imbued with the ideas of

[3]*Ibid.*
[4]Excerpts of a report by Hsiao Hua, then deputy director of the Political Department of the PLA, at an All-Army Political Work Conference, *Jen-min Jih-pao*, 22 January 1964.

Mao. Quite clearly, the objective of this Maoization was to bring the army under Mao's grip, an army loyal to him personally and an effective purveyor of his ideas, willing to listen to his command and ready to act at his bidding. Working through Lin Piao, Mao moved carefully, methodically, and relentlessly to enlist the support of the army and to secure complete control over it. In this task Lin Piao placed himself at the disposal of Mao, a willing agent and a pliant tool, making untiring efforts to push forward the process of the Maoization of the army.[5] Lin Piao's efforts on Mao's behalf were highly valuable and that should explain his steady rise in Mao's favour and his present enviably eminent position. With Lin Piao's assistance Mao "purified" the army, suppressed or purged unreliable elements, and ensured its allegiance at the time of reckoning. Once the army's support could be relied upon, it would be well-nigh impossible to challenge Mao's policies and programmes.

LEARNING FROM THE PLA

Having "fashioned" the army in the image of his ideas and strategic concepts and taken a firm hold of its allegiance, the next move was to raise the army above criticism and, what is more important, to make it a model for emulation by the rest of the country. The army became the pace-setter, the best "school for the thought of Mao Tse-tung" and a worthy example for others. The entire nation must learn from it and follow in its footsteps. A country-wide campaign to profit and learn from the PLA's experience in political and ideological work was launched with the characteristic thoroughness of Mao Tse-tung. A *Jen-min Jih-pao* editorial said that the PLA had carried on "the excellent traditions and working style" of the Communist Party, and that this could all be fundamentally ascribed to "the guidance of all its work by the thought of Mao Tse-tung." This "valuable experience" of the PLA should be studied widely in order to bring into fuller play the proletarian, militant, revolutionary spirit in the socialist revolution and all fields of socialist construction, for Mao's thought was the

---

[5]All the various directions on Mao-study and indoctrination in the thought of Mao were issued by Lin Piao.

guide for the revolution and socialist construction of the Chinese people.[6]

Thus, the PLA was held up as a model for the whole country and during the next two years every enterprise, factory, commune, educational institution, artistic and literary body was organized to study the PLA's methods and style of work, to compare and contrast their own with that of the PLA, and to consciously and consistently emulate the PLA. This "learn from the PLA" campaign had many dimensions. There was the exhortation to "hoist the red banner of the thought of Mao Tse-tung," as had been successfully done by the PLA and to treat the PLA as the teacher in the manner, method, and system of "penetrating" absorption of Mao's ideology. There was the need to learn the PLA's style of "plain, hard work," taking pride in undertaking difficult and complicated tasks and adhering to the working style of building the country and running all enterprises with thrift.[7] There was also the appeal to imbibe the "revolutionary tough-bone spirit" of the PLA.[8] The men of the PLA knew no rest, feared no hardships, and overcame all obstacles and problems. Countless stories were recounted and printed by Peking's mass media of communications and propaganda during the next three years showing the bravery and fearlessness of the men of the PLA, their courage and fortitude, their willingness to sacrifice their lives, their disregard of personal comfort and benefit, their resourcefulness and exemplary conduct. They were the teachers of the country and everyone was to follow their example.

Another dimension to this learning from the PLA was the creation of hero-images, ordinary soldiers who smothered all notions of personal advancement or comfort, diligently read and acted upon Mao's adages, believed they were working for world revolution while at their posts of duty, and sacrificed themselves in the fulfilment of their assignments. They also generally kept a diary in which they repeated to themselves the exhortations of Mao, lauded their efficacy in facing various situations and solving problems, and resolved to be faithful pupils of Mao. The process started with

---

[6] *Jen-min Jih-pao*, editorial, 1 February 1964.
[7] *Ibid.*
[8] *Ibid.*, editorial, 10 March 19 64,

Lei Feng.[9] Mao himself wrote the inscription in March 1963 calling upon the people to learn from the selfless spirit, the proletarian resoluteness, and the earnestness and sacrifice of Lei Feng. Then followed further inscriptions by Liu Shao-ch'i, Chu Teh, Teng Hsiao-p'ing, Lin Piao, and others in *Chieh-fang Chun-pao*. It is always possible to read unwarranted meanings in others' statements and writings but there does seem to be a difference in stress in these inscriptions. While Liu and Teng spoke about the "commonplace but great Communist spirit" of Lei Feng, Lin Piao asked the PLA soldiers to "follow the example of Lei Feng in order to be good soldiers of Chairman Mao."[10]

There was no walk of life, no branch of human activity, which was not required to develop a systematic mass campaign to imbibe all the qualities of the PLA and to follow its style of work and, above all, to be loyal like the PLA to Mao and his ideology. Even in literary and artistic work, the PLA began to promote its own writers and artists, and was soon praised for setting the pace in the creation of socialist art and literature. The economic enterprises, in particular, were asked to learn from the PLA in carrying out their work. In fact many army officers were transferred in 1963 to economic enterprises in order to guide the economic work of the country.[11] It was a significant move in the direction of acquiring a tighter grip over economic operations and to run them according to Mao's ideas and directions. Additionally, as one of the measures learnt from the PLA, economic enterprises also established political departments so that ideological work could take precedence over all other work, and a report in early 1964 mentioned that 23 ministries and bureaus of industry and commerce had set up political departments.[12]

It is now apparent that these moves had a certain meaning and significance, so far as Mao was concerned, even though the others did not realize their import. Having brought the army largely under his control, he was now establishing the political supremacy of the army over the rest of the country so that, like Caesar's wife, it would be

[9] *New China News Agency*, Peking, 6 March 1963.
[10] *Ibid.*
[11] See, for instance, *Ta-kung Pao*, editorial, 29 February 1964.
[12] *New China News Agency*, Peking, 23 April 1964.

above suspicion and above criticism, and so that the army could legitimately guide, supervise, and control all other work and all other organizations. The army could not any longer be subjected to political attack, nor its right to lead questioned. It could do no wrong, and since it was now established as a highly politicized force its leadership over other organs and groups could no longer be regarded as unwarranted. At the same time, the loyalty of the army to Mao of which, thanks to Lin Piao, he must have been quite confident, made the success of Mao's actions and whatever campaigns he had in mind almost a foregone conclusion. It may be argued that all these measures were being approved of by the entire leadership, but there is no doubt that the initiative in most cases came from Mao himself. Singly, those on whom the axe fell later on could not oppose any of these steps, nor could they perhaps have grasped the hidden meaning of these moves: only Mao knew all that he was doing and all that he was planning.

"SOCIALIST EDUCATION" AND MAO-STUDY CAMPAIGN

Simultaneously, a socialist education campaign was launched which had as its primary object of attention the peasant masses, but which was gradually broadened to include the workers and intellectuals, and the cadres of the Communist Party and the Government. This decision came shortly after the tenth plenary session of the Eight Central Committee. The Committee meeting in Peking (24-27 September 1962) repeated the Maoist doctrine that "throughout the historical period of proletarian revolution and proletarian dictatorship, throughout the historical period of transition from capitalism to Communism (which will last scores of years or even longer), there is a class struggle between the proletariat and the bourgeoisie, and struggle between the socialist road and the capitalist road." "Never forget the class struggle" was Mao's message to the country. The overthrown ruling classes were not reconciled to their doom; they always attempted to stage a comeback. Therefore, "among the people," there was a small number of persons who had not undergone socialist remoulding and who attempted to depart from the socialist road whenever there was an opportunity. Under the circumstances, class struggle was inevitable.

This class struggle is complicated, tortuous, with ups and downs, and sometimes it is very sharp. This class struggle inevitably finds expression within the Party. Pressure from foreign imperialism and the existence of bourgeois influence at home constitute the social source of revisionist ideas in the Party. While waging a struggle against the foreign and domestic class enemies, we must remain vigilant and resolutely oppose in good time various opportunist ideological tendencies in the Party.[13]

The communique evidently reflected Mao's ever-present fear of a departure from his policies and a reversion to the "revisionist" line both in domestic and foreign affairs. Subsequent references made the initiative of Mao behind this resolution quite clear. There were other reasons, too, adding to Mao's fears. The setback during 1959-60 had compelled the regime to tolerate "liberal" economic measures and allow what would normally be regarded as "capitalist tendencies" to grow—the private plot, the free market, etc. This situation was a constant source of anxiety for Mao and along with a number of steps taken to restrict the free market and private subsidiary occupations of the peasantry,[14] a nation-wide socialist education campaign was set afoot and developed in the next two years. The goals of this mass education movement were defined as: the use of proletarian ideology to educate and remould the peasants; to raise the class awakening of the broad masses of poor peasants and lower middle peasants; to improve the ideological work style of the cadres; to promote closer relations between the cadres and the masses; to overcome and prevent erosion by capitalist ideology; to "expose and smash the various plots of sabotage by the class enemies"; and to consolidate collective economy.[15] The socialist education campaign also came to be known as the "four clean-up" movement—to "clean" things up in the fields of politics, ideology, organization, and economy.

[13]Communique of the Tenth Plenary session of the Eighth Central Committee of the Chinese Communist Party, *New China News Agency*, Peking, 28 September 1962.

[14]For a detailed discussion of those measures, see Gargi Dutt, *Rural Communes of China: Organizational Problems*, Chapter V, Asia Publishing House, 1967.

[15]T'ao Chu, "The People's Communes are Making Progress," *Hung-ch'i*, No. 4, 26 February 1964.

Although the economic situation continued to call for caution and the socialist education campaign had to be generally confined to propaganda and persuasion, unaccompanied by any drastic administrative or economic changes, Mao's objective seemed to be to gradually build up an atmosphere and a climate for a sharp curtailment of the current economic policies, and for promoting once again greater collectivization. It is unlikely that most of the other members of the leadership were thinking in terms of a major switch in policies and, while they went along with Mao's proposals for certain restrictions on the growth of capitalist tendencies and for stepping up socialist propaganda, they could hardly be envisaging the revival of the big leap atmosphere and policies. It is possible that agreement on the measures that were adopted only screened a wider disagreement over their aims and intentions and over the future course of developments.

The next step was an active acceleration of indoctrination of the entire nation in the thought of Mao Tse-tung. The Mao-study movement was broadened from the ranks of the army to engulf the whole country. The movement was unfolded from one part to another and from one end of China to the other. It was, typically, whipped up as a mass movement in which there was participation by millions upon millions of people. To take a stray example, in the province of Liaoning alone, 70,000 teams were set up for promoting the Mao-study campaign.[16] To learn the thought of Mao Tse-tung "had become the pressing and craving demand of more and more workers, peasants, intellectuals and the broad masses of cadres." This was described as the sole method for "every one of us, every unit and every department to become more revolutionary."[17]

This mass movement was expected to yield a rich harvest in promoting Mao's ideology and to kill many birds with one stone. It was hopefully expected to change the "spiritual outlook" of the masses and make their view of life conform to the direction laid down by Mao. As it was put: "The moon will not shine without the sun, seedlings will wither without rainfall, and one will lose track of direction if one does not learn the thought of Mao

[16]"Strive to Learn the Thought of Mao Tse-tung," *Jen-min Jih-pao*, 26 March 1964.
[17]*Ibid.*

Tse-tung."[18] This spiritualization would facilitate Mao's task of carrying the country towards a higher stage of collectivization, in effectively combating trends contrary to Mao's wishes, and in perpetuating the line laid down by Mao. Above all, it would blunt the edge of any opposition to his schemes, policies, and future moves. The idolization of Mao would automatically shut out criticism. You could not regard the sayings and prescriptions of Mao as the higher truth and yet be able to stand against his policies. The idol may be struck down in a certain situation, but, as long as it stands, it sways and brooks no opposition. The idolization of Mao also had as its ultimate objective the smothering of any possible dissent and to make Mao irreproachable and omniscient. It would be inconceivable that after all this glorification anyone could successfully pose a direct challenge to his authority: his word was law, his utterances commandments.

Like a clever craftsman, Mao struck carefully. He did not hit directly. He was the master chess-player whose moves had a certain deceptivity about them, not revealing their true intention and keeping others guessing about their significance. He prepared the ground well and moved with his characteristic thoroughness and ruthlessness. Having ensured the loyalty of the army, and the political and ideological superiority and supremacy of the army over the rest of the country, the intensification of the campaign for ideological remoulding and his own dominance as the Leader and the Ideologue, he was now ready to initiate the struggle which was to reverberate throughout the world.

THE BEGINNINGS OF THE STRUGGLE

While the fury of the cultural revolution was let loose in 1966, Mao started the struggle in 1965. Significantly, 1965 was also the year of substantial economic growth, of full recovery from the economic losses of the bleak period, 1959-62; the year when economic prospects once again appeared rosy; the year when the "downward spiral" was no longer a haunting nightmare; on the other hand, the upward spiral had become a visible reality. Production levels in agriculture as well as industry had overtaken the pre-

[18]*Ibid.*

big leap figures and the momentum of growth was regained. Peking has not yet released any hard figures for these years, but it is generally believed that agricultural production had risen up to somewhere between 180 and 190 million tons and that industries again started working to near capacity. Officially, Peking claimed that by 1965 there was an "all round upsurge in agricultural and industrial production" and that the entire economy "took a turn for the better."[19] 1965 was also the year of preparation for the launching of the third Five-Year Plan beginning in 1966. China had also exploded its first nuclear device in 1964 which shot up the morale of the people. Evidently, Mao felt that the time was ripe for the struggle for which he had already prepared the ground-work.

The proletarian cultural revolution, or the campaign to weed out unreliable elements and dissidents (that is, those deemed unreliable for their total commitment to Mao's ideology) from all positions of power in the Party and the government and in the intellectual life of the country, the shaking up and overturning of authority and bureaucracy, driving out of all old and new ideas and instead the planting of "the red flag of the thought of Mao Tse-tung" in the minds of the Chinese people may be said to have begun with the attack on Wu Han by Yao Wen-yuan in November 1965, of which mention was made in the preceding chapter. The struggle was simmering even earlier. One later propaganda article said that the curtain of the cultural revolution was raised by the festivals of revolutionary dramas on contemporary themes on Peking and elsewhere in mid-1965.[20] This was the time when efforts to eliminate the old drama and the classical opera and to replace it by modern drama and modern themes for the opera reached a new peak. According to the materials released for the indoctrination of the army on the seventeenth anniversary of the establishment of the People's Republic of China (October 1966), Mao "personally" initiated and led the proletarian cultural revolution in the second half of 1965, but met with stubborn resistance from "those in power who followed the capitalist line" and from the "bourgeois reactionary academic 'authorities.' "[21]

[19]*Jen-min Jih-pao*, editorial, 1 January 1965.

[20]Selection from "Big Character Posters" in *Jen-min Jih-pao*, 10 December 1966.

[21]Material released by *Chieh-fang Chun-pao* and republished in *Jen-min Jih-pao*, 24 September 1966.

There is also evidence to show that a sharp struggle took place in 1965 in the Peking University between the Party authorities and those who resisted their policies, and stood for a more leftist line, and had the secret support of their close confidants in the Party's top echelons. A subsequent editorial of *Jen-min Jih-pao* revealed that from early 1965 there was a "brutal" struggle in the Peking University and that it was "precisely the conscious effort and defence" (of the leftist opponents) by the Central Committee and Mao (meaning really the Maoists at the top) which "opposed" the Party leadership of the University.[22]

Undoubtedly, the struggles that took place in 1965 at various places and in various fields were directly instigated and supported by Mao. There is also no doubt that Yao Wen-yuan's attack on Wu Han was similarly written at the instance of Mao. It was not fortuitous that the struggle first started in educational institutions and in literary and art circles. This was because Mao wanted to capture the minds of the Chinese people and reach out to where ideas originated and fertilized—among students and intellectuals. It was for the same reason that the Maoists ensured control over as much of the mass media of communication and propaganda— the radio and the press, etc.—as possible. Mao was also apparently anxious to remould the younger generation so as to secure their adherence to his policies and ideas and thus to leave behind what have been described as "proletarian revolutionary successors." The approach to intellectuals and the educational policy were crucial issues in the new struggle.

THE HIGH DRAMA OF THE POWER STRUGGLE

The storm of the proletarian cultural revolution gathered force with the attack on Party intellectuals and those in charge of educational institutions, of which the denunciation of Wu Han was the curtain-raiser. While Mao took all the steps to consolidate his position and to catch his victims, one by one, those in the Party High Command who were gradually falling out of step with Mao and who were to be the target of the struggle bestirred themselves

---

[22]*Jen-min Jih-pao*, editorial, 5 June 1966. English translation in *Peking Review*, 10 June 1966.

and prepared to protect themselves. The showdown was imminent. Perhaps they finally grasped the true meaning of Mao's moves and had to start fighting with their backs to the wall. The exact sequence and course of the drama of the struggle at the top will remain a mystery confined to the four walls of the Forbidden Palace in Peking. According to a Hong Kong Report, P'eng Chen and Liu Shao-ch'i during February and April gathered their forces in Peking for a meeting of the Central Committee to vote down Mao Tse-tung and his supporters, much in the manner that Khrushchov defeated his opponents in the Soviet Union. Possibly, Mao was in a minority in the higher councils of the Party. Mao left for Shanghai and made his base there, again possibly, to avoid being held to ransom by the P'eng and Liu forces in Peking, while Lin Piao marshalled his forces for the coming showdown. According to this account, Teng Hsiao-p'ing faltered at the critical moment and hesitated to agree to the convening of a meeting of the Central Committee in the absence of Mao. Teng's vacillation sealed the fate of the opposition; the dice was loaded against Liu, P'eng, and Teng, and bloodshed or civil war between Lin Piao's forces and those supporting P'eng and Liu was averted. P'eng fell earlier but Liu remained in command until Mao came back to Peking and was now ready to strike down his opponents which is what he did at the crucial eleventh plenary session of the Central Committee in August 1966.[23]

There were also persistent reports in wall posters about the so-called February military coup. From sketchy reports and indirect references in wall posters, it appears that there was an attempt in February 1966 by some of Mao's opponents to stage a military coup and seize power. The attempt, however, did not fructify. The existence of such a plot was categorically denied by Teng Hsiao-p'ing who reportedly said at a meeting in the People's University on 2 August:

...I must inform you that I have before me a few requests for my comment on the question of the February military coup. We have made inquiry into this matter because we have heard of it.

[23]*Ming Pao*, Hong Kong, 1-2 January 1967.

There was no such incident. We have made a formal inquiry for you, and are satisfied that there was no such incident. At that time, some armed forces units wanted to stay in Peking and requested for the allocation of barracks. Later, the comrades of these units felt that the school could not be released for their use, and that it was also not very good to get armed forces units mixed with a school. Therefore, that was all. I earnestly inform you that neither...nor other persons, nor I can move our troops."[24]

Nevertheless, allegations about such an attempt at a military coup have continued in Red Guard newspapers and wall posters.

Whatever the truth about the details, a fierce struggle was undoubtedly shaping in China and has continued right till now. A firm indication came with the dismissal of Lu Ting-i, Minister of Culture, and Chou Yang, the literary boss of the Communist Party of China. But Mao's first successful strike against a top-ranking Party leader came in June when the strategically placed Peking Municipal Committee of the Chinese Communist Party was dissolved and its powerful chief and member of the Politbureau, P'eng Chen, dismissed. This decision in the name of the Central Committee was broadcast to the country on the afternoon of 3 June. It was announced that Li Hsueh-feng, First Secretary of the North China Bureau of the Party's Central Committee, had been appointed concurrently First Secretary of the Peking Municipal Party Committee and directed to reorganize it with the assistance of Wu Teh, First Secretary of the Kirin Provincial Party Committee. Earlier actions had made this decision almost a foregone conclusion. One by one, P'eng Chen's deputies and assistants had been denounced and disgraced and it was apparent that the ring was closing in on the chief himself. Wu Han had already been axed; then came the turn of Teng T'o and his associates. The accusations against these leading functionaries of the Peking Party Committee was a prelude to an attack on their leader.

At the same time the struggle was reaching a climax in the Peking University. It began with a wall poster put up by "revolutionary

[24]For a report of this speech see *Current Background* (published by the American Consulate General, Hong Kong), No. 819, 10 March 1967, p. 7.

students" Nieh Yuan-tzu and six others on 25 May, attacking Party leaders like Sung Shuo of the Universities Department of Peking Municipality, Lu P'ing, President of Peking University, and P'eng P'ei-yun, Deputy Secretary of the Party Committee in the University, for "sabotaging the cultural revolution in the Peking University." The wall poster not only lit the "flame of the great cultural revolution" in the Peking University but also "started the fire of a great nationwide cultural revolution." That Mao's invisible hand was there behind the wall poster can be deduced from a reported statement by K'ang Sheng, another of Mao's close confidants and one who has also risen rapidly in the Party hierarchy, which reads:

On the afternoon of 1 June, Chairman Mao notified us, saying that the wall poster of Peking University was a Marxist-Leninist wall poster which must be immediately broadcast and published in the press. Chairman Mao's instructions were received in the afternoon. At 8 0'clock, the poster was broadcast and on 2 June it appeared in *Jen-min Jih-pao*. After the broadcast, all universities in the country and some middle schools were astir. They on the one hand voiced their support for Peking University, while on the other hand starting a revolution in their own schools.[25]

Thus, according to K'ang Sheng, did Mao "kindle the fire of the great proletarian cultural revolution."

One of the first decisions of the newly organized Peking Municipal Committee was to dismiss Lu P'ing and P'eng P'ei-yun from all their posts and to send a new work team, headed by Chang Cheng-hsien, which would function as the Peking University's Party Committee during its reorganization. The new Peking Party Committee also decided to dismiss the editorial board and its director, Fan Chin of *Pei-ching Jih-pao* (Peking Daily) and *Pei-ching Wan-pao* (Peking Evening News), to replace it with a new editorial board with Chai Hsiang-tung as editor-in-chief and Wu

[25]A speech reportedly made by K'ang Sheng on 8 September at a reception in People's Great Hall to some of the "revolutionary rebels" who had come to Peking from other parts to establish revolutionary ties, *Current Background*, No. 819, p. 22. Also, see the account in *Hung-ch'i*, editorial, entitled "Carry the Great Proletarian Cultural Revolution to the End," No. 1, January 1967.

Hsiang and Lin Ching as deputies, and the editorial board of the fortnightly *Ch'ien-hsien* (Frontline) and to suspend its publication pending reorganization.[26]

The official catalogue of the sins of the former Peking Municipal Party Committee (meaning thereby P'eng Chen) was a wide-ranging and comprehensive indictment whose veracity it is hard to determine. The leading functionaries of the Peking Municipal Party Committee were accused of erecting a "tight barricade" against the Party's Central Committee. They regarded the Peking Party Committee as an "independent kingdom," "watertight and impenetrable," in which no one dare intervene. The Party Committee was "like a tiger whose back side no one dared to kick." Its leaders were "a gang of conspirators and careerists." They recruited "deserters and mutineers," functioned like a "feudal guild," and formed "cliques" in order to "push through their revisionist political line" and restore capitalism. They opposed the "creative study and application of Chairman Mao's works by the broad masses of workers, peasants, soldiers, and cadres" and "intensely hated Mao's thought." They stood in opposition to Mao's educational policy and, instead, followed a "bourgeois and revisionist" educational policy. The Peking University under their control became "a typical stubborn stronghold of reaction."[27]

It was now admitted by official propaganda that "under the direct leadership" of Chairman Mao the Shanghai Municipal Committee started the criticism of Wu Han's *Hai Jui Dismissed from Office*, and "sounded the clarion call for the great proletarian cultural revolution." This greatly angered the "gang of revisionist lords" in the Peking Committee and they made "unscrupulous attacks" on the Shanghai Committee. Even after Mao had criticized the Peking Committee, they "continued to organize their planned resistance in an attempt to save the queen by sacrificing the knights." In other words, P'eng Chen and his associates tried to save themselves by criticizing a few of their followers who had come under fire, while continuing to pursue their basic policies. They were also accused of having opposed the socialist education movement

[26] *Jen-min Jih-pao*, 4 June 1966.

[27] "Thoroughly Criticize and Repudiate the Revisionist Line of Some of the Principal Members of the Former Peking Municipal Party Committee," *Hung-ch'i*, No. 9, 1966.

in rural and urban areas and protected the Party members "who were in power at the basic levels in the urban and rural areas and were taking the road of capitalism,"[28] and so on and so forth.

Chieh-fang Chun-pao (Liberation Army Daily), which because of Lin Piao's link with Mao, became the pace-setter during the crucial period of the struggle, spoke menacingly of enemies without guns who were more cunning, more dangerous than the overt ones, who were double dealing and who feigned compliance while in fact opposing Mao. They were "wolves in sheep's clothing," "man-eating tigers with smiling faces"; they spread "bourgeois poison" through the media of literature, films, music, the press and periodicals, etc. The paper warned that a high degree of vigilance was needed against these thieves in the house and that there could be no sitting on the fence in this struggle.[29] This was the clearest indication that the coming clash would be a comprehensive struggle and that there were many more marked men than had been exposed by that time. An editorial, few days later, in *Jen-min Jih-pao* also served notice that Mao's hidden or overt, real or fancied, opponents would not be allowed to escape. Those "representatives of the bourgeoisie who had wormed into the Party," and covered up "the true class nature of the struggle" and "twisted the serious political struggle into a purely academic affair" and an "exchange of different views" would be stripped of their disguise. There was no such thing as "everyone is equal before the truth"—an out and out bourgeois concept (and evidently the argument being put forward by the dissidents). The paper ridiculed the "tattered flag of liberty, equality and fraternity" carried by the opponents and affirmed the resolve of the Maoists to strike them down: "You cannot cover your retreat" and "our socialist system certainly will not allow freedom of speech to counter-revolutionaries."[30]

The fall of P'eng Chen while Liu Shao-ch'i was still in harness seems to suggest that Liu and Pe'ng had not coordinated their forces and fought back unitedly. Liu's acquiescence in the dismissal of P'eng at a time when Liu still commanded considerable influence and had not yet publicly come under a cloud suggests that he was

[28]*Ibid.*
[29]*Chieh-fang Chun-pao*, editorial, 7 June 1966; reproduced in *Peking Review*, 10 June 1966.
[30]*Ibid.*

unwilling or perhaps unable to offer a direct challenge to Mao's authority and to plunge the country into a virtual civil war. Possibly, Liu did not apprehend at this time that he would be the ultimate target of the cultural revolution and that Teng Hsiao-p'ing also did not realize that the axe would fall on him too. Or were they also attempting to follow the maxim of "saving the queen by sacrificing the knights ?" The failure of Liu, Teng, and P'eng to act in concert is suggested by the fact that, during June-August, Liu Shao-ch'i was in command in Peking and that Teng was also considerably active at this time and that both were subsequently accused of having attempted to derail the cultural revolution in the absence of Mao who had, rather surprisingly and significantly, repaired to Shanghai. That Liu Shao-ch'i was still in the saddle at this time is well known. An editorial in *Jen-min Jih-pao* quoted approvingly one after another, Liu Shao-ch'i, Teng Hsiao-p'ing, Chou En-lai, and Lin Piao, almost as if to assure the people that this top leadership was safe and stood united.[31]

Be that as it may, there is no doubt that Liu and Teng attempted to control the cultural revolution and direct it according to their lights. With the approval of the Party centre which they controlled at that time, they sent out work teams to various universities and colleges to conduct the cultural revolution there. These work teams functioned in close cooperation with the authorities in these institutions and this was the source of endless trouble, for these very Party committees were the real object of Mao's attack. They, therefore, came into conflict with the "Leftists" in these institutions who were already creating considerable trouble for the Party leadership and who were, as it came to light later, being secretly supported by Mao. This led to considerable turmoil and uneasiness in the university campuses. There were often violent clashes resulting in disruption of the normal life of the universities and colleges. The work committees and the Party committees treated the rebel students as counter-revolutionaries, and it was alleged later by the Maoists that they had prepared secret dossiers on the opponents and carried out a bloody suppression of them. The rebel students, enjoying clandestine support from high quarters,

[31]"Long Live Mao Tse-tung's Thought—In Commemoration of the 45th Anniversary of the Founding of the Communist Party of China," *Jen-min Jih-pao*, editorial, 1 July 1966,

looked upon the work committees and the Party leadership there as counter-revolutionary revisionists and did everything possible to undermine their prestige and overturn their authority. A very graphic account of this struggle and the forces ranged against each other, at least in one area—Sian—has been given by an unusually privileged onlooker, Watson, in *Far Eastern Economic Review*.[32]

The work committee in Tsinghua University, Peking, was directed by Liu's wife, Wang Kuang-mei, and her stepdaughter acting in close cooperation with Ho Lung's son.[33] A sidelight revealed by the current developments in China was the power and influence wielded by the children of high-ranking Party members in their respective units or institutions. The struggle in Tsinghua was particularly acute and bitter. It was at this time that a wall poster went up against Mao himself. The fierceness of the struggle was evident from the fact that in this *cultural* revolution Liu's wife was referred to as "the bitch" by the "revolutionary rebels."[34] In a subsequent denunciation of her father, Liu's daughter alleged that the work committee was directed by her parents and that their objective was to control the revolution and oppose the Maoist leadership and the thought of Mao Tse-tung.[35]

After Mao gained full control of the Party Centre in August 1966, these work committees were severely condemned by the Maoists and it was demanded that those who had been subjected to unjust condemnation and suppression by the work committees should be publicly rehabilitated and that the "black lists" prepared by them against the Maoist-supported students be publicly consigned to fire. Teng Hsiao-p'ing was highly apologetic about them in a meeting with the students in late August[36] and Liu himself in his subsequent "confession" (which he retracted soon after) owned the mistake

[32]See Watson's special articles in *Far Eastern Economic Review*, Hong Kong, Nos. 225-7, 229-30.

[33]Ho Lung was Vice-Premier, member of the Politbureau and the Central Committee's Military Control Commission, and one of the oldest members of the Party along with Mao Tse-tung, Chu Teh, Liu Shao-ch'i, and Chou En-lai.

[34]This is mentioned in Liu Tao's statement of confession and denunciation of her father.

[35]The statement of self-criticism and denunciation by Liu's daughter was published in the Red Guard newspaper, *Chingkanshan*, and was reproduced in *Current Background*, Hong Kong.

[36]See fn. 24.

of sending work teams but did not acknowledge that there was any sinister motive behind it. He put it down to lack of penetrating understanding of the cultural revolution and the thought of Mao Tse-tung and the continuing bourgeois influences over him.

STRUGGLE IN THE ARMY

In July, Mao issued a new directive to the Army[37] with renewed emphasis on the building up of the army in consonance with his ideas. The directive exhorted the army to become "a great school" which was interpreted by the Army daily to mean that it should become "a great school of Mao Tse-tung's thought." Mao said:

> The People's Liberation Army should be a great school. In this great school, our army men should learn politics, military affairs, and culture. They can also engage in agricultural production and side occupations, run some medium-sized or small factories and manufacture a number of products to meet their own needs or for exchange with the State at equal values. They can also do mass work and take part in the socialist education movement in the factories and villages as it occurs.... They should also participate in each struggle of the cultural revolution to criticize the bourgeoisie. In this way the army can concurrently study, engage in agriculture, run factories, and do mass work. Of course, these tasks should be properly coordinated, and a distinction be made between the primary and secondary tasks. Each army unit should engage in one or two of the three fields of activity—agriculture, industry, and mass work—but not in all three of them at the same time.[38]

This direction came after a fresh struggle in the army again on the vexed issue of professionalization and modernization as against politicization and ideological indoctrination. This problem had troubled the army's relationship with the Party and with Mao and continues to do so even now. Although Mao had secured a grip

[37]The directive was not directly published in the press but was referred to and quoted first in an editorial of *Chieh-fang Chun-pao* (Liberation Army Daily), on 1 August, on the thirty-ninth anniversary of the Liberation Army. English text in *Peking Review*, 5 August 1966.   [38]*Ibid.*

over the army and turned it into an instrument for the execution of his policies, trouble continued to crop up now and again. According to Peking's own admission, three times since the establishment of the new regime in 1949 this struggle broke out in the army. The first struggle came shortly after the termination of the Korean war when some leaders, keeping in view the experience of the Korean war, asked for a more rapid modernization and professionalization of the army. In the words of official propaganda, under the pretext of "regularization" and "modernization" the "representatives of the bourgeois military line" wanted to turn the army into "a complete carbon copy of foreign practice, vainly attempted to negate our army's historical experience and fine traditions, and to lead our army on to the road followed by bourgeois armies."[39]

The second struggle came in 1959 with Marshal P'eng Teh-huai, then Defence Minister, in the lead and has already been noted in the previous chapter. The third struggle came in the wake of the cultural revolution, and this time it involved another high-ranking army officer, Senior General Lo Jui-ch'ing, Vice-Premier and Chief of Staff and former Minister of Public Security. General Lo seems to have demurred at the extent to which politics was being allowed to take command in the army and, like P'eng Teh-huai, to have shown concern at the degree of the erosion of professionalization. Obviously, Lo was not alone in the army and his views were shared by some others. Whether there was any secret tie-up between Lo, P'eng and Liu is not known. What seems apparent is their failure to take concerted action, which facilitated Mao's task in picking them up one by one.

According to the Army daily, "exposed" in the recent struggle in the army were "representatives of the bourgeoisie who had usurped important posts in the army and were important members of the counter-revolutionary anti-Party, anti-socialist clique." They had opposed Mao's thought, had "overtly agreed to, but covertly opposed" Lin Piao's directive on giving prominence to politics, had "talked about putting politics in command but in practice put military affairs first, technique first, and work first," and they had "waved red flags to oppose the red flag." They had reduced the army's tasks to the "single task of training in combat skill in peace time and fighting in times of war." "In short, everything they did

[39]Ibid.

was diametrically opposite to Chairman Mao's thinking on army building."[40]

As the Maoists crushed the dissidents in the army, the political supremacy of the army was reinforced and Mao issued another directive to the people to learn from the PLA and to turn "all fields of work into great revolutionary schools" (which, as official pronouncements made it clear, meant turning them into "great schools of the thought of Mao Tse-tung") in the manner that the PLA had done.[41] The avowed objective was that all the people should "take part in both industry and agriculture and military as well as civilian affairs." For the peasants in the communes, Mao advised that along with agriculture as their main task they should learn to run industries; they should also study "military affairs, politics, and culture" and "when conditions permit, they should also engage in subsidiary agricultural production and side occupations." The students were similarly directed that "whilet heir main task was to study, they should in addition learn other things, that is, industrial work, farming, and military affairs. They should also criticize the bourgeoisie. The school term should be shortened, education should be revolutionized and the domination of the schools by bourgeois intellectuals should not be allowed to continue."[42]

As was to be expected and as is usual with Chinese propaganda, no sooner had Mao's directive been issued than people all over the country reportedly hailed the new "wise" instructions of Mao and pledged to turn their units into "a great school of revolution" in the fashion of the Liberation Army.[43] Reports from various parts of China were publicized showing the determination of workers, peasants, soldiers, and "revolutionary cadres and intellectuals" to read Mao's works, follow his teachings, and act on his instructions.

RED GUARDS AND THE WAR OF POSTERS

During this proletarian cultural revolution the students of middle schools, colleges, and universities were the primary objects of

[40]*Ibid.*

[41]See, for instance a despatch by *New China News Agency*, Peking, 2 August 1966.

[42]*New China News Agency*, 3 August 1966.

[43]Fn. 41 and 42.

Maoists' attention. A definite, systematic, and sustained effort was made to arouse the students, surcharge them emotionally in their loyalty to Mao, to make them the chief instrument of Mao's current political campaign, and to pit them against the victims of Mao's latest purge. The students were galvanized into action to "protect" Chairman Mao, to rebel against the established authority (wherever and whenever Mao wanted them to), and to carry out the objectives that Mao had aimed at in launching the so-called cultural revolution. It was they who first began the trouble against the Party leaders in various educational institutions and denounced the work teams in many places, who initiated the tumult that soon engulfed China, and who subsequently took to the streets to pull down all those and all that Mao disapproved. From May to August (1966), many "proletarian cultural revolutionary organizations" sprang up in China's educational institutions comprising students and "revolutionary" teachers and staff. There was often more than one organization in one institution, sometimes each department establishing its own "branch association." These so-called "revolutionary rebels" were later called the Red Guards. (The term Red Guards was first used in Communist Chinese terminology for the peasant militia for local defence in the Communist-held areas during the war against Japan and the civil war against the Kuomintang.) The Red Guards established their own work teams and were led, controlled, and directed by the Maoist leadership. The invisible but unmistakable hand of Mao was behind them. The Maoists sought to bring discipline and order into the ranks of their student supporters and advised them to establish revolutionary organizations and hold "Paris Commune type elections" so that greater supervision could be exercised over them through election" of their leaders and control over these leaders. Each cultural revolutionary organization selected its representatives who exercised effective control over their members and in turn were subject to the instructions issued by the higher level cultural organizations reaching right up to the top where the proletarian cultural organization of the Central Committee of the Chinese Communist Party, completely dominated by the Maoists, had been set up to direct the activities of the cultural revolutionary organizations of the subordinate units.

To take one instance of the "Paris Commune type elections,"

a report from Hupeh University stated that the "revolutionary teachers and students of the law faculty," employing the method of direct election, set up a proletarian cultural revolutionary branch association.   Soon the other faculties and units followed suit and all the various classes established their revolutionary groups.   This was followed by discussions among these "work groups" for the establishment of a proletarian cultural revolutionary committee of the university and it was decided that student members should not be less than 80 per cent of the total membership, the rest being filled by the revolutionary teachers and staff.   Staff candidates would be "elected" by "secret ballot" of the staff, workers, and cadres while the student candidates were to be elected by secret ballot in each faculty, their number being dependent on the size of each faculty.[44]   But, of course, in line with the usual practice, there was a single slate of candidates arrived at after "mass discussions," no doubt ensuring that only those who were active Maoists and could reasonably be relied upon were elected.   And thus the "Hupeh University's proletarian cultural revolution provisional committee," owing complete allegiance to the Maoists, came into being and it was this committee which selected the heads of various subordinate cultural revolutionary groups.   Similar committees   and groups were organized in other institutions.

Who and what kind of people should be elected to these committees and groups?   It was made quite clear that only those should be elected "who are faithful to Mao Tse-tung's thought, believe in Mao Tse-tung's thought, and support Mao Tse-tung's thought." They were the real successors to Mao and should be particularly cultivated in these "prerequisites."   They should be "equipped with Marxism-Leninism,"   meaning equipped with Mao Tse-tung's thought, be imbued with "revolutionary working spirit," and be "fearless of difficulties."   There was no use electing persons who "do nothing but act as good people."[45]

Subsequently, such "revolutionary" committees and groups bearing different names and not confined to students mushroomed all over the country.   Soon the youngsters took the name of Red Guards for themselves and the name gained wide currency throughout

[44]Wuhan Radio, 21 August 1966.
[45]*Ibid.*

the country. The first Red Guard organization sprang up at Tsinghua on 29 May[46] and within a matter of months they had mushroomed in all major cities and towns of China and were gradually brought under central direction of the Maoists in Peking. Thus a network of a parallel organization—parallel to the Communist Party and the government—came into existence, looking directly to Mao for command, ever at his beck and call, destined and designed to play a crucial role in the struggle that was already under way. The creation of such a rival organization can only be explained by Mao's need for a reliable instrument through which to realize his objectives and his rejection of the Party organization as the requisite agency. He had created this organization, by and large, to topple the existing authority and to bring up a new leadership. He could not use the Party to struggle against the Party officials, the Party bureaucrats to beat down the Party bureaucrats, the Party organization to demolish the Party establishment. The avowed aim of the current struggle was to "drag out" and overthrow all those "who had wormed their way into the Party and were taking the capitalist road" and since this category included a very large number of influential leaders at all levels, it was hardly possible to ask them to be their own executioners. They had to be pilloried and punished by an outside force. It cannot also escape notice, and perhaps it speaks volumes by itself, that Mao could not rely on the workers and peasants to be the mainstay of his latest revolution, but had to fall back on youngsters and teenagers (with the army in the background as the ultimate support) to browbeat the dissidents and to carry out a vast purge in all walks of life.

Moreover, the Party and government apparatus were under considerable control of the very people against whom Mao was aiming his shots—Liu Shao-ch'i, Teng Hsiao-p'ing and others. Mao had himself passed over direct control of the Party to them; he had earlier named Liu as his successor, and the rise of Teng as Secretary-General had his approval, if it was not on his initiative. It would but be natural that over the years these people tightened their grip over the Party and administrative machinery and placed their trusted men in various strategic positions in the Party and the administration. These people might not have thought of chal-

[46]*New China News Agency*, Peking, 12 October 1966.

lenging Mao's authority, but faced with a threat to their own positions and apprehending a collapse of the entire establishment, they had no choice but to give battle. Mao could not depend on them for the realization of his goals. For that he needed a different instrument. The army's loyalty had largely been ensured, but, in the nature of things, Mao could not straightaway use the army and thus condemn his revolution from the start—thus the need for another political force and hence the Red Guards.

Spurred on by the Maoists, the Red Guards and "revolutionary" students went into battle and in July and August the country was already in a big tumult. They pledged eternal loyalty and unquestioning obedience to Mao and became his fierce and fearsome knight-errants. Already on 6 June a letter came, addressed to Mao and the Central Committee, from students of the "fourth class of the Senior Third grade" at Peking's No. 1 Girls' Middle School suggesting abolition of the old college entrance examination and its substitution by a new revolutionary system.[47] "Warm tears welled up" in the eyes of another group of students on reading this letter and within a little more than a month (12 July) another letter came suggesting shortening of the college term for the arts faculty, early graduation and assignment to take part in the "three great revolutionary movements of class struggle, the struggle for production and scientific experiment."[48] Knowing as these authors do from personal experience in China something about the real nature of such "spontaneous" acts and gestures, there could hardly be any doubt that these letters were written at the instance of mightier men in Peking. In any case, the schools and universities were closed indefinitely, pending reorganization of the system, so that the students could plunge themselves into the storm of the cultural revolution. Significantly, however, the reforms suggested were for the arts faculties and not for the sciences, and the science students were not drawn into the tumult to the same degree.

The youngsters were thus thrown into action. They were reminded of Mao's instructions that the youth were "one of the most active and vital forces in society," the "most anxious to learn," the "least conservative in their thinking."[49] Had not Mao said

[47]Text in *Peking Review*, 24 June 1966.
[48]Text in *Peking Review*, 22 July 1966.
[49]*Ibid.*

to them: "The world is ours, the country is ours, and society is ours. If we don't say so, who will? If we don't act, who will?" With this direct encouragement from Mao, the students spread their net far and wide. They went for the Party bosses in various institutions one after another. The first wall poster went up in Peking University in June denouncing the university's Party leadership and within days and weeks a veritable poster war developed in the schools and universities of China. Soon the struggle spread to other fields and units. In this general assault fell many presidents and vice-presidents and Party secretaries of universities and other educational institutions, famous litterateurs and historians, economists and theoreticians, novelists and dramatists, all generally high-ranking Party functionaries who had hitherto ruled the roost in their own institutions and units. People were freely dragged out, insulted publicly and beaten up. Homes were broken into and despoiled and household goods and properties exposed to public view. Even Madame Sun Yat-sen's house was not spared. There were also cases, admitted by Chou-En-lai,[50] of Red Guards appropriating watches and other valuables of the houses broken into in the name of the cultural revolution.

It was not surprising that the powerful and entrenched authorities should resist this onslaught and fight back. Many of them were not even aware initially that there were more powerful forces behind this assault. They regarded the rebellious students as counter-revolutionary and their revolt against them as a revolt against the Party. Inevitably, there were bitter clashes. The authorities sought to suppress them and reacted strongly against the hostile posters. But the cover support from the real initiators in Peking was soon made clear. *Jen-min Jih-pao*, while welcoming the action of the "revolutionary students and staff and faculty members" of Nanking University in "dragging out" the "anti-Party, antisocialist counter-revolutionary" Kuang Ya-ming, president of Nanking University and first secretary of the Party committee, gave the call to "freely mobilize the masses and completely defeat the sinister counter-revolutionary gangs,"[51] giving

[50]Speech to representatives of Red Guards on 1 September, *Current Background*, No. 819, p. 16.
[51]*Jen-min Jih-pao*, editorial, 16 June 1966.

blanket approval to the youngsters in pulling down the Party
bosses from their high pedestals and liquidating their authority
and power. These party bosses and their supporters were described as "royalists," a rather suspicious term which could only be
referring to their allegiance to higher and more influential bosses
in the Party.

At the same time it was emphatically emphasized that no suppression of "big character posters" would be allowed. These wall
posters had the support of Mao who regarded them as "an extremely useful new type of weapon." They were "magic mirrors"
to show up "monsters of all kinds" and with everybody putting
up such posters it was possible quickly to "reveal the true face of
the sinister anti-Party and antisocialist gangs."[52] It was acknowledged that "counter-revolutionary" posters were also being put
up but it was believed that these would help in catching the enemies
and settling accounts with them.

A fierce struggle was thus developing between "those in authority"
and the Maoist youthful supporters which continued to snowball
throughout the year, but with the help of the Red Guards and the
background shadow of the army, Mao was already by August in
a dominant position, had come back to Peking from Shanghai and
was able to push his line through the Party's Central Committee
which met in early August for a marathon session lasting twelve
days. By then, Liu Shao-ch'i and all the other dissidents had practically lost the battle. Although unable to challenge Mao directly,
they took devious measures to protect themselves and fight off the
attack on them. The Central Committee rubber-stamped the
measures that Mao had already taken; it also attempted to lay down
some guidelines for the "revolutionary rebels" in conducting the
cultural revolution and the meeting was also significant for the
changes that had taken place in the hierarchical structure of the top
leadership of the Chinese Communist Party.

THE AUGUST CENTRAL COMMITTEE MEETING

With Mao Tse-tung himself in the chair, the Central Committee
went into a prolonged huddle on 8 August. The first thing about
it that needs to be noticed is the composition of this meeting.

[52]*Ibid.*, 20 June 1966.

Participating in the meeting were not only regular members and alternate members and Party leaders from regional bureaus and from provincial, municipal, and autonomous Party committees as well as members of the cultural revolution group of the Central Committee but also, most unusual, "representatives of revolutionary teachers and students from institutions of higher learning in Peking." It was in fact a packed meeting in order to ensure a big majority for Mao. In an unparalleled act in Communist history, Mao invited Red Guards to a meeting of the Central Committee and the dice was loaded against any possible dissenters. That he was compelled to adopt this most extraordinary procedure provides the clearest evidence that Mao's majority in the top echelons of the Party was not secure and comfortable.

This eleventh plenary session of the Eighth Central Committee issued a communique on 12 August which formally proclaimed Mao as the "greatest Marxist-Leninist of our era" and the intensive study of Mao's works by the whole Party and the whole nation as being "an important event of historic significance." It also officially condemned the Soviet leadership as deserters and renegades to the cause of socialism and of the "oppressed peoples" of the world and declared China's determination to wage an uncompromising struggle against the Soviets.[53] Earlier, on 8 August, the Committee passed the "Decision of the Central Committee of the Chinese, Communist Party concerning the Great Proletarian Cultural Revolution." The decision outlined the objectives of the revolution and also laid down a 16-point guideline for the future course of the cultural revolution.

The decision made it clear that the current objective was "to struggle against and crush those persons in authority who are taking the capitalist road, to criticize and repudiate the reactionary bourgeois academic 'authorities' and the ideology of the bourgeoisie and all other exploiting classes and to transform education, literature and art and all other parts of the superstructure that do not correspond to the socialist economic base, so as to facilitate the consolidation and development of the socialist system."[54]

It was emphatically declared that the "anti-Party, anti-socialist Rightists must be fully exposed, hit, pulled down and completely

[53]English text of the Communique in *Peking Review*, 19 August 1966.
[54]English text in *Peking Review*, 12 August 1966.

discredited and their influence eliminated." They should, however, be "given a way out so that they could turn a new leaf" (by completly obeying the Maoist instructions). That the new political groups that had sprung up with the blessings of Mao were intended to practically supplant the Party organizations was evident from the declaration of the Central Committee that the cultural revolutionary groups, committees, and congresses were "organs of power of the proletarian cultural revolution." Thus, power was formally invested in these groups almost parallel to the Party organization. They were "excellent new forms of organization" whereby under the leadership of the Communist Party meaning really only the Party centre which had now passed under the control of the Maoists, "the masses are educating themselves." They should not be temporary organizations but permanent, standing mass organizations and were suitable not only for schools, colleges, and government organizations but also for "factories, mines, other enterprises, urban districts and villages." The authority of the Party organizations was thus whittled down, for they had to bow before the new instruments of Maoist revolution.

The Maoist-dominated Central Committee meeting called upon the people to organize criticism of "typical bourgeois representatives who have wormed their way into the Party" and "typical reactionary bourgeois academic authorities." Again, significantly, the leadership instructed that the scientists and technicians be left alone as far as possible. For scientists, technicians, and ordinary members of the working staff, the decision was that "as long as they are patriotic, work energetically, are not against the Party and socialism, and maintain no illicit relations with any foreign country, we should in the present movement continue to apply the policy of 'unity, criticism, unity,'" and that "special care should be taken of those scientists and scientific technical personnel who have made contributions."

While giving the call for ruthless struggle against "those in authority taking the capitalist road," the decision made a distinction between four categories of leaders and cadres. There were some Party leaders who were swimming with the tide and were "good pupils of Mao," fully associating themselves with the revolution. They were acceptable and should be kept in their positions. There were some who had a very "poor understanding" of their duties in the cultural revolution and were neither conscientious nor effective. Then there were some others who had made "mistakes of one kind or another," and who were apparently possessed by fear of what was taking place. However, both these groups were not beyond redemption provided they made "serious self-criticism" and accepted the "criticism of the masses." But then, there were others "who had wormed their way into the Party" and were taking "the capitalist road." They were the targets of the current struggle. They were resorting to various "tactics" to "turn black into white" and to "lead the movement astray." They resorted to "intrigues," "stabbing people in the back," and "spreading rumours with the purpose of attacking the revolutionaries." The Central Committee "demanded" of Party committees at all levels to give "correct leadership," "boldly arouse the masses" to encourage those who had made mistakes to shed their fear and join the struggle and to dismiss from their leading posts "all those in authority who are taking the capitalist road," and so make possible the recapture of the leadership by the proletarian revolutionaries.[55]

The Maoist leadership showed some concern at the clashes that were taking place and, while declaring that it was "absolutely impermissible" to deliver blows on "revolutionary activists" and to incite the masses to struggle against each other, it also advised the "revolutionary activists to conduct the struggle through persuasion and not force, and to distinguish between the anti-Party, anti-socialist Rightists" and those "who support the Party and socialism but have said or done something wrong or have written some bad articles or other works." The Central Committee resolution said that the method to be used in debates was to "present the facts, reason things out, and persuade through reasoning" and that the minority should be protected, for "sometimes the truth is with the minority" (as was the case even now when the Maoists were clearly in a minority!). The "revolutionary activists" were also advised not to punish those poor scholars with "ordinary bourgeois academic ideas" along with the reactionary bourgeois scholar despots and "authorities."[56] Mao wanted the blows to be concentrated on Party authorities and famous personages in the academic

[55] *Ibid.*
[56] *Ibid.*

fields for having shown a certain tolerance towards competent scholars, even though ideologically somewhat backward, and for having produced works which showed some concern for artistic standards at the expense of complete subservience to Mao's doc-trine on art and literature. Once they had been taken care of, the lesser scholars and artists, who did not show sufficient obedience to Mao's line, would immediately crawl back into their lairs and shout fulsome praise for Mao's doctrine in order to save their skins.

CHANGES IN THE POWER STRUCTURE AT PEKING

One of the most important results of the Central Committee meet-ing was that it signified the breakdown of the old power equation and its substitution by a new one. It signified the unmistakable fall of Liu Shao-ch'i and the rise of Lin Piao. It indicated a major shake-up at the summit, a developing purge at the top, and the rise of new stars on the political firmament. This became evident immediately after the meeting. There is indirect evidence to suggest that Liu Shao-ch'i was taken to task in the meeting for following a "bourgeois" line and opposing Mao Tse-tung and that Mao Tse-tung practically, if not formally, named Lin Piao as his successor. The Central Committee was followed by mammoth mass demonstrations one after another in which the "great Leader, great Supreme Commander, great Chief Helmsman and great Teacher," Mao Tse-tung, gave *darshan* accompanied by other top leaders and his followers. The rostrum of names published officially indicated the shift that had taken place at the top.[57] Soon, Lin Piao became Mao's "close comrade-in-arms," to be singled out from others and mentioned along with Mao. Liu Shao-ch'i was dropped to the seventh place. Chou En-lai was ranked second (after Lin Piao) and recent events once again confirmed his amazing capacity to survive at the top. Equally notable was the rise of T'ao Chu, Ch'en Po-ta, and K'ang Sheng. T'ao Chu suddenly shot up to number three (Mao excluded) in the hierarchy. His rise and fall have been meteoric—and his fall was only a little

[57] See for instance, reports of mass demonstrations *Jen-min Jih-pao*, 19 August and 16 September 1966.

more mystifying than his rise. T'ao Chu, with his base in the Kwangtung province, rose into prominence and power during the great leap forward and besides being the Party boss of Kwangtung was appointed Chief of the Central-South Bureau of the Central Committees. He was brought to Peking around the time of the cultural revolution and, with the fall of P'eng Chen, Liu Shao-Ch'i, and Teng Hsiao-p'ing, he was promoted to the third place, apparently as a more loyal member of the Maoist group. But, within months, T'ao Chu was also removed and disgraced for the usual crime of opposing Mao and attempting to restore "capitalism" in China.

Ch'en Po-ta, with the fall of T'ao Chu occupied the third position in the galaxy below Mao. One of the closest confidants of Mao, Ch'en Po-ta had been Mao's ideological storm-trooper for years. It was he who wrote the most ferocious articles denouncing the "rightists" during 1957-58 and the Yugoslav "revisionists." The present writers personally heard Ch'en in 1957 at a meeting in Peking University arrogantly denouncing intellectuals, particularly the more famous among them like Feng Yu-lan, for their inadequate self-reformation. Ch'en is also believed to be Mao's ghost writer. Similarly, K'ang Sheng, also close to Mao, rose rapidly and became the fourth most important member of the top leadership after Mao. Both of them were also admitted into the Standing Committee of the Politbureau. The new hierarchical order below Mao was: Lin Piao, Chou En-lai, T'ao Chu (very soon eliminated), Ch'en Po-ta, Teng Hsiao-p'ing (also eliminated shortly afterwards), Kang Sheng, Liu Shao-ch'i (subsequently denounced as the "top person in authority taking the capitalist road"), Chu Teh, Li Fu-chun, Ch'en Yun (being there only for form's sake but otherwise under a cloud since his opposition to the extremist policies of the big leap), Tung Pi-wu, Ch'en Yi, Liu Po-ch'en, Ho Lung (also subsequently purged), Li Hsien-nien, T'an Chen-lin, Hsueh Hsiang-chien, Nieh Jung-chen, Yeh Chien-ying, Li Hsueh-feng, and Hsueh Fu-chih.

Another notable rise from the relative obscurity and anonymity of domestic life was that of Mao's wife, Chiang Ch'ing. Formerly an actress and Mao's fourth wife, Chiang Ch'ing after having retired into domestic obscurity suddenly came back into public view and became the *enfant terrible* of the proletarian cultural revolution, particularly in the field of art and literature.*   She came to be one of the most prominent members of the cultural revolution group of the Central Committee, of which T'ao Chu was the Chairman, replaced shortly afterwards by Ch'en Po-ta.   It was this group which now wielded effective power and directed the various cultural revolutionary groups and the Red Guards.   Chiang Ch'ing thundered against leading figures in literature, the drama and theatre, the movies and the opera, and gave a more and more left-wing twist to the proletarian cultural revolution and encouraged the Red Guards to go to the extremes and to catch hold of more and more leaders.   Many observers have commented on the jealousy between Chiang Ch'ing and Wang Kuang-mei, wife of Liu Shao-ch'i, who had held the limelight until then, and have ascribed much of the acrimony of Chiang Ch'ing's actions and utterances to feminine jealousy.   Chiang Ch'ing herself was reported to have told a Red Guard gathering that she had requested Wang Kuang-mei not to wear ornaments during a visit to Indonesia where she accompanied her husband, President of the People's Republic of China, on a State visit, but that Wang Kuang-mei had disregarded her advice and disgraced the fair name of Chinese Communism by wearing a pearl necklace in Djakarta. However, womanly jealousy is too easy and too simple an explanation to provide all the answers.   The more plausible explanation is that in a situation in which his chief lieutenants were falling by the wayside, found wanting in their loyalty to him, Mao did not trust many people. He could depend on the loyalty of his wife, and, therefore, pushed her to the forefront of the struggle to take charge, to keep Mao informed, and to see that his wishes were respected and his commands followed.

RED GUARDS ON THE RAMPAGE

The Central Committee resolution and other Maoist utterances paid lip-service to the role of the Party but quite clearly Mao had discarded the Party as his main instrument and was relying mainly on the Red Guards and other proletarian cultural revolutionary

*Chiang Ch'ing had become active in the early sixties in the struggle to reform and replace the classical Peking Opera with modern themes and instruments.

groups in the current struggle. In fact the struggle was directed against the leading lights of the Party at the centre and in the provinces, and Party leadership in other units of work, like art and literature, education, even athletics, and for that purpose he had created the new organizations which were controlled by the Maoists through the Central Committee's Cultural Revolution Committee. Even the Central Committee resolution had described them as "organs of power," and asked the Party leaders and committees to submit themselves to the criticism and supervision of the "masses" (which meant the Maoists in the cultural revolution groups). Although the Central Committee's decision on the cultural revolution injected a note of caution and appealed for conducting the struggle through methods of reason and argument and not of force, everything was done to incite the Red Guards to assault the citadels of power, to drag out leading Party figures in various units and publicly humiliate them. And this the Red Guards did with a vengeance.

Within days of the conclusion of the Central Committee meeting, the young Red Guards of Peking, "detachments of students," were out on the streets, destroying customs and beliefs, property and street signs and shop name-plates at will. They launched "a furious offensive to sweep away reactionary, decadent, bourgeois, and feudal influences, and all old ideas, culture, customs, and habits."[58] Beating drums and singing revolutionary songs, "holding aloft big portraits of Mao and quotations from Mao's works, they held street meetings, put up big character posters" and distributed leaflets in their attack against all the old ideas and habits of the exploiting classes. They changed street names, "tainted with feudalism, capitalism, or revisionism," removed shop signs and gave new names to streets, lanes, parks, and schools. They closed down "beauty parlours"[59] and came down heavily against odd hair styles and western-style dresses. Not to be left behind, the youngsters of Shanghai and Tientsin and other cities picked up the gauntlet and took to the streets. *New China News Agency* reported gleefully from Shanghai and Tientsin that the Red Guards were holding demonstrations from dawn to

[58]*Peking Review*, 2 September 1966.
[59]During their stay in China for three years (1956 to 1958), the present writers never saw a "beauty parlour."

dusk and "making a clean sweep of all the shop signs and the old customs and habits that reek of feudalism, capitalism, and revisionism."[60]

The objective of this war on the old and the ancient was made clear with the declaration that every family "should have three things and do away with four things." To have three things meant: a portrait of Mao on the wall, quotations from Mao's works on the walls, and Mao's books on the desk. The first of the four don'ts was that no family should keep an altar for the worship of gods or preserve ancestral tablets. Secondly, couplets and tablets propagating feudal superstitions should no longer find a place in any house. The third injunction was that no family should keep pictures or clay models of ancient and famous kings, emperors, generals, prime ministers, and beauties. And the fourth don't was that there should be no pictures in the house of oneself dressed in "bizarre clothes or posed in a low taste and vulgar fashion."[61] There were also cases reported of Red Guards desecrating graves, pulling down statues, and destroying old books and ancient works of art and decoration.

The Red Guards broke into people's houses to unearth "hidden wealth" and gold and ornaments. The Maoist leadership sent up three cheers for them for their meritorious acts. *Jen-min Jih-pao* in a "salute" to the Red Guards proudly called them the "shock force" of the cultural revolution that "makes bold frontal attacks." The sharp blade of their struggle, it said, was "mowing down all resistance." The Red Guards were "pulling out these bloodsuckers, these enemies of the people one by one" and their "concealed gold, silver, valuables and other treasures are being taken out and put on exhibition, and their various kinds of murderous weapons are being put on public show by the Red Guards."[62]

More seriously, the Red Guards made a general assault on the Party leadership in the educational institutions and attempted to carry the revolution to factories and villages and other units, struggling against the Party leadership there. They went to various places and various units and enterprises trying to stir up trouble

---

[60] *New China News Agency*, Peking, 24 August 1966.
[61] *Yang-ch'eng Wan-pao*, Canton, 31 August 1966.
[62] *Jen-min Jih-pao*, editorials, 26 and 29 August 1966.

and activate those places. Inevitably, they met with resistance, the Party leaders hit back at this challenge to their authority. The workers also resented the interference of the teenagers and refused to acknowledge their authority to tell them what to do and what not to do. At many places the workers beat back the students and blood was shed profusely in some places. The Party leaders in the educational institutions and various other units raised the slogan of "defend the Party" and rallied support from loyal followers. They said that an attack on the Party branch was an attack on the Party itself and they dubbed the trouble-making students as "anti-Party counter-revolutionaries." The clashes that took place on an ever wider scale caused concern in the Maoist headquarters at Peking and their propaganda organs issued sharp warnings to all those who were resisting their youthful storm-troopers. *Jen-min Jih-pao*, for instance, directed that the Party organizations of every locality and unit must accept "mass supervision and criticism" and must not reject or suppress criticism. It certainly was not allowed to brand their critics as "counter-revolutionaries," for after all if a Party organization went against the Central Committee headed by Mao, why should it not be criticized and opposed?[63]

The Maoists affirmed the right of the "revolutionary students" to rise up and "make revolution and oppose the overlords"; they had the right to parade and demonstrate on the streets, the right to assemble and form associations and the right of speech and publication (a right which had hitherto been denied and was now being extended only to enable the students to struggle against Mao's targets). They complained that those in authority who were taking the capitalist road were trying to "shift the targets for attack," inciting students to struggle against each other, and that they had even "stirred up a few workers and peasants to struggle against the students." They appealed to the workers and peasants not to listen to "the nonsense of these overlords" but to take a firm stand in support of the students. The revolutionary students might have "certain shortcomings," it was acknowledged, but their "general direction" was correct and, therefore, they must be whole-heartedly supported. The workers, peasants, and PLA men were also advised not to go to schools and universities to take

[63]*Ibid.*, 13 August 1966.

part in debates, for they might not know the actual situation there.[64]

Typically, the Maoists soon began to claim that the nation was responding to their call to support the Red Guards.[65] Armymen were reported pledging themselves to learn from the Red Guards,[66] and all other sections of the people were enthusiastically admiring the actions of the Red Guards.

Some observers of the Chinese scene have claimed that Mao was taking the country towards direct democracy, appealing to the people over the heads of leaders and throwing the whole issue into the lap of the masses. The Maoist pronouncements in this regard have rendered this claim completely indefensible. As the Red Guards of the Middle School attached to the Tsinghua University said in a poster:

> Bourgeois Rightist Gentlemen, we rebels have leadership, weapons, organization, "ambition," and powerful backing. We are not to be taken lightly.... You find it hard to bear and you too want to "rebel".... No wonder there has been this recent queer phenomenon of both the Left and Right shouting "rebel" in unison.... Let us tell you frankly that the eyes of a fish cannot be confused with pearls. We are permitting only the Left to rebel, not the Right ! If you dare to rebel we will immediately suppress you ! This is our logic. After all, the State machine is in our hands.[67]

This attitude was reaffirmed many a time in public pronouncements and the bourgeois reactionary concept of freedom for all was duly denounced. There could be freedom only for those who obeyed Mao. T'ao Chu, while he had not yet fallen out of grace, also made it clear in a speech in Peking that Mao Tse-tung and Lin Piao were not subject to criticism—all the others could be condemned.[68]

[64] *Ibid.*
[65] "In China of the Red Guards," *Hung-ch'i*, No. 12, 1966.
[66] *New China News Agency*, Peking, 4 September 1966.
[67] Reproduced in *Peking Review*, 16 September 1966.
[68] T'ao Chu's talk to the Propaganda Department of the CCP Control Committee on 25 August 1966, *Current Background*, No, 819, 10 March 1967, p. 13.

The enthusiasm of the Red Guards was also raised to a frenzied pitch through the public appearance of Mao. First on 18 August and then on 15 September, Mao came out on the T'ien An Men square in Peking to be seen by shouting, screaming, chanting students going wild with joy and enthusiasm. Each time there were a million people present—"a vast sea of people and a forest of red flags."[69] Each time Lin Piao and Chou En-lai spoke to the mammoth gatherings. The difference in tone and emphasis in the speeches of the two leaders has been generally noted. Lin Piao made hard-hitting, uncompromising speeches and gave militant calls, while Chou En-lai appeared to show concern for the disorder that was being created and for its impact on production, appealing to the Red Guards to take organized action and to spur production. In his 18 August speech, Lin Piao thundered against the dissidents and declared that the Maoists "will strike down those in authority who are taking the capitalist road, strike down the reactionary bourgeois authorities, strike down all bourgeois royalists, oppose any act to suppress revolution, and strike down all ghosts and monsters." He served notice that the cultural revolution was a "long-term task" in between which there would be "big campaigns" and "small campaigns" and would last a very long time and called upon the Red Guards to "thoroughly topple, smash, and discredit the counter-revolutionary revisionists, bourgeois Rightists, and reactionary bourgeois authorities and they must never be allowed to rise again."[70]

Chou En-lai, in his speech that followed, stressed the 16-point decision of the Central Committee "adopted under the personal leadership of Mao" and asked the revolutionaries to "set themselves firmly against monopolizing things which should be done by the masses themselves, against acting as high and mighty bureaucrats, standing above the masses and blindly ordering them about."[71] The 15 September rally was also attended by representatives of the revolutionary students from north, southeast, east, and central-south China. Lin Piao in his speech at this huge demonstration congratulated the Red Guards for "creating consternation"

[69] *Jen-min Jih-pao*, 19 August and 16 September 1966.
[70] *Jen-min Jih-pao*, 19 August 1966; English text in *Peking Review*, 26 August 1966.
[71] *Ibid.*

among the victims of the cultural revolution and among bloodsuckers and parasites, and once again he declared emphatically that they would not tolerate the reactionary bourgeois element, trying to "bombard our headquarters of the proletarian revolution" and must "smash" their plots. But he admitted that "some people" were going against Mao's instructions and "creating antagonism between the masses of workers and peasants and the revolutionary students and inciting the former to struggle against the latter." On the other hand, Chou En-lai in his speech talked about the third Five-Year Plan (which began officially in 1966) and about Mao's call to take a firm hold of the revolution on the one hand and of production on the other. He appealed to the "masses of workers, commune members, and technical personnel and functionaries of Party, of government and public organizations and enterprises" to remain at their posts and promote production. He also advised the Red Guards not to go to factories and communes for "establishing revolutionary ties" and to let the revolution take its own course there.[72]

The note of caution sounded by Chou has led many observers to conclude that Chou represents the moderate view within the surviving top leadership. No doubt Chou's influence seems to have been exercised on the side of moderation and a healthy concern for keeping the production lines open. It should, however, be recognized that Chou's capacity to act independently is extremely limited. His record shows that he generally sided with the Left within the Party but that does not necessarily mean that his head and heart are with the extreme Left this time too. But Chou has never been an independent force in the Party; like Mikoyan, his survival at the top through all the vicissitudes and fluctuations of fortune among the leadership has depended on his ability to swim with the current. His subservience to Mao is complete and he even paid public homage to Lin Piao, indicating that he accepted Lin's leadership. Whatever brakes he has applied to the galloping horse of the cultural revolution, he has done so with Mao's approval. He has so far been trusted by Mao because he did not pose a threat to the Maoist leadership, nor did he stand in its way in the pursuance of its policies. On the other hand, he is a remarkable diplomat, an able and useful technician in the execution of

[72]*Ibid.*

Maoist policies and has displayed extraordinary administrative skill and resilience and flexibility of mind, a prodigious memory, and a high degree of capacity for hard work. Chou En-lai may not be a weather cock but he certainly is a good barometer of the mood and temper in Peking. It is another matter that when Mao is gone and the struggle for succession brings about new alignments, Chou En-lai might switch allegiance and try for the top position if backed up by powerful forces within the Party who might be lacking an eminent and acceptable spokesman of their own.

The Red Guards had been given the green signal by Mao to revolt against the established authority and to spare only those who were considered their own men by the Maoists. Many of their actions had been directly instigated by Mao and his confederates. Between June and September they caught many a big fish and their net haul was impressive as well as frightening. Apart from P'eng Chen and his deputies, and Chou Yang and Lu Ting-i, who fell early in the present upheaval, those who were denounced and dismissed included the president and first secretary of the Communist Party branch of the Peking University, the president and first secretary of the Party branch of Nanking University, of Cheng Chow University, president of Wuhan University, and Li Ta, a veteran Communist, in the educational field. The axe also fell heavily on propaganda commissars who had been found wanting in pushing the indoctrination of the people in Mao's thought and who had protected many rightists, including Ch'en Ch'i-t'ung, deputy director of the Cultural Section of the General Political Department of the PLA in charge of cultural work in the army, Lin Mo-han, Vice Minister for Culture and deputy director of the Propaganda Department of the CCP Central Committee, and Tseng Tun, director of the Propaganda Department of CCP Hupeh Provincial Committee, and Sung Yu-hsi, director of the Propaganda Department of the CCP Honan Provincial Committee; such eminent Communist economists as Sun Yeh-fang, Communist historians like Chien po-tsan and dramatists like T'ien Han. Indeed, practically the entire range of artistic and literary works, movies and plays and the opera produced during the early sixties except those sponsored by the PLA and its artists was declared to be "revisionist," objectionable, and "big poisonous weeds."[73]

[73]*Jen-min Jih-pao, Kuang-ming Jih-pao, Chung-kuo Ch'ing-nien Pao,* and

THE DEIFICATION OF MAO

The proletarian cultural revolution was accompanied by the exalta-tion of Mao to new heights. The study of Mao's works, learning and remembering them by heart and reproducing quotations from them at a moment's notice became one of the social verities of con-temporary China. From the highest to the lowest, from the top to the bottom, from Lin Piao and Chou En-lai to the ordinary peasant, worker and student, everyone carried Mao's works in his pockets and was required to be able to reproduce the best-known quotations from them. A separate booklet of quotations from Mao was printed and sold in millions. *Jen-min Jih-pao* hailed the "revolutionary measures" adopted to print within a year thirty-five million volumes of *Selected Works of Mao Tse-tung* and a large number of *Selected Readings of Mao Tse-tung's Works*—a record for any book in history.[74] The Peking National Library set aside a "spacious and well-lighted hall" for displaying Mao's works in Chinese and foreign languages. This example was soon followed by other places. Mao's sayings became commandments and in any situation a quotation from him supplied the answer. Indeed, like *mantras* his sayings were chanted in groups with the refrain taken from one person to another.[75] One person would recite a line and the second would take up the refrain and chant a second line, followed by the third person with the third line, and so on.

To quote from Mao all the time and in all the talks and articles, even by the leaders, became the current vogue. To take one instance, out of a total of nineteen paragraphs in a speech of Kuo Mo-jo at a Peking rally in support of American Negroes, eight paragraphs started with quotations from Mao.[76] It even became the current

---

Hung-ch'i for this period may be consulted for the details of these denuncia-tions. The points made against such eminent Communist functionaries and and their implications will be considered in greater detail in the next chapter.

[74]"A Big Joyful Event for the People of the Whole Country," *Jen-min Jih-pao*, editorial, 7 August 1966.

[75]See, for instance, a report entitled "The Sunlight of Mao Tse-tung's Thought Illuminates Peking," *Peking Review*, 30 September 1966.

[76]See the text of the speech in *Peking Review*, 12 August 1966.

fashion to quote from Mao in diplomatic *demarches* and official statements on various international issues. Every conceivable achievement in any field, including the international win in ping-pong, was ascribed to the thought of Mao Tse-tung. Whether it was the nuclear bang or a fire put out in a factory with courage and heroism, the inspiration of it all was said to have come from the thought of Mao Tse-tung. And everybody was being indoctrinated into the belief (how seriously they took it one does not know) that it was all for world revolution. An armyman who had been assigned the task of duck-raising first thought that it was too lowly a job but suddenly realized and took comfort in the belief that he was doing it for world revolution. The ducks that he raised thereafter with this consciousness were "big and fat."[77]

Mao became the "reddest of the red sun" in the hearts of the people and his pictures (not the real photographs) glowed with a slight halo. Thinking of him people were reportedly driven to acts of supreme courage. Patients, even tubercular ones, looking at his picture drew succour and determination and got well. A woman who had the rare fortune of shaking hands with Mao in one of the mammoth gatherings at Peking to celebrate the "great proletarian cultural revolution" went wild with joy and with tears profusely running down her cheeks, refusing to wash her smutty hands, she shook hands with her children and all the inmates of her household. The boys and girls, particularly, thought of nothing else except of Mao Tse-tung and his instructions. They swore eternal allegiance to him and pledged themselves to hold aloft the banner of his thought and his policies for a thousand years.

It was also around this time that the Chinese announced that Mao Tse-tung, "the most respected and beloved leader of the Chinese people," had a good swim in the Yangtse River on 16 July. Why Peking took nearly a month to announce Mao's feat is mystifying. Mao was reportedly in the water for sixty-five minutes and covered a distance of fifteen kilometers downstream.[78] The Chinese propaganda apparently showed no embarrassment in making a claim which was a near physical impossibility for a man above seventy, and one who was known to be suffering from gout; but, perhaps the news was meant more for home consumption than for

[77]*Hung Wei-pao*, 20 October 1966.
[78]See the report in *Peking Review*, 12 August 1966.

international circulation. As was to be expected, the Chinese propaganda machine immediately went into action and the "good news" spread through the country and was reportedly greeted with "unprecedented enthusiasm." People expressed their "heart-felt wish for a long, long life for their most venerated and beloved leader," and "their determination to follow forever the revolutionary road charted out by Chairman Mao."[79] One of the aims of the rallies being organized in Peking was also to create a psychological atmosphere for driving an artificially created enthusiasm of the Red Guards to a feverish pitch and to promote the deification of Mao. Ironically, however, it seems, *Jen-min Jih-pao* claimed while narrating the virtues of Mao that he was "most modest"! He was "best at learning from the masses, summing up their experience and bringing together their wisdom."[80]

THE AUTUMN PAUSE

The developing clashes between Mao's teenage army and the workers and peasants as well as Party functionaries and their supporters have been noted above. This conflict was causing some worry in the Maoist headquarters. But a far more important cause for worrying was the approaching autumn farming season. If those clashes developed into a widespread conflict, agricultural production would be seriously affected and factory production would also feel its impact. With the experience of the disastrous setbacks resulting from the big leap still fresh, even the Maoist leadership could not take chances and allow the cultural revolution to seriously interfere with production. Rice was still more important than ideology. The first call was given by *Jen-min Jih-pao* to take "firm hold" of the revolution in order to stimulate production. The material front could not be headed by "leading cadres of all factories, mining enterprises, people's communes, and units of capital construction and scientific research." They were asked to practise division of work and establish two groups, one for promoting the cultural revolution and the other production, while giving overall leadership to both. The autumn harvest was drawing

---

[79] *Ibid.*
[80] *Jen-min Jih-pao*, editorial, 20 August 1966.

near and the farming season must on no account be missed. All efforts should be concentrated on it and if necessary the political-ideological struggle might be suspended in order to make a good job of the autumn farming season.[81]

Jen-min Jih-pao followed this, a week later, with another emphatic assertion that "production must not be interrupted." The Red Guards from schools and universities were now told that it was "not necessary" for them to go to factories and rural areas and the rural areas were once again advised that the cultural revolution might be suspended there during the busy farming season. The workers and peasants were also told that they could not emulate the student Red Guards and go to other places to exchange revolutionary experience." There were no vacations for them for this purpose. They must stick to their posts of production.[82] The same day Chou En-lai had issued a similar call at the mass rally of the Red Guards.[83] He had also instructed the Red Guards "not to go to the factories and enterprises and to Party, government, and public organizations of county level and below, and people's communes in rural areas." The revolution there was to proceed in a "planned and systematic manner in accordance with the original arrangements for the 'four clean-up' movement."

The requirements of the autumn harvest season and of industrial production apart, Peking also had to contend with the germs of civil disturbances, with Red Guards clashing on an ever wider scale with not only party functionaries but also their supporters. Enjoying their licence, the Red Guards were freely attacking all and sundry, posing the threat of a general conflagration. The Maoist objective in the so-called cultural revolution was to purge the Party of all those in leading positions at various levels who had shown the slightest reservation with regard to Maoist policies and doctrines—without, if possible, leading to a conflict of mass proportions. But it was just such a conflict that the situation was leading to. They, therefore, had the contradictory task of keeping the enthusiasm of the teenage Red Guards undampened without precipitating a mass conflict.

The problem that the Maoist leadership faced was threefold.

[81]*Jen-min Jih-pao*, editorial, 7 September 1966.
[82]*Ibid.*, 15 September 1966.
[83]See fn. 70.

The Red Guards were coming into collision with the party machinery generally in all the big cities and towns of China. Even more grave, from the point of view of Peking, was the growing hostility between workers and peasants on the one hand and student Red Guards on the other—and at many places the workers had beaten up the students. Worse still was the antagonism between different groups of Red Guards which was already creating serious difficulties for the leaders. Each Red Guard group considered itself superior to others and was somewhat contemptuous of the other's ideological purity and fighting capacity. Chou En-lai himself acknowledged in a talk to the Red Guards that this was causing the greatest disquiet among the Maoist leadership.[84]

Instructions and advice from the Maoist headquarters was that the struggle should be continued and that the Red Guards must not allow themselves to be deflected into a self-stultifying conflict among the masses themselves. The main orientation was to attack and drag out those in leading positions in the Party and government and in other units and institutions whose subservience to Mao and his policies had not been proved beyond doubt, and some of whom had even demurred at some of these policies. The youthful storm-troopers of Mao should not go astray and should concentrate their forces against the fourth category of cadres mentioned in the 16-point decision of the Maoist-dominated Central Committee meeting, that is all those "counter-revolutionary revisionists" who were against Mao's thought and were occupying leading positions in the Party and the State.[85]

At the same time the masses must not start fighting among themselves: those ordinary cadres who had "some shortcomings" should not be made the main target of attack. They should be "persuaded" and "educated" and the methods employed in this regard should not be simple and crude. They were not the principal enemies, and Mao's dictum about distinguishing between enemies and friends must be faithfully observed. Additionally, among the masses there would be differing views about various matters concerning

[84]Speech by Chou En-lai on 10 September at an oath-taking rally of those going out to establish revolutionary ties, *Current Background*, No. 819, 10 March 1967.

[85]"Hold Fast to the Main Orientation in the Struggle," *Hung-ch'i*, editorial, No. 12, 1966.

the cultural revolution. These should not be handled as if they were the views of the antagonists. They should be appropriately resolved through reasoning and argument. It was "impermissible" to use any pretext to attack "revolutionary activists" or to "incite the masses to struggle against the masses."[86]

REVOLUTION CONTINUES IN SCHOOLS AND PARTY ORGANIZATIONS

Despite the autumn pause and the attempt to isolate the factories and industrial enterprises from the interference of the Red Guards and the exhortation to prevent civil strife among the masses themselves, the cultural revolution continued in schools and universities and Party organizations, and, as the autumn harvesting season drew to a close, the flames of the cultural revolution burst into a conflagration in December and January.

In order to keep the frenzy of the student Red Guards at its feverish pitch and to keep them busy, they were encouraged to a long march in the far-flung territories of China to "exchange revolutionary experience" and to establish "revolutionary ties." Thousands of students trekked across the plains and mountains of China into Peking, Canton, Shanghai, Tientsin, and other cities. They were following the tradition of the Long March and toughening themselves in order to become worthy soldiers of Mao. The pioneers in this regard were fifteen students of the Dairen Mercantile Marine Institute, who were said to have covered a distance of 1,000 kilometers on foot within a month. They were immediately lionized, and the leaders expressed the hope that other students would follow their example.[87] Their feat caught on and "with the support of Mao" thousands of students were soon following in their footsteps. During their long march it was their task to contact the masses and give them the message of Mao and propagate Mao's thought: they recited Mao's sayings and told stories about the earlier Long March of Mao. Many of them poured into Peking and were often received by high-ranking leaders.[88]

---

[86] *Ibid.*

[87] *Jen-min Jih-pao*, editorial, 22 October 1966.

[88] For instance, on 15 September, Chou En-lai, T'ao Chu, Ch'en Po-ta, Li Fu-chun, and other leaders received over thirty long march detachments

Similarly, students from Peking were sent out to other areas to stir the embers of the cultural revolution, although they were still required to avoid factories and enterprises and not to try to interfere with arrangements about the cultural revolution in the communes. Generally speaking, the students went only to big cities and towns. There was a definite attempt by the Maoist headquarters to plan these trips of the students and to keep some control over their activities, and they were still discussing what to do about small towns and *hsien* and communes. The Red Guard units had PLA instructors to guide and direct them and they were asked to carry out the instructions of their PLA instructors. Many of those who had gone out from Peking were middle school students. Chou En-lai in his 10 September speech to the Red Guards gave some break-up of the members being sent out. Nearly 2,000 went to Shanghai. Chou admitted that the situation in Shanghai was highly complex and confusing and wanted the Red Guards going there to be very careful. He could not say which group there was better than the others—the Red Guards would have to investigate it for themselves.

About 400 student Red Guards were sent to Sinkiang—one of the most sensitive and strategic areas of China. Chou En-lai wanted those who were going there to be particularly vigilant. Under no circumstances must they go to frontier posts or cities and towns on the frontier. That was the season for the ripening of grapes and melons and while they may not be impolite in refusing all offers, they should not eat too much either! Another batch of eighty was going to the northwest—the craddle of China's civilization. Chou described the struggle there as "very violent," with "different views" among the people and even among the Red Guards, and advised the Red Guards going there to "investigate the situation calmly." Still another group of 350 Red Guard students were being despatched to the central-south, 250 to the southwest, and 350 to the northeast.[89] Thus there was a certain method in the madness that seemed to be engulfing China.

---

organized by more than 430 revolutionary students and teachers and Red Guards who had walked all the way from their home towns in Liaoning, Anhwei, Shantung, Hopei, Shansi, Honan, and Inner Mongolia, see *Peking Review*, 25 November 1966.

[89]See fn. 84.

FURTHER MAOIZATION OF THE ARMY

The army was generally under the control of the Maoists, but all was still not well with it. Although the open adherents of P'eng Teh-huai and Lo Jui-ch'ing had already been purged, the old problems raised by these top army men continued to trouble the functioning of the army and the Maoist control over it. As Air Force Commissar Yu Lin-chin admitted at a mass rally of 11,000 officers and men of the Air Force in late October, that there were "many weak links" in the Maoization of the army, and the Air Force was "still lagging far behind" other units of the armed forces in the study and absorption of Mao's works and prescriptions.[90] So, in order to step up Maoization (as if the saturation point had not already been reached), Lin Piao issued a new directive to the army calling upon it to intensify the mass drive for the "creative study and application" of Mao's works. These "extremely important" instructions were first communicated through General Hsiao Hua, now the director of the General Political Department of the PLA, to a meeting of officers of the Air Force.[91]

Lin Piao was quoted as saying:

Mao Tse-tung's thought is the science of revolution. It is the proletarian truth which has stood the test of prolonged revolutionary struggles. It is Marxism-Leninism closest to the present-day reality. It is a programme for united action by the whole party, the whole army and the entire army. The whole party, the whole army, and the people of the whole country must be imbued with Mao Tse-tung's thought and our thinking must be unified with it.

Those people who were armed with Mao Tse-tung's thought were "the most courageous, the most intelligent, and the most revolutionary." The armed forces "equipped with Mao Tse-tung's thought" would be "ever victorious" and "invincible."[92]

The theme was immediately taken up by the Army daily, *Chieh-fang Chun-pao*, and *Jen-min Jih-pao* and other propaganda

[90]Peking Radio, 25 October 1966.
[91]*New China News Agency*, Peking, 9 October 1966.
[92]*Ibid.*

organs. The Army daily warned that there must be no complacency and that the army must forge ahead in further indoctrination of Mao's ideology.[93] Meetings and rallies, attended by top officers as well as by the ordinary soldiers, were held throughout the armed forces units and political commissars and army officers went to naval vessels, air fields, army warehouses, army hospitals, and frontier outposts to explain Lin Piao's instructions and to intensify the Mao-study campaign.[94] At the same time, Lin Piao also sought to further entrench his position and strengthen his hold over the army. Side by side the deification of Mao, there was also high praise for Lin Piao in the propaganda in the army. He was Mao's "closest comrade-in-arms," his "best student," and the "best example in creatively studying and applying Chairman Mao's works." All the army men "must learn from Comrade Lin Piao."[95] This intensification in the indoctrination of the army took place while the country was being placed further and further under the direction of the army and the Red Guard organizations were being passed under the control of the army which itself was being directly guided from Maoist headquarters.

FURTHER DEIFICATION OF MAO

There was another spurt in the idolization of Mao which was carried to new heights. There seemed to be no limit to which this deification could be taken. Thousands of young Red Guards streamed into Shaoshan, the birth-place of Mao, to pay homage and derive inspiration. They left "refreshed and inspired" and were quoted as saying: "We have come to the place from which the sun arose to shine for the people all over China."[96] New acts of valour in the name of Mao were related and broadcast throughout the country, particularly by model heroes of the PLA.[97]

Literally, to use the English phrase, "a song," was made of Mao's sayings. The words and music of nine new songs, eight of them

[93]*New China News Agency*, 11 October 1966.
[94]*Ibid.*
[95]*Peking Review*, 14 October 1966.
[96]*New China News Agency*, Ch'angsha, 23 November 1966.
[97]See, for instance, the report on model PLA hero, Tsai Yung-hsiang, *Peking Review*, 4 November 1966,

based on key quotations from Mao and one on Lin Piao's latest directive on Mao-study, were carried by the Army daily, *Chieh-fang Chun-pao*, and *Jen-min Jih-pao* simultaneously on 25 October.[98]

At the same time, more massive demonstrations were organized in Peking for Mao's review and for further pushing the idolization of Mao. For the sixth time on 3 November and again on 10 and 11 November, and still again on 25 and 26 November, Mao took his stand on the T'ien An Men rostrum to be seen by millions of Red Guards and others. Moved to frenzy, the Red Guards leapt with joy, waved their books of quotations in "boundless excitement," and shouted and screamed:

What is the reddest thing in the world? The sun on the T'ien An Men gate. Who is the dearest person in the world? The great leader Chairman Mao! What is the greatest happiness in the world? To see the great supreme commander Chairman Mao! What is the most glorious task in the world? To study, implement, propagate, and defend Mao Tse-tung's thought![99]

Also present at these mammoth rallies were thousands of students from other parts of China who had left their "small classrooms" to walk into the "big classroom" of society. *New China News Agency* reported that when the student Red Guards from various middle schools were leaving for Peking, their schoolmates and teachers pinned their own badges with portraits of Chairman Mao on their coats and asked them to take them to Peking and some even gave their own coats to be taken so that Chairman Mao might see them. "When we wear them again, we shall feel infinitely happy and be filled with boundless strength," they said.[100]

Lin Piao in his speech at the 3 November rally had a word of cheer for those travelling on foot to exchange revolutionary experience and wanted such foot-marches to be undertaken in a planned and organized way. "Chairman Mao was the greatest proletarian revolutionary," he said, and he was always with the masses and had set "the most glorious example" for all the Party members and for

[98] *New China News Agency*, 25 October 1966.
[99] See reports of the 3 November rally in *Jen-min Jih-pao*, 4 November, and *Peking Review*, 11 November 1966.
[100] *New China News Agency*, Peking, 21 October 1966.

the younger generation. He exulted over the recent successful guided-missile nuclear weapon test as a great victory for Mao Tse-tung's thought, and described the situation of the cultural revolution as "excellent." However, with the growing concern over the developing conflict among various sections of the population and among the Red Guards themselves at the back of his mind, he exhorted the Red Guards to be "good at mutual consultations, at listening to dissenting views, at presenting facts and reasoning things out" and at "uniting the great majority" in order to isolate the "handful of bourgeois rightists."[101]

Quite clearly the aim of the continuous idolization of Mao was to place him above reproach, to ensure unquestioned obedience to him, and to supplant all other ideas and ideologies by his ideas and his ideology in the minds of over seven hundred million Chinese. Putting in the mouths of the Red Chinese, a Hsinhua correspondent expressed this determination in this manner:

China today is a China that works energetically to achieve the complete ascendency of Mao Tse-tung's thought.

The world today is a world in which Mao Tse-tung's thought shines in all its splendour....

We shall turn heaven and earth into the realms of Mao Tse-tung's thought and arm all the people with it....

The sun is the brightest thing in the sky, but not as bright as Chairman Mao's writings. The sun can only shine on one's body whereas Chairman Mao's writings light up one's heart.[102]

Meanwhile, the student Red Guards, let loose by Mao, caught more "anti-Mao" and "anti-socialist" Party functionaries and Party litterateurs and academicians. They were joined in the foray by *Chieh-fang Chun-pao*, *Jen-min Jih-pao*, *Kuang-ming Jih-pao*, and other propaganda organs, and "revolutionary cadres" in the government and other units. The latest catch included Ch'en I-hsin, Vice-Governor of Hupeh and member of the Standing Committee of the CCP Hupeh Provincial Committee, Wang K'uang, K'uang Ya-ming, First Secretary of the Party Committee

[101]See fn. 99.
[102]*Peking Review*, 9 December 1966.

of Nanking University, Wei Tung-ming, Vice-President of the
University of Hunan, Hsia Yen, a prominent Communist figure on
the literary and film world of China, writer Wang Yuan-chien
(who was branded as Chou Yang's "faithful disciple" and whom
Chou Yang was reported to have praised as the "most successful
writer of rare accomplishment"), academician Hou Wei-lu, member
of the Committee of Department of the Academia Sinica, deputy
director of its Institute of Historical Studies and member of the
editorial board of *Historical Research*, Li-shih Yen-chiu, and many
others. A large number of well-known and not-so-well-known
figures were disgraced and dismissed. People were freely dragged
out of their homes and offices, made to wear dunces' caps on their
heads and paraded around in the streets with excited crowds of
young Red Guards shouting at them, abusing them, and even spit-
ting at them. Many were mercilessly beaten or subjected to other
indignities. There was no security of office or occupation, no sanctity
of home, no respect for human dignity. Indeed the Maoists had
made it crystal clear that the violation of the human dignity of
those who were held guilty of having opposed Mao and his thought
was a good thing, not to be regretted or criticized.[103]

By December 1966, the cultural revolution snowballed into a
huge struggle, a conflict of massive proportions between the various
groups involved. It was at that time that Mao's planning, which
had worked superbly until then, broke down and the situation got
out of hand. But before we consider the crucial developments of
December-January, it is time to pause and take stock of the issues
involved in the so-called cultural revolution so far as the Maoist
leadership and the victims of its purge were concerned.

[103]"Tear Aside the Bourgeois Mask of Liberty, Equality, and Fraternity,"
Jen-min Jih-pao, editorial, 4 June 1966.

CHAPTER THREE

ISSUES IN THE CULTURAL REVOLUTION

THE UNDERLYING FACTORS in the cultural revolution are many and are not so mysterious as a superficial reading of current news may give the impression. The issues are identifiable and cover a whole gamut of policies and attitudes. It is not just one problem or some differences of opinions here and there, but a set of differences, a basic divergence of opinion on the strategies and tactics to be adopted by China in her future development, an assessment of the mistakes of the past and the lessons to be learnt from them—a way of looking at things and judging and evaluating developments, and, above all, the familiar historical phenomenon of a dominant, ageing, capricious, and impatient leader demanding absolute and unquestioning obedience from his associates and followers. All these reasons, suspicions, clashing viewpoints and contradictory approaches have coalesced to give rise to the cultural revolution. The different strands can he picked up but they are not isolated, and they form one whole fabric. Mao's evolving cosmology, his view of himself and of his place in China and the world, of the direction which the future generations of China might take, of the attitude to be taken towards intellectuals, of the form and content of art and literature, of the press and other mass media of communication, of education and professional competence—all these have played a definite role in prompting Mao to unleash the cultural revolution. They are directly related to the developments of the past few years producing serious rifts within the Chinese leadership.

THE IMPACT OF THE FAILURE OF THE BIG LEAP AND ITS AFTERMATH

A constant refrain in the catalogue of accusations against the so-called "bourgeois rightists" in authority (that is, those holding positions in the Communist Party or in the administration) is that during the period of "temporary economic difficulties" in 1959-62, they denigrated the experiment of the big leap and the people's communes and criticized the assumptions behind it and the speed at which it was tried. Chinese propaganda, true to form, tries to portray a person once denounced and purged as having been a born rogue and a lifelong opportunist who had all along harboured *mala fide* intentions, and every possible crime is ascribed to him. This necessitates a certain caution in evaluating Peking's charges against those who have fallen from grace, but the policies of the big leap certainly came to be the subject of sharp and critical review in the period that followed the reverses caused by their adoption. The failure of the big leap caused heavy tremors and shocked many in the country.

Mao was the author of the philosophy of the big leap and although leaders of the eminence of Liu Shao-ch'i, P'eng Ch'en, and Teng Hsiao-p'ing were highly enthusiastic about it, its failure started a process of critical examination which reached up to the top echelons of the Party. The reverses were so agonizing, the setback so great that it led to serious questioning even within the Party. It was like a long, dark, starkly cold night and the shadows did not disappear for many years. It took China nearly five years to emerge out of it, during which period the country teetered on the brink of disaster and breakdown. There was widespread hunger and starvation. The privations the people endured were painful enough to shake even hardened Party leaders. The Vice-President of Hunan University, Wei Tung-ming, used poetical and allegoric words of the ancient poet Tu Fu to express their state of mind:[1]

Carefree and fond of wine, I hate injustice
For I am upright
Common people are filled with anxiety in a calamitous year
I sigh and feel sorrow in my heart
A new pine tree wants to grow to a thousand feet
An evil bamboo tree should be cut to two thousand pieces.

Already in 1959, doubts were expressed by some Party functionaries about the wisdom of the policies being enforced by the Party

[1]Ma Hsing-wu, "Thoroughly Expose and Criticize Wei Tung-ming's Anti-Party, Anti-Socialist Crimes," *Hung-wei Pao*, Canton, 9 October 1966.

leadership under Mao's inspiration, but these doubting Thomases were roundly condemned and punished at the time. The harrowing experience of the frightful failure that came shortly afterwards caused apparent ripples of discontent on a large scale among Party members. The image of an infallible Mao was badly tarnished and many Party members expressed their dissatisfaction with the practice of following one man's subjective wishes. For instance, the Communist, and more significantly, PLA writer Wang Yuan-chieh, who was the object of much praise in the earlier period, wrote a novel entitled *Party Dues* in which he was alleged to have "openly laid the blame for the escapist errors of left opportunism" of the great leap forward on Mao himself.[2] "In this way," it was said, "he not only twisted historical facts but also directed the spearhead of attack against the red sun in our hearts, Chairman Mao."

The veteran Communist cartoonist Hua Chun-wu, who went to join the Communists in Yenan in 1929, also pointed an accusing finger at Mao for the set-back in 1959-60. In 1961, his "attention to the rudder regardless of the wind" implied a sarcastic reference to the "great helmsman," Mao. In another work, *Silkworm*, he was alleged to have pictured the Party leadership (meaning Mao) as a silkworm enmeshing itself in its own net. His other works, such as *A Short Flute without a Melody*, *A Reed Floating on the Broken End of a Thread*, and *Fruitless Labour* were all branded during the cultural revolution as "vicious attacks against the general line and the great leap forward."[3]

From the angry denunciations of Mao's detractors in the cultural revolution it is obvious that there were many others in the Party who shared the views of Wang and Hua with regard to Mao's responsibility for the terrible time that China had had. The big leap was subjected to caustic comments, and was considered responsible for China's miseries during the sixties. The big leap and the people's communes were the result of subjective fancies and not based on objective realities. Even those who were in charge of propagating Party policies became sceptical and openly critical. Tseng Tun, a member of the Standing Committee of the CCP Hupeh Provincial Committee and director of its Propaganda Department, was reported

[2]Extract from *Chieh-fang Chun-pao* quoted in *Jen-min Jih-pao*, 17 October 1966.

[3]*New China News Agency*, Peking, 11 January 1967.

to have described the big leap as a "head-on dash in a great hurry" with the result that "our life has been rather miserable." He also remarked that "our difficulties are so grave that the situation is touch-and-go, which will plunge both urban and rural areas into ruin." The people's communes had been introduced "too soon" and had "ended in a mess." He pithily summed up the situation: "Both imperialists and revisionists are supplied with food, but Marxist-Leninists are not."[4]

Wang K'uang, member of the Central Committee's Central South Bureau and director of its Propaganda Department, was subsequently accused of launching "frenzied attacks" on the big leap calling it the product of subjectivism and describing the "temporary economic difficulties" as an "economic crisis." He similarly ridiculed the experiment of the people's communes.[5] Chung Lin, Editor of *Kwangsi Jih-pao*, spoke harshly about the mistakes made in the great leap forward and about the cloak of bravery donned by the leadership and described the Maoist attempt to belittle the difficulties as "rash words of those who regard themselves wise heroes and who do not recognize the difficulties," and as "chest beating" and "hollow shouting."[6] Communist writer Ouyang Shan was denounced by his own son in the cultural revolution for having attacked the great leap forward as "petty bourgeois fanaticism" and "a big mess"—phrases that were frequently used in the aftermath of the failure of the big leap.

Among the most direct and forthright criticisms of the assumptions behind the philosophy of the big leap and the havoc they caused was that of veteran Communist economist Sun Yeh-fang. Sun said in 1964 that "the great demolition of 1958 had brought about a sorry mess." Production and productivity declined in the past few years while production relations "ceaselessly leapt forward." Instead of getting finer, he said in 1962, the economic work became cruder and cruder. Economic accounting was ignored and all the emphasis was placed on political accounting. In the great leap forward, because there was "deviation in our opposition to revi-

---

[4]"Bourgeois Rightist Element Tseng Tun Dragged Out and Denounced by Members of the CCP Hupeh Provincial Committee and Officers," *Hung-wei Pao*, Canton, 5 September 1966.

[5]*Hung-wei Pao*, 16 October 1966.

[6]*Ibid.*, 24 September 1966.

sionism and mechanical materialism, we went to the other extreme."
Regarding the people's communes, they constituted "a mistake of
rash and reckless advance, a mistake of subjective idealism or
subjective will."[7]

He accused the leadership of "indulging in empty talk about
production relations in recent years, turning production relations
into something metaphysical." There was hardly any study of the
concrete problems of production relations such as systems of management and forms of organization of labour with a view to relating
them to productivity. Production relations were viewed in isolation from productivity. "We want to reach heaven in one step,"
was Sun's indictment. Indirectly, he called Mao Tse-tung a lazy-
bones in economics and his theory of the "general line" of "exerting
the utmost, aiming high, and building socialism with greater, quicker,
better, and more economical results" as a sheer abstraction. The
general fault in the past, he said, was the placing of politics and
ideology in the primary position. The excessive emphasis on the
role of thought—something passionately advocated by Mao—
led to the upsetting of "distribution according to labour" and the
"development of productivity." How could politics be divorced
from the economy of the country? He paid the Maoists in their
own coin and said that the substitution of the "mass line" and putting
politics in command for objective economic laws was an "idealistic
viewpoint" and "a lazy man's idea." Obviously hitting Mao,
Sun charged the leadership with ignoring productivity and exaggerating man's subjective initiative.[8] The prerequisite for the transition
to Communism was not, Sun Yeh-fang asserted in contrast to Mao's
viewpoint, ideological education and Communist consciousness, but
the development of productivity and a great increase in material
wealth. The real "red" line of writings on socialist political economy
should be "planned production, with the least expenditure of social
labour, of the largest quantity of products that satisfy social needs."
Sun said, the "law of value" must be applied to the socialist economy
of China. The "general line" of China's economic development
must be the "creation of maximum use-value with the least expense."
Planned and proportionate development of the national economy

[7]Kung Wen-sheng, "Sun Yeh-fang's Theory is Revisionist Fallacy," *Jen-min
Jih-pao*, 8 August 1966.
[8]*Ibid.*

could only be realized on the basis of the "law of value." All socialist enterprises must be put on a profit basis and be judged by the yardstick of whether or not they reach a profit target. Profit was the "most important comprehensive standard for checking on enterprises." As soon as profit was grasped, it may be said that "the cow is led by the nose, and the cow's legs (meaning other targets) will naturally follow. Otherwise, it will be like carrying the cow by her legs." Sun admitted that in this respect he had something "in common" with Liebermann, the Soviet economist. In fact, Sun went so far as to urge the abolition of the target of product output and in this he claimed to be "even more thorough than Liebermann." And committing the greatest sacrilege in Mao's China, Sun said that it was imperative to criticize revisionism but not necessary that "we must discard anything adopted by revisionism."[9]

A very large number of writers, historians, artists, and other academicians were given the "Red Guard treatment" during the cultural revolution for their alleged dissatisfaction with Maoist policies of the big leap and the communes and for using fictitious characters to criticize Mao. Historian Hou Wai-lu, deputy director of the Institute of Historical Research and member of the Editorial Board of *Li-shih Yen-chiu* (Historical Research), was accused of being "particularly active, around 1960, during the period of temporary economic difficulties," attacking the general line and "cursing" the people's communes. In volume 4 of *General History of Chinese Thought*, compiled by him, Hou was alleged to have picked out a bureaucrat of the Southern Sung dynasty, Ch'en Liang, who dared to "rebuke the emperor." "The Ch'en Liang depicted by Hou Wei-lu is fictitious, just as the Hai Jui depicted by Wu Han is fictitious." The Maoists claimed that "through the mouths of dead men, both give vent to their deeply ingrained hatred for the Party and socialism [meaning thereby Mao Tse-tung, for Hou was himself a Party member of some distinction]. They are false in advocating 'rebuking the emperor.' They are genuine in attacking the Party's Central Committee headed by Chairman Mao."[10] Not only did Hou create a fictitious Ch'en Liang who dared

[9]*Ibid.*

[10]Shih Wei-tung, "Expose Reactionary Substance of Hou Wei-lu's Advocacy of Heresy," *Jen-min Jih-pao*, 22 November 1966.

"rebuke" the emperor but he also collected from the "rubbish dump of history" a large number of 'heretics' who dared to rebuke the emperor. He eulogized their "spirit of rebellion," calling them "heroes" who "pleaded the cause of the people." Hou Wei-lu was alleged to have encouraged people to "leave the classics and rebel against the doctrines."

Similarly, Tsai Ho-jung, "Chieftain of the art circles," was reported to have said: "People talk about greater, faster, better, and more economical results everywhere, but everywhere there is a mess." But, it was alleged, he was all praise for Khrushchov who was "doing a lot of good, correcting Stalin's mistakes." He even went so far as to praise Tito as an "anti-fascist guerrilla hero."[11] Most of the "bourgeois rightists" who were subjected to attack in the cultural revolution were accused of criticizing the establishment of the communes as "a manifestation of petty bourgeois fanaticism" and with having pleaded for the continuance and extension of the concessions given to the peasantry for restoring agricultural production, like the private plot and the free market and a system of guaranteed output and guaranteed rewards for overfulfilment of the quota.

These select accusations, from innumerable people, against those who were "struggled against" show the extent of disillusionment with the failure of the big leap. Even though the words put into the mouths of the critics were not faithfully reproduced, there was considerable disappointment and discontent within the Communist Party ranks at the unprecedented economic decline and consequent hardship in the wake of the failure of the great leap forward, the responsibility for which was quite squarely placed by many Party functionaries and intellectuals on the top leadership and on Mao himself. It is noteworthy that all this bitter questioning came not when the big leap was initiated, at that time only a few voices (like those of P'eng Teh-huai and Ch'en Yun) were raised against Mao's policies while most of the Party leaders and members gave unqualified endorsement to them, but during the subsequent period when those policies proved bankrupt and led to actue hardship. It was then that loud murmurings were heard and Mao himself was not spared for the plight in which China found itself. The Maoist pro-

[11] *New China News Agency*, Peking, 11 January 1967.

paganda itself generally places most of the utterances of the critics between 1961 and 1963. The venom with which these critics have been attacked during the cultural revolution shows that the philosophy of the big leap was still a live issue.

The big leap ended in a foxtrot, putting the economy back by many years and compelling the leadership to introduce many drastic changes in methods of organization and remuneration, particularly in the rural areas. An unusually large number of Party members, even at higher levels, perhaps including Liu Shao-ch'i, Teng Hsiop'ing, and P'eng Ch'en, were no longer enamoured of Mao's prescription for a short cut to Communism and for catching up with the great powers. The fact that the sharp break with the policies of the big leap, the re-establishment of the primacy of material incentives and of agricultural production and the subordination of heavy industry to agriculture and even to the production of consumer goods, in order to supply urgent needs of the people, paid quick dividends and set the country on the course of economic restoration and expansion strengthened the critics in their belief in the efficacy of alternative economic policies and in the need to go step by step and not to drive the people too hard and not to push through extremist policies. On the other hand, Mao had not learnt the same lessons from the fact that his policies had gone awry. He had not reappraised the soundness of his policies. He continued to believe doggedly and equally passionately in the earlier policies. Others had revised their opinions and changed their viewpoint—but not Mao. He had been forced to give concessions in order to overcome the crisis but he did not regard the period of retreat as a normal time or a long-term perspective. He was worried lest these should breed complacency and was anxious to circumscribe them and to end this period as soon as possible. The bitterness of the denunciation in the cultural revolution of those who raised doubts about the big leap policies during the period of "temporary economic difficulties" and the emphatic reassertion of the "achievements" of the big leap and the correctness of Mao's policies is an indication of Mao's mood and convictions.

Clearly, also, accustomed as he had become to unquestioned obedience from his associates, no less than from his followers, Mao reacted sharply against the carping criticism of his policies — a phenomenon which was unique. He was obliged to mark time because of the economic difficulties the country was faced with but the passage of time did not soften his resolve to strike back forcefully and decisively and to cripple his critics. Everything said and done by them was entered in the ledger, so to say, and they were all called to account as soon as Mao believed the suitable time had arrived. No mercy was shown; no quarter given. The punishment was swift and unambiguous. Whether or not among the top leadership—in the Politbureau—such misgivings were expressed and criticism made openly, there is not enough evidence to say anything with finality. It is notable that those, who were accused of having "slandered" the big leap and the people's communes, occupied fairly important positions in the Party or in their respective occupations, and evidently had not incurred the displeasure of people like Liu Shao-ch'i, P'eng Chen, and Teng Hsiao-p'ing who largely controlled the Party machinery. All the indirect evidence suggests that while these people did not wish to start opposing Mao frontally and were also prepared to put some curbs on the concessions given in the period of retreat, and to increase the propaganda about socialist consciousness, they were averse to taking a "big leap" again and to switch back to the old policies, even though in a modified form.

Mao, on the other hand, was entirely taken up with his pet ideas and displayed less and less patience with the slow pace of the transformation that he wanted to bring about and with the resistance that he was encountering in effecting the changes. There is evidence to show that this in all its wide ramification had become a major issue in the struggle that Mao now launched. For Mao, the mistakes made in the great leap forward were entirely of a different kind. The real problem was that insufficient ideological groundwork had been done and that there were some minor mistakes of extreme direction given to the movement, but Mao remained a total convert to the effectiveness of ideological education and subjective determination in transforming the political outlook of the people and the economic face of the country.

Mao was also concerned at the partial consumer orientation of the economy since 1960. The unprecedented economic difficulties had led to the equally unprecedented change in the pattern of investment—from heavy industry, agriculture, and light industry to agriculture, light industry, and heavy industry in this descending order. Agriculture now claimed top priority but even light industry moved up one step ahead of heavy industry. For the first time, the needs of consumption were given some attention and living standards showed a slight rise. It was believed that in the fertile areas a peasant family was earning annually as much as 350-400 yuan. The necessities of life were provided in greater measure. This situation was anathematical to Mao. It not only carried the danger of "embourgeoisment" of the Chinese society and the perpetuation of a consumer-oriented economy, but it also made difficult rapid achievement of Mao's goals of world leadership and power. Mao's objectives could be realized only if the Chinese people tightened up their belts and the living standards kept at the barest minimum level in order to concentrate attention and investment on the sinews of power. The opponents were not averse to putting some curbs on consumption and to developing China's power but their experience of the breakdown in 1960 made them wary of exclusive emphasis on heavy industry and brought them round to the view that living standards must also rise, even though modestly, along with the growth of the economy.

It also appears that Mao in his seventies is a worried and impatient man. He is impatient that he has not been able to accomplish all that he wanted to and he is worried that his policies might be discarded by his successors and he himself might be repudiated by them. The dreams that he saw in his youthful days remain distant and faded; the millennium is nowhere in sight. Mao is unhappy with the slow change. He is not satisfied with the pace of progress. He is worried that the momentum of revolution was being lost. The humdrum process of economic development in the normal course was sounding the death-knell of revolutionary zeal. The country was sliding back and the younger generations were being corrupted by the lure of material incentives and worldly ambitions. Mao hopes to recover the revolutionary elan through a terrific shake-up. Mao's greatest anxiety seems to be that the course he had charted out for the country would be abandoned after he is no more. He is possessed by the haunting fear that those who were going to take over from him would disown him and his policies. The history of the Soviet Union must not be repeated in China and China must not go "revisionist." The example of Stalin was there for all to see. He is afraid that his successors might also do a Stalin to him and he wants to prevent it. He intends doing so by ruthlessly weeding out all those who might have shown the slightest hesitation in proclaiming full-throated allegiance to his ideas and policies, no matter how high their position or how long their record of service to the cause of Communism, and by intensifying the indoctrination of the younger generation. By encouraging blind and emotional adherence by the youth to the "thought of Mao Tse-tung," he proposes to leave behind "millions of revolutionary successors" who would carry forward his policies and prevent any regression from them. Through a combination of ideological fanaticism and terrorization of the dissidents, he hopes to perpetuate his name and his ideas.

THE CULT OF MAO'S PERSONALITY

Quite clearly, the cult of Mao's personality had become a vital issue, perhaps the most important one, in the political upheaval in China. The idolization of Mao had been taken to fantastic lengths. No other person in human history had received the same adultation in his own lifetime. Mao had been raised to the status of God. He was omniscient and his "thought" was omnipotent. No derogatory remark about him could be tolerated, nor the slightest deviation from his "instructions" permitted. He had become the living Buddha. Every word of his was the truth and equal to ten thousand words uttered by others.* His sayings should be memorized, to be reproduced, just like the scriptures, in any difficult situation to provide the answer. Lin Piao declared in a speech to the Red Guards that Mao was "even greater than Marx and Lenin." While Marx and Lenin had only solved the problem of seizure of power by the proletariat, Mao had resolved all the problems and shown the way for the consolidation and maintenance of this power and blazed the trail for all other countries to follow. His experience was, therefore, even "more profound" than that of Marx and Lenin. It was for the first time that a claim was being made on behalf of a Communist that he occupied the same position as, in fact a higher position than, that of Marx or Lenin. Even for Lenin, the claim

*See Lin Piao's foreword to the second edition of *Quotations from Chairman Mao Tse-tung*; also see *Chieh-fang Chun-pao*, editorial, 19 December 1966, circulated by *New China News Agency*, Peking, 19 December 1966.

was never made that he was greater than Marx. Such claims would in the past have been regarded as downright sacrilege and hereticism. It reveals something about the tenacity of the Chinese traditions that the first such claim has been made by the Chinese for their own leader.

There can be no doubt that a great deal of the trouble arose because many of Mao's colleagues and followers looked askance at the extent to which the cult of Mao was being carried, and resisted this. It would be natural that those who had worked with him most of their time took the propaganda about the "thought of Mao Tse-tung" with a pinch of salt. They could not be charmed into a belief about the infallibility of Mao and the omnipotence of his thought and sought to circumscribe the propaganda about him and prevent it from going to ridiculous extremes. In this, they incurred the wrath of Mao who was ready to strike down any one who stood in the way of his deification. In his lifetime, he wanted to create the myth of an impersonal Mao who had no peer now or in the past. Opposition to the thought of Mao Tse-tung and the belittling of his achievements is the constant burden of the account of crimes of all "those in authority and taking the capitalist road." A study and a recapitulation o fthe charges against Teng-Hsiao-p'ing by the Red Guards of Tsinghua University and their comparison with the pronouncements of Lin Piao are highly instructive in this regard.[12]

Teng Hsiao-p'ing was accused of having said after the revelations made by Khrushchov about Stalin that "the cult of personality will surely be reflected to a certain extent in our Party life and social life" and that "an important achievement of the 20th Congress of the CPSU is that it tells us what serious, calamitous results would be produced by deifying an individual." Teng, therefore, warned: "Our task is to continue to implement the guidelines of the Party centre to oppose the bringing to the fore of any individual and eulogizing individuals." Thus, Teng "maliciously objected to Chairman Mao being a great leader" and said: "What will remain unchanged forever is that the Communist Party is the leader and the only one." Another crime of Teng was, that after 1959 (signifi-

[12]"One Hundred Examples of Teng Hsiao-p'ing's Utterances and Deeds Contrary to the Thought of Mao Tse-tung," *Ching Kang-shan*, Peking, 15 February 1967.

cantly, after the failure of the big leap) he never made a report about his work to Mao. In 1961, Teng approved a report by the Central Propaganda Department entitled "Report on Examination of Some Problems of Propaganda of the Thought and the Revolutionary Deeds of the Leader" in which he "vigorously attacked" the study of Mao's works by workers, peasants, and soldiers, calling it "philistine," "oversimplified," and "formal." Teng "never mentioned" the teaching of the thought of Mao Tse-tung to "cadres and Party members."[13]

In contrast to Teng's lack of enthusiasm, Lin Piao was applauded and quoted for his idolization of Mao. "Chairman Mao is the most outstanding leader of the proletariat of the present era. He is the greatest genius of our time," Lin Piao was quoted as saying. "Chairman Mao's experience is more profound than that of Marx, Engels and Lenin. . . . His vast store of revolutionary experience has never been excelled by any one." And "Chairman Mao enjoys the highest prestige in the whole country and the whole world. He is the most outstanding, the greatest person." Lin also said: "The Thought of Mao Tse-tung is the peak of contemporary Marxism-Leninism, the highest and most dynamic Marxism-Leninism. Chairman Mao's books are the supreme directive for all work in the PLA. Chairman Mao's words belong to the highest level. They carry the greatest weight and are most powerful. Every sentence is a truth, and each sentence is worth ten thousand other sentences." Lin also advised the people that "in studying classical works of Marxism-Leninism, we must devote 90 per cent of our time to the study of Chairman Mao's works"[14] (and only ten per cent to Marx, Engels, and Lenin!).

Thus, it is obvious that the attitude towards the deification of Mao had been a major factor in Mao's struggle against his colleagues. It is not accidental that with the exception of Chou En-lai, most of the surviving leadership which had been with the Party for as long as Mao — like Chu Teh, Liu Shao-ch'i, Ho Lung, and Li Ta — have been denounced with varying degrees of venom for opposing the deification of Mao. It is a measure of the length to which the cult of Mao's personality has been carried that the topmost leaders were told by Red Guard mobs to prove their loyalty by reciting Mao's

13 *Ibid.*   14 *Ibid.*

works extempore; and to escape the dragnet of the Red Guards, many leaders, high and low, must have spent hours upon hours committing Mao's writings to memory. Liu Shao-ch'i was dragged out by the Maoists and publicly humiliated and made to recite Mao's works from memory. A most serious charge against Ho Lung was that he had "never studied Chairman Mao's works, except once, during the Lushan Conference in 1959, when he did bring with him a set of Chairman Mao's works. But it was kept at the bottom of his suitcase and never taken out."[15] It need hardly be pointed out that the Red Guards had no sources of information of their own about such matters and that they were supplied such "information" right from the top.

Ho Lung, who was Deputy Premier and in charge of the Sports Commission, was also accused of making fun of the cult of Mao. He was reported to have said at a reception he gave to the leading functionaries of the Sports Institute of Peking in 1965: "In our era, failure to learn Chairman Mao's bag of tricks is for a Party member a sign of an impure Party character." He was also reported to have told members of the Hunan physical culture committee: "Hunan [Mao's native province] is the home of our Emperor. It won't do to bungle things there." Even before liberation, when Ho Lung was in northwestern Shansi, every time a directive came from Mao, he would say sarcastically: "Heh, hey! Generalissimo Mao has issued another order."[16] Whether Ho Lung really did make all these jokes (which would hearten one in the knowledge that Chinese leaders at the top do have a sense of humour!) is doubtful, but what is undoubted is that Mao's oldest colleagues could not stomach the fantastic idolization of Mao and tried to put some brakes on it, and that Mao viewed them with suspicion and found them wanting in blind obedience to him. Li Ta, one of the oldest and founder members of the Communist Party and President of Wuhan University, was accused of dismissing Mao's works as "platitudes" and of daring to say that some of Mao's concepts "may not necessarily be correct." When a fourteen-year old girl, an "activist" in the Mao-study campaign, was sent to Wuhan University to deliver lectures, Li Ta was amused and declared it a

---

[15]"Towering Crimes of Ho Lung, Anti-Party Element and Army Usurper," *T'i-yu Chan-hsien* (Sports Front), Peking, 28 January 1967.
[16]*Ibid.*

joke: "A 14-year old girl does not even understand what matter and consciousness are. How can she talk about philosophy?"[17]

This disbelief in the incredible limits to which the cult of Mao was sought to be carried and resistance to this cult was found at various levels and the accusation of opposition to its spread runs like a thread through all the current propaganda of the Maoists. Party members of some standing seemed to have objected to this deification and attribution of all positive developments in China—and the world to the thought of Mao Tse-tung as "oversimplification" and "vulgarization." Chou Yang, the Commissar for Literature, and Lu Ting-i, the Propaganda Chief of the Central Committee, fell partly for this crime. A discordant note crept into the attitude of many Party leaders after the failure of the big leap when Mao's infallibility stood exposed and the subsequent retreat provided some scope for the expression of divergent views. Many winced at the way the thought of Mao Tse-tung was being spread and treated like the holy scriptures. As Chung Lin, Editor of *Kwangsi Jih-pao*, reportedly exclaimed, in a fit of rare rectitude and frankness, "Chairman Mao's books are not heavenly books. They cannot possibly produce such great effect." The study of Mao's works could not be "like praying to the gods that you get immediate results."[18] Lin Mo-han, a Vice-Minister for Culture and deputy director of the Propaganda Department of the Central Committee, was denounced for having complained that it was "simplification" and "vulgarization" to "attribute all achievements in concrete work and scientific invention to the thought of Mao Tse-tung."[19] He was also accused of having predicted indirectly in June 1961 the fall of Mao. "The Empire of Ch'in fell only 14 years after its establishment" (Mao's empire had had a lifespan of only ten years till then).

Or take the case of Wang K'uang, director of the Propaganda Department of the Central Committee's Central South Bureau. Among the various crimes of Wang K'uang, a particularly serious

---

[17]*Chieh-fang Chun-pao* Correspondent's report, *New China News Agency*, Peking, 6 September 1966.

[18]Chao Ch'un-sheng, "Chung Lin's Crimes Against the Party, Socialism, and the Thought of Mao Tse-tung Must be Thoroughly Reckoned With," *Hungwei Pao*, Canton, 24 September 1966.

[19]"Thoroughly Overthrow Lin Mo-han, Chou Yang's No. 1 Accomplice," *Kung-jen Jih-pao*, 23 September 1966.

one was that he changed a newspaper headline which had originally proclaimed, "the Thought of Mao Tse-tung is the teacher of the revolution of the peoples of the world," and made it look as if Mao's teachings were meant only for the Chinese people. He said that Mao's thought was only a "Chinese version of Marxism-Leninism." He also "opposed the propagation of the thought of Mao Tse-tung" and said that "to publish quotations from Chairman Mao in the newspapers is formalism and waste of space." About splashing the walls with quotations from Mao, he objected, saying that they "spoil the walls and waste ink." He "even went to the extent of forbidding the newspapers from publishing articles and news concerning the study of Chairman Mao's works." "Who would read these things," he had blasphemed.[20] Inevitably, Wang K'uang was now discovered to have come from a "bankrupt landlord family" and to have been a rightist for decades. Meetings were held in Canton by seamen, engineers, and technicians back from foreign countries condemning Wang K'uang for disparaging "the red sun in the hearts of the people of the world." Mao Tse-tung's, thought, they claimed, "had become universal language, and foreign visitors came to China to seek revolutionary truth."[21]

Sung Yu-hsi, director of the Propaganda Department of the Honan Provincial Committee, was put on the mat for having resisted the cult of Mao and trying to limit the study of Mao's works to Party cadres alone. He and his accomplices in the Party Committee ruled that only Party organization, militiamen, and youth should be organized to study Mao's works — the "broad masses" of commune members and citizens need not be organized for this purpose. They left the question of Mao-study to the volition of the people and they believed that masses of workers and peasants could not understand Mao's works. Sung Yu-hsi also forced *Honan Jih-pao* to re-examine its calls for Mao-study which he and his supporters described as "vulgarization" and "oversimplification."[22] Tseng Tun, director of the Propaganda Department of the CCP Hupeh Provincial Committee, was also one of those who felt uncomfortable at the frequent and strident accounts and broadcasts on the international significance of the thought of Mao Tse-tung and believed that this

[20]*Hung-wei Pao*, Canton, 16 October 1966.
[21]*Ibid.*, 27 September 1966.
[22]*Ibid.*, 27 September 1966.

was a case of unnecessary "bragging." His advice reportedly was that "there was no need to promote the idea in a big way that Comrade Mao Tse-tung is the greatest contemporary theoretician of Marxism-Leninism."[23] It was also his crime that he laid down regulations exempting cadres below the cultural standard of junior middle school from theoretical studies but requiring cadres of a higher grade to study 30 volumes of classical Marxist-Leninist writings (encompassing a much broader study than merely that of Mao's works). This was put down as a conspiracy on the part of Tseng Tun to discourage people from reading Mao's works.[24] Similarly, Ch'en I-hsin, a Vice-Governor of Hupeh and Secretary of the Party Committee for *Hunan Jih-pao*, was also found guilty of *lese-majeste* and of wishing to include in the propaganda arsenal of the Party something more than just Mao's sayings.[25] During the socialist education campaign, he prepared 31 documents for the use of the work teams but not one of Mao's works was included in this material.[26]

Scores of others—some well known, others less known figures—in the Party hierarchy were hauled over the coals for similar exhibition of uneasiness and annoyance at the manner in which the deification of Mao and his thought were being carried on and for their incredulity and scepticism about the infallibility and omniscience of Mao, all of which adds up to the irresistible conclusion that the cult of Mao was a crucial factor in the so-called cultural revolution. Mao was determined to achieve an unparalleled transformation of men's minds and to drive out all old and new ideas and ideologies from the minds of the Chinese people and instil in their place his own thoughts. Mao's "thought" must be the supreme and the sole reigning ideology. It would not share its position of primacy with anything else, nor would it brook a rival ideology. It must be accepted totally and unconditionally. On the one hand were Mao's visions of his own glory and on the other his ambitions for world leadership and a world power status for his country. As he advances in age, his visions and ambitions grow and so do his suspicions,—

[23]*Ibid.*, 5 September 1966.

[24]*Ibid.*

[25]"Bourgeois Rightist Ch'en I-hsin Dragged Out," *Hung-wei Pao*, 13 September 1966.

[26]*Ibid,*

suspicions about his associates, about the men around him, about his followers. There has been a steadily decreasing coterie of colleagues as more and more leaders around him have excited his suspicions and have been cast aside. This may explain the general "massacre" at the top in Peking.

History is replete with instances where a highly strong-willed leader or king, verging on senility, but accustomed to enjoying, in lonely grandeur, the plenitude of power, was possessed by illusions as well as suspicions leading to fratricidal wars, extermination of his own followers, and other irrational acts. In recent Chinese history, Hung Hsiu-ch'uan, the great T'aiping leader, was subject to such megalomaniac hallucinations and some of these not only proved his undoing but made him fall upon his own colleagues and followers. Stalin's case in contemporary history is too well known to need elaboration. Of a different kind, but still significant, was the fact that Churchill also suffered from delusions of grandeur in the last few years of his life and it was quite a job for his household members to keep him away from public view. In sum, Mao's advancing age, his unchallenged position at the summit of power for such an incredibly long time, his expanding ambitions about his manifest destiny as the greatest leader of the world, his visions of the grandeur of his country, and his suspicion of all those who might stand in the way have combined to prompt him to launch the cultural revolution.

MAO AND LIU—THE PERSONAL EQUATION

An important though surprisingly neglected factor is the personal equation between Mao Tse-tung and Liu Shao-ch'i, the personal struggle between the two, and the impact of the cult of personality on this struggle. These two men who have been in the Communist movement in China almost from its start and, until recently, seemed to have pulled together rather harmoniously, have fallen out and, along with policy differences, a personal struggle between the two also seems to have taken place on a gigantic scale. Once considered to be Mao's lieutenant, Liu built independent and rival power and has now become a victim of the cult of Mao's personality. There has been a fierce clash of wills and personalities at the top in Peking. This clash had been building up since the end of 1959, and the present upheaval in China is in some ways a direct consequence of the power duel between Mao and Liu (a struggle that was further accentuated by a tussle for influence and power between their wives).

The catastrophic failure of the big leap and the upsetting resulting from the extremist features of the people's communes in 1958 saw a reduction in Mao's power and prestige and a retreat from his pet ideas. The ideas and concepts that formed the nexus of Mao's philosophy of development came under sharp criticism within the Communist Party, and Mao himself did not escape blame for the resulting mess. The policies the Party was now obliged to adopt represented a substantial departure from the Maoist ideas and strategies of economic development and ideological progress. The field was left relatively free for Liu Shao-ch'i and his men to clear the mess and through pragmatic and flexible policies achieve economic recovery. While Mao receded from the stage, Liu and his associates occupied it and entrenched themselves in the Party and the bureaucracy.

Since 1962, at least Mao has been engaged in a gradual but ever-sharpening struggle to wrest back power and pull down Liu Shao-ch'i. Mao did not show his hand fully until he was ready, but the last phase of the cultural revolution has demonstrated how intense the personal struggle between Mao and Liu has been. Mao is not ready to forget and forgive anything. The cup of bitterness, accumulated over the years when Mao was in the sidelines and was slowly working his way back to unchallenged power, is full and thousands of words of denunciation of Liu have already been written in China. There is also a striking amount of petty jealousy in the attacks on Liu. The former Head of State has been accused of attempting to build up personal prestige and fame and of, *ipso facto*, belittling Mao's achievements. Liu got published millions of copies of his work, *How to be a Good Communist*, which was now given the dirty name of "self-cultivation" in order to "hang" the author, while the publication of Mao's works was neglected.

Or take the case of the film, *The Prairie Fire*. It was subjected to severe criticism because "this black film was made to perpetuate the fame of the general back-stage manager of these counter-revolutionary revisionists" (Liu Shao-ch'i). The film was about the struggle of the Anyuan coal-miners way back in the twenties. In the film the chief character obviously personifies the "top person in authority taking the capitalist road." He was "elevated to the exalted status of 'leader,' a 'hero' of great courage and a big 'saviour' of the people." This had now aroused the wrath, no doubt prompted by the proper quarters, of the Maoists Red Guards. They averred that the big Anyuan strike, which occupied a "shining page in the history of the Chinese workers' movement," was "personally led by our much respected and great leader Chairman Mao." It was Mao who on "numerous occasions" visited the pits and worksheds and "ignited fierce revolutionary flames." The strike "in reality" was carried out under the "concrete guidance of Chairman Mao" and the victory of the strike was "a victory of the great thought of Mao Tse-tung."[27] But the film, under the "signboard of allowing 'artistic licence' and under the pretext of casting a brilliant image of the Party," ascribed the "great services" performed by Mao to Liu Shao-ch'i. In fact, the accusation now was, that Liu carried on "secret talks" with the capitalists in order to sell out the workers.[28]

This intense personal struggle between the big two of China and the clash of two tough, strong-willed, and determined individuals is an important development revealed by the cultural revolution and should be weighed carefully in evaluating the causes of the cultural revolution. Many important and not-so-important figures in China have fallen by the wayside because they were believed to be proteges of Liu Shao-ch'i, Teng Hsiao-p'ing, and P'eng Chen.

IDEOLOGY VS. PROFESSIONAL COMPETENCE

How much should a person be "red" and how much "expert" has been a matter of controversy and a source of trouble for years now. The Maoists have insisted that a person must first be "red" before he can claim to be an expert and that, in fact, the quality of his expertise would be determined by the intensity of his "redness." Experts are worse than useless if they are not thoroughly red; indeed, "redness" is a passport to expertise, a merchandise not fully available

[27]"The Prairie Fire is a Black Film For Perpetuating the Fame of the No. One Ambitionist" (Tungfanghung Joint Combat Detachment, Shanghai Tungfanghung Film Studio), *Kuang ming Jih-pao*, 20 April 1967.

[28]"The Prairie Fire Cannot Deny Its Crime of Tampering With History" ("Three-Red" Literary Army and Light Cavalry of Chinese People's University to the Congress of the Capital's Red Guards), *Jen-min Jih-pao*, 28 April 1967.

to those who have yet to master the thought of Mao Tse-tung. This was the dominant view within the Chinese Communist Party during the period that the great leap forward was the order of the day, but the ensuing fiasco forced a retreat on this front also and it was conveyed to the intellectuals through Ch'en Yi that a little less "redness" and a little more expertise would be tolerated and would not be frowned upon. This experience of the policy of deriding professional competence and substituting it by ideological militancy induced second thoughts among leading Party functionaries, but Mao stuck to his view that politicization must come first, that doctrinal purity must take the pride of place, and that the intellectuals could not be allowed to escape thought-reform in the name of professional competence. Only those who held firmly the one end of the thought of Mao Tse-tung could hold the other end of expertise. And as soon as conditions permitted, Mao insisted again on the enforcement of this concept and the purging of all those who did not fall in line.

A significantly, but perhaps not unsurprisingly, large number of Party leaders have been revealed to have shown notable consideration for professional competence. Obviously, they were convinced that the country's uninterrupted progress depended on turning out in large numbers technically skilled and professionally competent persons in various fields and in order to encourage professional proficiency, they were not averse to turning the blind eye on ideological deficiencies. Even those whose function it was to supervise the intellectuals and secure the implementation of Party policies in education were infected by this partiality to professional competence and showed a soft corner for those who gave evidence of promise in their field of study or work. Even while delivering themselves of ferocious statements on ideological conformity, they seemed to have protected those who were competent. The Commissar for Literature, Chou Yang, for instance, besides being guilty of a host of other "crimes," was also attacked for having held on to the view that the leadership in the professions must come from the experts. "Science must be led by scientists, art by artists, and music by musicians,"[29] rather than by ignorant ideologues whose only qualification was an ability to quote the scriptures.

[29]Tung Feng, "Chou Yang's Counter-Revolutionary True Face in Class Struggle," *Jen-min Jih-pao*, 27 October 1966.

The same issue was put a little differently but equally effectively by Kuang Ya-ming, First Secretary of the Party Committee in the Nanking University, who reportedly said: "In judging whether a teacher is good or not, the first thing is to see whether or not he teaches diligently, is responsible for the students and has attained a relatively high academic level." In short, a teacher was a "good teacher" if he was good professionally, and a student was a "good student" if he obtained high marks.[30] It was also held against Kuang Ya-ming that whenever new students were admitted into the university, he would specially cultivate those students who had obtained high marks and would spur them on for better academic performance by encouraging in them "bourgeois concepts" of personal fame. He would even give them the lure of Party membership if they achieved meritorious results in their studies.[31]

Kuang Ya-ming asked the younger generation to rely on four things in their period of probation: first, on "realistic and diligent learning and practice"; second, on "guidance from well-known teachers"; third, on "assistance from the collective"; and, fourth, on "satisfactory arrangements of inspection by the leadership." The Maoists charged that Kuang was asking the younger generation to rely on "bourgeois" specialists and scholars and not on Party leadership and on the thought of Mao Tse-tung.[32] The trend towards specialization was particularly encouraged by Party leaders in education and art and literature during the comparatively liberal period of 1961-63 when the Party was in retreat, recuperating from the losses of the big leap, but many of these leaders were now "dragged out" and made to account for this deviation from the thought of Mao Tse-tung. Lu P'ing, a well-known Communist leader and the President of the Peking University, was also among those who had favoured the encouragement of specialization and expertise. The Lu P'ing "black gang" was accused in the cultural revolution of assuming a contemptuous attitude towards children of workers and peasants, describing them as "stupid eggs" and "lazy fellows," "pampering" sons and daughters of the bourgeoisie and giving them intensive training saying, "to cultivate an all-round

[30]Chiang Su-wen, "Refute Kuang Ya-ming's 'Intellectual Education First,'" *Jen-min Jih-pao*, 13 October 1966.
[31]*Ibid.*
[32]*Ibid.*

student is preferable to cultivating a hundred half-baked students."[33] Similarly, Li Ta, veteran Communist and President of Wuhan University, wanted the students to occupy themselves primarily with "book reading." "If all students go to labour," he said, "what would a university be like?" The loss was greater than the gain and he was afraid that teaching would be "placed in a passive position."[34]

The issue has sometimes been defined as a conflict between the ideologues and the professionals. This is not quite the correct perspective in which this problem should be looked at. Liu and Teng and others now in the shadows have themselves been ideologues. They are not the natural leaders of technocrats and managers. It would be more relevant and realistic to describe this conflict of views as a struggle within the Communist Party between those who, at the instance of Mao, insisted that professional competence was a secondary matter and must conform to the thought of Mao Tse-tung, and those who believed that porfessional skill and expertise could not be sacrificed at the altar of ideological conformity. It is one of Mao's objectives in the cultural revolution to pull down and demolish the prestige of the "experts" and "academic authorities" and "masters."

The problem that has plagued the Chinese Communist army is also an extension of the same issue — the issue of the relationship between professionalization and politicization. Mao has insisted that ideology must take command here as elsewhere and that professionalization must come after the army is thoroughly indoctrinated in the thought of Mao Tse-tung. First Marshal P'eng Teh-huai and later Senior General Lo Jui-ch'ing and many of their followers in the army were purged for advocating the creation of a first class, modern, professional army, even with Soviet assistance if necessary, and for resisting the Maoization of the army. It is the belief of the present writers that Marshal Ho Lung, too, besides being a victim of the cult of Mao, fell because he was a votary of a realistic balance between professionalization and politicization of the army. The "army professionals" seemed to have made common cause with those others within the Party who also believed in the need for fostering and treasuring

[33]*Ibid.*, 15 August 1966.
[34]"Wrathful Denunciation of Black Gangster Li Ta's Towering Crimes" (report by a *Chieh-fang Chun-pao* correspondent), *New China News Agency*, Peking, 6 September 1966.

professional competence and expertise in various other fields. They are being picked one by one in the cultural revolution.

An allied issue is the problem of the growth of bureaucracy and Mao's anxiety to prevent its entrenchment. Whenever a society settles down to peaceful economic development, the bureaucracy tends to grow and develop its own momentum, or rather inertia, as well as vested interests. In a Communist country like China, the Party bureaucracy has grown phenomenally, becoming, in Mao's view static and gravitating towards *status quo*. The Party cadres, having become bureaucratic, naturally dread change and unsettling conditions. Mao hopes to give a terrific shake-up to the bureaucracy through the cultural revolution and thus solve the problems created by the growth of bureaucracy. The Party bureaucracy has reacted sharply to this threat to its entrenched position, and, therefore, a violent struggle has followed.

THE INTELLECTUALS

It has not generally been realized how much the intellectuals figure in the cultural revolution. The attitude towards the intellectuals, the demands made on them, have been extremely live issues in the cultural revolution. Himself a poet and writer of some distinction, Mao believes that this field is his special preserve, and he has laid down the line in it which he expects all the intellectuals to observe faithfully. More than twenty years ago, Mao gave a talk at Yenan for the intellectuals on art and literature, and since then it has become a sacrosanct document to be followed to the letter by every intellectual on pain of excommunication from the fraternity. In this task, Mao asked the intellectuals to integrate themselves with the workers and peasants, go deep among them, and to serve them and write about them. As a general guideline, Mao's prescription was not unworkable but the hub of the problem came to be the intolerable demands made on the intellectuals in the name of serving socialism and adherence to the "class line."

One problem was that Mao practically denied and repudiated the view that different branches of scholastic and artistic activities had their "special laws" and problems which must be taken into account even while adopting the socialist standpoint in the work in these fields, and punished those who upheld this view. Mao regarded all such views with suspicion—as attempts to reject the ascendency of the thought of Mao Tse-tung in every field of activity. For instance, Chien Po-tsan, the doyen of Chinese Communist historians, was denounced for having said that, in the study of history, "apart from the concept of class, there should also be historicity." If one had only the concept of class and forgot historicity, according to Chien, one tended to give a one-sided interpretation and negate everything—an approach which amounted to nihilism. This was held up by the Maoists as evidence that Chien Po-tsan "employed reactionary bourgeois historicity," to oppose the thought of Mao Tse-tung.[35]   It was claimed by the Maoists that "in the course of the revolution in the field of history," historians and students of history, following the instructions of Mao, left their students to "participate in practical struggles." They "integrated" themselves with the workers and peasants and learned from them and worked with them in writing the four histories (the histories of the commune, the factory, the village, and the family). This, according to the Maoists, was "the way" in which historians could become both "red" and "expert." But Chien Po-tsan,* and obviously many others in the Party, had grave misgivings about this policy and had said: "In the study of history, books are the principal source of knowledge." Typically, Chien Po-tsan, who had spent much of his life with the Communist Party, was now discovered to have been a "filial son of the landlord class" who had all along been a "counter-revolutionary."

The crucial difficulty has been that Mao had no more use for anything ancient or foreign. He wanted the repudiation of the ancient Chinese classics as well as foreign works of art and literature, whether Soviet "revisionist" literature or French "bourgeois decadent" classics. Shakespeare was a reactionary writer and Beethoven's music was corrupting, decadent stuff; so was Tu Fu's poetry, not to mention the Confucian classics. The entire gamut of China's cultural handiwork was disowned and all those who showed a soft corner for the ancients were "dragged out" for struggle and

[35]*Yang-ch'eng Wan-pao*, Canton, 19 July 1966.
*These writers had an opportunity of meeting Chien Po-tsan in Peking in 1957 and were no less impressed by his modesty and personal affability than by his erudition.

denunciation. From Chou Yang to Chou Shu-li, and from T'ien Han to Hsia Yen, all were subjected to a withering attack for opposing Mao's policy of "destroying the old to let the new emerge."[36] The amazing aspect of it is that resistance came from well-known Communist figures in the literary and art circles. Even Liu Shao-ch'i was attacked for being the real boss behind this "black line" in art and literature which venerated the old and the foreign.[37]

What did Mao really want and what did he like to substitute in the place of the old and the foreign? First of all, no doubt, he wanted the arts and literature of China to show complete conformity to the "thought of Mao Tse-tung." No deviation, open or indirect, could be tolerated. He was unhappy at the respect in which the classics, including classical literature, were held by many people in China and he was keen to demolish thoroughly their prestige. He wanted the elimination of the old drama and the ancient opera and opted for its substitution by modern drama and revolutionary opera themes. Most importantly, all the writers and artists must confine themselves to revolutionary themes. They could only portray light in which there must not be the faintest impression of a shade. There was only one side of the coin; in the present Chinese society there was only brightness, no darkness. The writers must portray "positive" characters, socialist heroes who were dauntless against hardships, who conquered all difficulties, and who were all inspired by the thought of Mao Tse-tung. These revolutionary heroes had no weaknesses and if they had, they quickly overcame them with the help of the thought of Mao Tse-tung and their subjective determination. The camera could not stay very long on their seamy aspects and certainly no dwelling on individual idiosyncracies or petty foibles, which enliven man's relations with society, were permitted. Writing about "middle" characters who might have some evil mixed with good or who exhibit various kinds of personal struggles, people whose class consciousness was not boldly clear, was absolutely taboo under the Maoist instructions.

It was not fortuitous that Mao's greatest worry came during the period of economic setback. It all fits into the same pattern—which

[36]See, for instance, criticism of T'ien Han, *New China News Agency*, 23 January 1967.

[37]"Thoroughly Criticize and Overthrow the Head Boss of the Black Line in Literature and Art," *Kuang-ming Jih-pao*, 10 May 1967.

these writers clearly discern — that of the failure of the big leap inducing second thoughts in every field among a large number of Party
members with Mao not only stubbornly sticking to his views but
becoming more adamant in securing their implementation. The
precipitous economic crisis brought forth concessions all along the
line and the intellectuals, too, profited from the retreat. There were
fewer meetings, less demands, and greater scope for work coupled
with a little more freedom and a healthier respect for learning and
literature. The liberal interlude did not last long, but, while it lasted,
the intellectuals did their work with comparative ease of mind and
less fear of offending the authorities. We have already noted that
the failure of the big leap and the retreat caused grave questionings
among the Party leaders about Mao's policies, and direct as well as
indirect criticism. Unobtrusively, it would appear, they loosened the
control on the intellectuals, softened the rigours of Party policies,
and tried for a new balance in which the ideological strait-jacket
would not stifle artistic expression or professional excellence and a
new synthesis of the old and the new — a new balance in the preser-
vation of China's cultural heritage and the development of a socialist culture.

All this Mao watched with increasing dismay and a rising temper.
While he could not do much during the period of acute economic
distress, he went into action as soon as conditions permitted. He
issued a directive in November 1963, closely followed by another
one in June 1964, on literary and artistic work. The texts of the
directives were not published in national newspapers at the time
but there were constant references to them, in subsequent literature
and even excerpts from Mao's directives were repeatedly quoted.
Only Mao could have the authority to say that in the last seventeen
years, the Party and the intellectuals had failed to carry out, in the
main, reform in art and literature. In a "written observation on
art and literary work," he said that "in many departments the results
achieved in socialist transformation are microscopic to this day.
In many departments, it is still the 'dead' who are ruling."[38]   In
his second directive of June 1964, he again criticized the literary
and art circles and said: "Most of those associations and their publications (it is said that a few of them are good) have basically (but

[38] "Struggle against Anti-Party Element T'ien Han," *Jen-min Jih-pao*, 6 December 1966. The text of Mao's directives is now available.

not all of them) not carried out the Party's policy in the last 15 years. They are officials and conduct themselves like lords, neither going near workers, peasants, and soldiers, nor reflecting socialist revolution and construction. In recent years, they have even slid down the brink of revisionism. Unless they are seriously reformed, they will one day, in future, merely become organizations like the Petofi club of Hungary."[39] No wonder that with this view of Communist China's efforts in literary and artistic creation, practically the entire literary and artistic output during the sixties was suspected and was denounced and discarded. There was not a Communist writer or artist who did not come under suspicion for writing revisionist or bourgeois decadent stuff and for non-conformity to Mao's directives.

Beginning in 1963, Mao made a conscious and systematic effort to control art and literature and other allied fields and to "purify" them in the image of the "thought of Mao Tse-tung." He first turned his attention towards the classical opera which to him seemed to be an important source of decadent art and a den of unrepentant escapists. The thousands of years old opera must be thoroughly purged and its content changed beyond recognition. He directed that the old themes of the traditional opera must be thrown out lock, stock, and barrel, and in their place must be injected modern, revolutionary themes. He entrusted the work to his wife, Chiang Ch'ing, who went about it with despatch and Mao-like ruthlessness and who later earned in the cultural revolution the reputation of being the *enfant terrible* of the literary and artistic circles in China. There is no doubt that there was a bitter struggle involving a large number of Party functionaries in charge of literary and artistic work who resisted such a drastic measure about a traditional art form which had delighted and captivated Chinese audiences for centuries upon centuries.[40] It is quite probable that even the hard-boiled Party commissars entrusted with work in this field, starting with Chou Yang, balked at the prospect of its immediate implementation and tried to slow down the pace of change.

[39]"Hsia Yen's Heinous Crimes Cannot Be Covered Up," *ibid.*, 10 December 1966.

[40]That, a struggle was going on, was even admitted by the Chinese press during the period of the cultural revolution. *New China News Agency*, Peking, 23 January 1967.

Not only must the writers not occupy themselves with the dead and the ancient, but they must also not touch upon the seamy side. They must paint only a bright picture, positive characters, and forward-looking situations. Whether they write well or not, whether the inspiration is present or lacking, whether or not the forms of art had been mastered, whether the technique was engaging or not, was immaterial — the only criterion of judgement was whether it portrayed heroic characters in the era of Mao Tse-tung. An acute controversy developed on whether any attention could be given to the "middle" characters; and all those, who were guilty in the eyes of the Maoists of showing a soft corner for middle characters were suitably punished and divested of their position and power in their fields. The middle characters comprised not only those whose class origin was dubious, but those who did not stand up to the test of being Mao's revolutionary heroes, even though they might be Communist Party functionaries or of worker-peasant parentage. According to one of Mao's chief lieutenants in the literary field now, Yao Wen-yuan,[41] "whether heroic characters among the masses of the revolutionary peasants and soldiers or corrupt images of the bourgeoisie are to be praised is the watershed between proletarian and bourgieois artists, and the touchstone for distinguishing between socialist and capitalist art and literature."[42]

Yao made it clear that any theory of "writing about people in the middle" is a serious violation of Mao's directives on art and literature. All talk of writing about middle characters for the purpose of "diversification" and as "more profound expression of reality" was unacceptable. Two lines from Mao's "magnificent poetry" were quoted as the final justification: "In this holy land of six hundred million people, everybody is a sage," and "Evening smoke seeks the retirement from work of heroes everywhere." Only a "glorious picture of revolutionary people's heroes" must be the subject-matter of art and literature.

Scores of Party leaders in the field of art and literature, and Party artists were thrown out for failure to, observe faithfully, Mao's

[41]Yao Wen-yuan, an important figure in the Central Committee's Cultural Revolution Group sounded the first salvoes of the cultural revolution with his broadside against Wu Han.

[42]Yao Wen-yuan, "A Theory which Causes Socialist Art and Literature to Degenerate," *Kuang-ming Jih-pao*, 20 December 1964.

directives in this regard. These people, many of whom were leading Party members in their own fields and artists and litterateurs of some renown, were not enamoured of "bourgeois" characters; but what they wanted was to write about people in depth, to portray their struggles and hopes and disappointments, their courage and their frailties, their strength and their foibles, to evolve complex characters and to invest their stories with interest, meaning, and a touch of humanism. All this was rejected out of court by Mao. We should create types, not real persons, was his exhortation. There was no such thing as "truthful writing"—that was merely a smoke-screen for perpetuating "bourgeois literature"—so was all the talk about opening the "wide path of realism" and the "deepening of realism." Those who were tired of the "smell of gunpowder" in Communist Chinese literature were also denounced.[43]

Chao Shu-li, who until the other day was one of the most popular writers of Communist China, was now attacked for resisting Mao's thinking on art and literature, spreading "big poisonous weeds," obstinately writing about "middle-roaders," "frenziedly assailing the three Red banners and a series of policies and principles of the Party," and "directing the spearhead against our great leader, Chairman Mao." Chao's record as a writer for the past twenty years or more was "one in which he brandished black pens to oppose the party and the people."[44] Vice-Minister for Culture, Lin Mo-han, was accused of ignoring Mao's directives on literary and artistic work and opposing the idea of "writing about the 13 years only,"[45] the period since the founding of the Communist regime. The famous writer T'ien Han and "his friends" were similarly denounced for "using their official positions and powers . . . to oppose the revolution in the Peking opera and to sabotage the reforms in opera."[46]

Hsia Yen, a prominent Party figure in the film world, was denounced for inciting the writers to ignore Mao's instructions and urging them to "think independently" so that they might not "follow

[43]*Chieh-fang Chun-pao*, editorial. (English text in *Peking Review*, 29 April 1966.)

[44]*Chieh-fang Chun-pao*, 9 January 1967, reported by *New China News Agency*, Peking, 9 January 1967.

[45]*Kung-Jen Jih-pao*, 23 September 1966.

[46]See f.n. 37; also see Hsiang Chung, "Exposing T'ien Han's Reactionary Character," *Yang-ch'eng Wan-pao*, 28 July 1966.

whoever happened to lead them."[47] Sung Yu-hsi, director of the Propaganda Department of Honan CCP Provincial Committee, was charged with stifling revolutionary drama. In the second half of 1961, he was reported to have "audaciously" notified the dramatic troupes that dramas on contemporary themes would not be performed for the next two years and that "forces should be concentrated on unearthing of traditional dramas." After that, he successively called forums of famous actors and old artists telling them to remove their worries, not to fear, but to "unearth" traditional dramas "boldly." A "gust of ill wind" to rescue "the traditions" began to blow, complained the Maoists. Even after Mao's directives, dissidents within the Party "continued to propose frantically" that equal importance be attached to traditional drama, modern drama, and historical drama.[48] In 1964, Sung Yu-hsi still opposed the "total non-performance of traditional dramas" and said that a "total switch to modern dramas would cause damage to dramatic work." In this way he "overtly resisted Chairman Mao's directives."

It was also held against the Party leaders among the intellectuals that they were propagating and promoting the adulation of the literature of the 1930s. Once regarded as highly progressive and deeply humanistic as well as a ruthless expose of the cruelty, the degradation and the exploitation of the old system, it was treated and viewed with considerable reverence and taken as a model for imitation. Now, with the exception of Lu Hsun and his works, most of it was rejected by Mao as decadent, reactionary "bourgeois" literature. The Party intellectuals, however, continued to admire these works and to adopt some of their methods and forms. This led to a great deal of struggle and Mao came down with a heavy hand on all those who gave evidence of any preference for the literature of the thirties. To take just one instance, Hsia Yen was accused of giving permission for the publication of many works that "advertised the tradition of the films of the thirties." He also "distorted history and openly whitewashed Wang Ming's left opportunist line," spreading the word that China's film industry got on the road of correct development way back in the thirties "in a vain attempt to obliterate the great significance of Chairman Mao's epic, brilliant

[47] Chieh-fang Chun-pao, 10 December 1966; New China News Agency, 10 December 1966.

[48] Hung-wei Pao, 27 September 1966.

'Talks at the Yenan Forum on Literature and Art.'" He also "ran counter" to Mao's line on art and literature.[49] Still another instance, Chou Feng — secretary of the All-China Musicians' Association, secretary of the Party Committee and vice-president of the Central Music Conservatory, and president of the Central Opera and Dance Drama Theatre — advocated, so ran the charges against him, "national defence music" of the thirties, "worshipped and publicized the reactionary art and literature of feudal China, of the bourgeoisie in Western Europe, and of modern revisionism"[50] (that is, Soviet art and literature). He has, therefore, been dismissed and purged.

Evidently, it was also not permissible now to find any virtue in Soviet art and literature. From Sholokhov to Siminov, the entire range of Soviet literature stands condemned as decadent, poisonous material which should not be allowed to besmirch the ideological purity of Chinese literature and Chinese intellectuals. In pursuance of this new understanding of the Maoists all those Party intellectuals, commanding influence in this field, who betrayed any sign of being attracted by Soviet literature or having propagated it among the people, paid with their reputation and their positions. This was a part of Mao's campaign against the foreign and the ancient, and the justification was that this was necessary to uproot slavishness among Chinese intellectuals, that is slavishness to things foreign and old.

Although the basic direction was said to be provided by Mao's discourse at Yenan in 1940, the fact is that what he demanded now from the intellectuals was a far cry from what he himself had been saying in his younger and more moderate days. In 1938, he had enjoined upon Party members the important task "to study our historical legacy and sum it up critically from the Marxist approach." He had said: "Our nation has a history of several thousand years, a history which has its own characteristics and is full of treasures. But in these matters we are mere school boys. The China of today has developed from the China in history; as we are believers in the

[49]See fn. 44.
[50]Under banner headlines reading, "Hold High the Great Red Banner of Mao Tse-tung's Thought and Thoroughly Uproot the Counter Revolutionary Revisionist Line on Art and Literature," *Kuang-ming Jih-pao* (22 January) devoted a whole page to Chao Feng's denunciation.

Marxist approach to history, we must not cut off our whole historical past. We must make a summing up from Confucius down to Sun Yat-sen and inherit this precious legacy. This will help much in directing the great movement of today."[51] Mao was also more modest in his approach to cultural problems and the intellectuals. In 1940, he said in his talk *On New Democracy*:

Being a layman on cultural problems, I hope to make a study of them, and I am just beginning. Fortunately, many comrades in Yenan have written exhaustive articles on this subject, so my sketchy treatment may serve as the beating of gongs and drums that precedes a theatrical performance. To the advanced cultural workers of the whole country, our writings serve only as a brickbat thrown to induce them to cast precious stones, and the heaps of our suggestions may contain a grain of truth; we hope that they will join us in the discussions so that correct conclusions will be reached and the needs of our nation will be met.[52]

About the study of history, Mao had complained in 1942 that only a few party members and sympathizers had taken up this work which was not being done in an organized way. "Many Party members are completely in the dark about Chinese history either of the last hundred years or of ancient times. Many of our Marxist-Leninist scholars are always dragging ancient Greece into their discussion. But as to their own ancestors, I am sorry to say, they have clean forgotten them. There is no lively atmosphere of studying seriously either the present or the past.... There are comrades who feel pride, instead of shame, in their ignorance or scanty knowledge of our own history." Mao confessed that he never entered any Marxist-Leninist school but was taught only such stuff as: "The master said, 'How pleasant it is to learn and practise constantly what one has learnt,'" but Mao asserted that although "such stuff is out-of-date as teaching material, yet it did me some good because it is from this that I learned to read."[53]

[51]"The Role of the Chinese Communist Party in the National War," *Selected Works of Mao Tse-tung*, Lawrence & Wishart Ltd., London. 1954, Vol. II, pp. 259-60.
[52]*Selected Works*, Vol. III, p. 106.
[53]"Rectify the Party's Style of Work and Reform Our Study," *Selected Works*, International Publishers New York, Vol. IV, pp. 12-20 and 30-45.

Such talk by anyone else would now be considered blasphemous. The new commandments to the intellectuals were: the study of history and all literary studies also must slight what is ancient and concentrate on the modern revolutionary period—the policy of *po ku, hou chin* is being pursued to extremes and in fact the study of history as of most other studies must minimize the reading of books and maximize participation in life. All those who thought that books and learning must take precedence over manual work and going out to the farms and factories were branded as bourgeois rightists aiming at the restoration of capitalism in China. The educational system (except the teaching of sciences) must be completely revamped to reduce the stress on the study of books and increase it on the integration with actual life and on manual labour. The curricula must be changed and study of the thought of Mao Tsetung should be the main preoccupation of the students. The intellectuals had no business writing about complex characters and complex situations. Socialist literature demanded the writing only about heroes of the new society and virtues of the new system. An impression of light and shade, of grey and dull colours, of personal idiosyncracies and weaknesses, of mixed characters and situations would not be tolerated. Only those publications and works of art would be permitted which took a positive approach. Professional competence of an artist or writer was altogether a minor matter, a skill which could be gradually acquired once the mind had been purged of all wrong and bourgeois notions: the content was the crucial thing. The "dead" and the ancient and the foreign in art and literature must be generally rejected; in their place must come revolutionary, contemporary themes. The "authority" of classical works of art and literature and thought and philosophy and of ancient writers and poets and thinkers must be completely toppled. Above all, artists, writers, historians, dramatists, movie-makers, and musicians must strictly adhere to the thought of Mao Tsetung and abide by his instructions and directives.

What is significant is that Mao ran into so much resistance from the very men he had appointed as what might be called "intellectual overseers." The Party commissars in art and literature, high-ranking Party intellectuals, and those whose job was to act as watchdogs over the intellectuals themselves seemed to be aghast at the extremities to which Mao was carrying his line on intellectual work and tried, directly and indirectly, overtly and covertly, to soften the rigours of this policy. They were averse to this complete break with the past; they looked askance at this attempt at the total rejection of the ancient and classical works, and forms of art. They showed consideration for professional skill and for competent intellectuals. They wanted the students to concentrate on studies and attain a high level of proficiency in their subjects and not to waste their time on political movements and manual labour. They appeared to believe in gradualism in change and in thought reformation. Some of them at least showed disenchantment with Mao's policies after the fiasco of the big leap and expressed their doubts over it. They also proved to be a stumbling block in the propagation of the cult of Mao. A large number of them were, therefore, given the sack in the cultural revolution.

CULTURAL REVOLUTION AND FOREIGN POLICY

It is beyond the scope of this work to deal with China's foreign policy in a thorough and systematic manner. But foreign policy in so far as it is an issue in the cultural revolution cannot be left out and must be taken note of. The impact of the cultural revolution on foreign policy and its likely consequences must also be touched upon. Therefore, there will be no attempt here to enter into a detailed discussion of China's foreign policy, but a few observations may be made about some of the implications of the cultural revolution on this policy.

Quite clearly, one of the most important implications of the cultural revolution is the spilling over of the cult of Mao into the field of foreign policy of China's relations with other countries. Not only is Mao Tse-tung the greatest leader of the Chinese people, but he is positively the greatest leader of the entire world, and woe be to those either within China or outside who dare question it. Two years ago, it could be said that the primary objective of China's foreign policy was the acquisition of a world power status and parity with the other super powers. That objective remains, but it is no longer the sole guiding force. To this has now been added another objective: recognition by the entire world of Mao Tse-tung as the mentor and the guide. Mao Tse-tung's thought is now being described as the "never-setting sun" and its "brilliant light" is proclaimed to be illuminating "the revolutionary path of the people of the world." Mincing no words, *Jen-min Jih-pao* declared boldly and frankly:

Comrade Mao Tse-tung is the greatest leader of our times. Rarely has history seen such a revolutionary leader as Comrade Mao Tse-tung, a leader who has gone through struggles of such duration, such complexity, such intensity, and such many-sided-ness. Comrade Mao Tse-tung stands on the most commanding height and sees the farthest. He makes the most penetrating analysis of problems, is the first to detect new problems and work out the most thorough solutions. Mao Tse-tung's thought is not only the greatest treasure of the Chinese people, it is the common treasure of the revolutionary people of the whole world.[54]

The reason why Chairman Mao enjoys extremely high prestige among the revolutionary people of the world is because he has, with the gifts of genius, creatively, thoroughly, comprehensively, and systematically developed Marxism-Leninism. Mao Tse-tung's thought is not only an integration of the universal truths of Marxism-Leninism with the truth of the Chinese revolution but also with the concrete practice of the world revolution. It has summed up not only the experience of the Chinese revolution but also the experience of the world revolution in the present epoch. It is an encyclopaedia both of the Chinese revolution and of the world revolution. It is the acme of Marxism-Leninism in our epoch; it is living Marxism-Leninism at its highest.[55]

The beginning of the cultural revolution also saw the beginning of the claim by the Maoists in Peking that Mao was the "red sun" in the hearts of the people of the world, that the "brilliant light" of Mao's thought was shining throughout the world and that the people all over the world "firmly believe that relying on Mao Tse-tung's great thought, they can certainly overcome all difficulties and march from victory to victory."[56] The trumpets of the cultural

[54] *Jen-min Jih-pao*, editorial note to a report by the *Hsinhua* correspondents entitled "The Brilliance of Mao Tse-tung's Thought Illuminates the Whole World," 16 June 1966.

[55] See report in *Peking Review*, 3 June 1966.

[56] *Ibid.*

revolution also blew the cult of Mao far and wide and declared his unchallenged pre-eminence as a world leader and indeed as the only spokesman and teacher of the people of the world. The Chinese press began to fill its pages with stories of the affection and regard in which he was held by the people in other countries and the Chinese correspondents abroad vied with one another in sending reports about how the people abroad looked up to him for guidance and leadership. People throughout the world, it was claimed by them, entertained "boundless love" for him. People everywhere say, according to Peking: "Chairman Mao is the great teacher of all oppressed people. The masses of the people keep him in their hearts all the time." They proclaim: "The radiance of Mao Tse-tung's thought has not only lighted up all China but is lighting up the whole world."[57] The Chinese press devoted a lot of space to reports, features, and statements showing the ardent love of the world's people for Mao and their "high appraisal" of Mao's thought.

Generally, the reports carried pronouncements made by known pro-Chinese politicians in other countries to Peking's reporters or statements made to them by obscure and unnamed workers and peasants and others in various parts of the world. To take one instance, a *Hsinhua* correspondent from Hungary reported that the Chinese pavilion in the 1966 Budapest International Fair created a "sensation" in the city and that many visitors "poured out their hearts in a most sincere and moving manner." One Hungarian worker came to the pavilion with a badge bearing Mao's portrait and told the Chinese reporter: "I stand by Mao Tse-tung; I don't stand by men like Khrushchov."[58] Man's capacity for self-delusion or self-deception, and in this case, perhaps, the desire to please and flatter the Maoists in Peking, is unbounded, otherwise it is almost unimaginable that Hungarian workers, an isolated case apart, would feel enthused over Mao's line in world affairs. Similar reports about what ordinary workers or intellectuals said in Poland, Rumania, France, Britain, Nepal, Burma, Vietnam, Cambodia, the UAR, Algeria, Mali, Madagascar, and so on, were publicized in the Chinese press.

Copious statements by pro-Chinese elements in Asia and Africa and elsewhere were also given prominence. Medjaher Abdul Kader,

[57] *Jen-min Jih-pao*, 4 June 1966.
[58] *Ibid.*

leader of the delegation of the General Union of the Algerian Workers, which visited China in May 1966, was quoted as saying: "We regard Mao Tse-tung as a great statesman. There should be a guide for the world revolution and Mao Tse-tung is the guide now." A.B. Nageobo and Peter Roborocko of the Pan-African Congress of Azania (South Africa) said in an interview with *Hsinhua* that Mao's thought was "an inexhaustible source of inspiration to the oppressed people." Alfred Binghan, a member of the delegation from the Canada-China Friendship Association, told *Hsinhua* that "Chairman Mao is a great revolutionary leader, a second Lenin. His thought is a lighthouse guiding the revolution in China and the whole world. The people all over the world like to read Chairman Mao's works. They take them as the truth."[59] Mlinda of the Afro-Shirazi Party of Zanzibar was quoted as saying: "Chairman Mao Tse-tung is a great and brilliant leader. His works represent truth. Everyone who wants to understand the truth must study Chairman Mao Tse-tung's writings and grasp his ideas."[60]

Mao's birthplace Shaoshan became a shrine not only for the Red Guards but also for visiting "foreign friends" who went there to pay homage to the "red sun in the hearts of the people of the world." *Jen-min Jih-pao* commented editorially:

> The East is Red and the sun rises; in China there emerges Mao Tse-tung; Shaoshan is sacred soil which all revolutionary people aspire to visit, because Comrade Mao Tse-tung, the great leader of the Chinese people and the great standard-bearer in the revolutionary struggle of all the people of the world, was born there. Many thousands of foreign friends have expressed their boundless love and admiration for Chairman Mao during their visits to Shaoshan over the last few years. They have gone to Shaoshan not just to recall the history of the Chinese revolution, but also to seek the revolutionary truth. All people who desire revolution draw inspiration and encouragement from Comrade Mao-Tse-tung's revolutionary activities."[61]

[59]See *Peking Review* report on the Chinese press accounts of such statements and features entitled, "Mao Tse-tung's Thought: Beacon of Revolution for the World's People," 17 June 1966.

[60]*Jen-min Jih-pao*, 1 June 1966.

[61]English text in *Peking Review*, 10 November 1967.

It was claimed that revolutionaries from different countries expressed "in most vivid terms" their "boundless love" for Mao and "infinite faith" in Mao's thought. "We love him more than we do our own lives," they were reported as saying.

The three main strands in Peking's new world outlook—the validity of China's experience for the rest of the world, the claim for Mao's unchallenged supremacy as the world leader, and the need for other countries to repeat China's cultural revolution—were authoritatively restated in Peking on the occasion of the 50th anniversary of the October Revolution in the Soviet Union.

Speaking at a mass rally in Peking on 6 November 1967, and flanked by other top leaders like Chou En-lai, Ch'en Po-ta, K'ang Sheng, and Chiang Ch'ing (Mao's wife), Lin Piao summed up China's experience for the seizure of power which was now regarded in Peking as relevant for the entire world: "Under the leadership of the political party of the proletariat, to arouse the peasant masses in the countryside to wage guerrilla war, unfold an agrarian revolution, build rural base areas, use the countryside to encircle the cities and finally capture the cities." This was the only path now for emancipation of the other countries. Secondly, Lin Piao gave a clarion call for the establishment of the hegemony of Mao Tse-tung's thought:

Once Mao Tse-tung's thought—Marxism-Leninism at its highest in the present era—is grasped, the oppressed nations and people will, through their own struggles, be able to win liberation.

Once Mao Tse-tung's thought—Marxism-Leninism at its highest in the present era—is grasped, the countries that have already established the dictatorship of the proletariat will, through their own struggles, be able to prevent the restoration of capitalism.

Once Mao Tse-tung's thought—Marxism-Leninism at its highest in the present era—is grasped, the people of those countries where political power has been usurped by revisionists will, through their own struggles, be able to overthrow the rule of revisionism and re-establish the dictatorship of the proletariat.

The same theme was further elaborated by a joint editorial of *Hung-ch'i*, *Jen-min Jih-pao*, and the *Chieh-fang Chun-pao* (Liberation Army daily) on this occasion.

The revolutionary people of the world have come to understand more and more clearly that Comrade Mao Tse-tung is the greatest teacher and most outstanding leader of the proletariat in the present era.... The world has now entered a revolutionary new era, with Mao Tse-tung's thought as its great banner. France was the centre of the revolution in the late 18th century, and the centre moved to Germany in the mid-19th century when the proletariat entered the political arena and Marxism came into being. The centre of revolution moved to Russia early in the 20th century and Leninism came into being. The centre of world revolution has since gradually moved to China and Mao Tse-tung's thought has come into being. Through the great proletarian cultural revolution, China, the centre of world revolution, has become more powerful and consolidated.[62]

The importance of the proletarian cultural revolution was not confined to China alone. Its significance was in no way less than that of the October Revolution. The October Revolution opened the way for the proletariat to seize power while the cultural revolution has opened the way for the consolidation of the dictatorship of the proletariat. The joint editorial stressed:

Like the October Revolution, China's great proletarian cultural revolution is not merely a revolution "within national bounds"; it is likewise a revolution of an international order. This great revolution has won the enthusiastic support of the proletariat and revolutionary people throughout the world. Its great victory has opened a new era in the international Communist movement and will assuredly have a far-reaching influence on the course of human history.

The real significance of all these Peking-based and Peking-inspired statements and the daily affirmation of Mao's leadership over the world lies not only in the fact that Mao wants his line to be accepted by the international Communist movement and the struggling people of Asia, Africa, and Latin America but that he must be acknowledged as the mentor, the guide, the instructor, and the leader. It is

[62]*Ibid.*

not sufficient that other countries or Communist parties or left movements follow broadly the Chinese strategy or borrow features of the Chinese practice, but they must acknowledge the debt to Peking. The homage must be paid ungrudgingly and handsomely. There is, for instance, the case of Cuba which has recently moved considerably away from the Russian position and is following policies that normally should have Peking's approval, but—partly at least—because Fidel Castro does not own the debt to Peking and refuses to acknowledge Mao as the leader, there is no love lost between Havana and Peking. On the other hand, Fidel sets himself up as the leader of the Latin American people and the inspirer of the revolution in Latin America. Apart from other reasons, this is also one reason why Peking is using such vituperative language against the Left Communist leaders of India. The Maoists are not satisfied with sympathy or approval for their line; with it must come unqualified tribute to Mao as the leader. Unless this acknowledgement is made, Peking would not be pacified and accept it as genuine. Peking continues to belabour the theme that nothing can stop the spread of Mao's thought around the globe until the entire world is swayed by it and comes under its influence. The insistence on acceptance of the Chinese line in toto and on establishing the supremacy of Mao Tse-tung in the international Communist movement has also fouled China's relations with North Korea and the Japanese Communist Party.

Communist China's foreign policy has generally alternated between the two extremes of "sweet reasonableness" and apparent ideological dogmatism coupled with ultra-nationalist responses. The pendulum has been swinging back and forth since 1949. The crusading zeal of the initial revolutionary period, encouraged and influenced by Stalinist rigidity in Moscow, determined early formulation of Chinese foreign policy and relations with the outside world. Gradually, the Chinese realized the importance of widening their contacts and cultivating Afro-Asian and even European countries. The need to break through U.S.-imposed encirclement, the defiance by India, followed by many other Asian-African countries, of the Western powers, and the demands of internal consolidation—all these and various other factors brought about a thaw and a milder approach. The "Bandung spirit" continued to govern Chinese foreign policy until 1957. Then the smile faded and the scowl returned. A stiff posture was adopted and China's relations with a large number of countries deteriorated. But the new policy soon became bankrupt and China's growing isolation as well as Soviet refusal to accept the Maoist world view compelled a retreat to more moderate positions. Although the struggle with Moscow and New Delhi (and with Washington and Belgrade too) continued unabated, a suitable change was made in policies towards other countries. Particularly, towards China's smaller neighbours, Peking extended the mantle of benign protection, tolerance, and a measure of non-interference, if they agreed to stay away from hostile alliances and professed a policy of friendship with Peking. Again by 1966, Peking, or rather the Maoists, were switching their foreign policy stance to aggressive, provocative, and chauvanistic attitudes in their relations with other countries. They could take the whole world in their stride—so they seemed to believe. A threatening posture was adopted towards a number of countries, with some notable exceptions (like Pakistan).

There is little evidence to suggest that foreign policy was a direct issue in the initial stages of the struggle in China. More likely, the conflict arose out of domestic issues and as a consequence of the cult of personality, but, as is usual in such circumstances, once the struggle developed, it became an across-the-board conflict. Foreign policy also came within the purview of this struggle and wide-ranging differences appear to have developed. One usual crime of the opponents continually harped upon by the Maoists is that they wanted to limit the "assistance" given by China to the struggling, revolutionary people of the world. If correct, this means that those who were sceptical about Mao's line wanted to limit China's interference in other countries and advocated the continuation of the policy of moderation and large-heartedness in relations with Afro-Asian countries, particularly, with China's smaller neighbours. More specifically, sharp differences seem to have characterized the discussions on alternatives over a Vietnam policy. The divergence of opinion over the question of modernization and professionalization of the army has already been noted. This was now overlaid by the problem of China's response to the escalation of the war in Vietnam. As the fighting was intensified in Vietnam, the danger of China's involvement grew, and so did the threat to China's security. What should be China's response and how should Peking meet the developing situation? As on other domestic issues, the leadership seems to have been split on this too.

The initial Maoist reaction was reflected in Mao's statement to Edgar Snow in February 1965 that he saw no cause for alarm regarding the danger of a Sino-U.S. war. Since the Americans had delcared that they had no intention of attacking China and since China had made it equally clear that it would not intervene and would fight only if attacked, there was no need to be unduly worried—Mao told Edgar Snow. The Vietnamese situation, however, continued to grow more serious and could no longer be adequately met by such statements. The conflict had become far more critical and Mao's statement had lost some of its relevance. The steady escalation of the war increased the dangers facing China and sharpened the controversy over policy alternatives before China. From indirect evidence, and from the repeated charges about the alleged advocacy of slavish reliance on others by the "top person in authority taking the capitalist road" and his associates, it seems fairly certain that a group in the higher echelons of the Party was gravely concerned about the increasing American presence in Vietnam and believed that in order to meet the American challenge it was necessary to slightly modify the stance towards the Soviet Union and arrive at least, at a limited understanding with the Kremlin. This group which possibly included Liu Shao-ch'i, Teng Hsiao-p'ing, P'eng Chen, Lo Jui-ch'ing, and Ho lung was not necessarily pro-Soviet in the accepted sense of that term, and some of them at least were militantly nationalistic, but they appeared to have come to the conclusion that in the interests of safeguarding China's security and containing the American challenge, some dialogue and accommodation with Moscow was called for, and that, in the face of a present and immediate threat, China's army must be modernized as speedily as possible with whatever assistance that could be secured from Moscow. This was not only totally unacceptable to Mao but seemed to fly in the face of all that Mao stood for and had preached to his followers. In Mao's view it was nothing short of rank heresy and was further proof that these people whom he had earlier entrusted with power and responsibility were unreliable pupils and unworthy successors. It needs to be noted in passing that the attitude towards the Soviet Union in the context of the struggle in Vietnam was precisely the issue on which Pyongyang and the Japanese Communist Party began parting company with Peking. It is also probable that even though the ensuing struggle of the cultural revolution was inevitable and was being carefully prepared by Mao, the showdown came somewhat suddenly in the wake of the conflict of opinion over the war in Vietnam.

Within the army, the crisis in Vietnam once again sharpened controversy over the pattern of development. Lin Piao continued to be loyal to the Maoist formulations but others like Marshal Ho Lung and Senior General Lo Jui-ch'ing appeared to be exercised over the state of the Chinese army and wanted primary stress on modernization. Once again, the hydra-headed monster of professionalization of the Chinese army raised its head which Mao thought he had struck down in 1960. Despite the helmsmanship of Lin Piao, powerful voices in the army command arraigned themselves on the side of quicker modernization and more thorough professionalization and once again doubts were expressed about the policy of putting politics (the thought of Mao Tse-tung) in command at the expense of completely professional training of the army equipped with the latest weapons. By the same token, and as a response to the deepening crisis in Vietnam, the dissenters seemed to be prepared to play the dispute with Moscow at a lower key and make use of modern Soviet weaponry. They made common cause with those within the top leadership of the Party who were also in favour of some kind of a joint action with the Soviet Union in Vietnam. In a way, therefore, the opponents of the Maoist line in China were more acutely disturbed by the American challenge in Vietnam and were more consistently anti-American than Mao and his followers. The Maoist policy of total rejection of cooperation with Moscow even in Vietnam and an intensification of the struggle against the Soviet Union enabled the United States to escalate the war in Vietnam without unnecessarily worrying about Sino-Soviet intervention.

It was significant that a renewed campaign began against P'eng Teh-huai in 1967 and that for the first time the Party resolution against P'eng adopted on 16th August 1959 at the 8th Plenary Session of the 8th Central Committee at Lushan was released in summary form—eight years after its adoption. The publication of the indictment of P'eng Teh-huai at this time and the spate of articles that followed in the Chinese press provided evidence of the strength of the opposition to the Maoist line in the higher ranks of the army command. An editorial published in *Chieh-fang Chun-pao* (Army daily) the day following the release of the Lushan resolution accused P'eng of opposing Mao's military line, of setting himself against the study of Mao's works and of resisting Mao's theory of the people's war and his concept that everyone should be a soldier. P'eng was described as a "wild dog in the water" who produced an 80,000-word document in 1962, aimed at reversing the judgement (of 1959) against him and launching a "revengeful counter-attack" against Mao.[63] A subsequent article in the same paper quoted P'eng as having said, "What is the use of relying entirely on political and ideological work? It cannot fly."[64] Similary, it was alleged that Lo Jui-ch'ing "stubbornly opposed" giving prominence to politics and tried to stress military skills over political and ideological training. While paying outward homage to Mao's line, he spread the notion of "giving equal emphasis to military affairs and politics" and was also credited (discredited?) with having uttered such nonsense as this": "If political work is not well-done, the soldiers will retreat in battle. But if soldiers have no military skill and their shooting is inaccurate, when the enemy rushes at them in battle, will the soldiers not then retreat?"[65] Inevitably, the further accusation was made that P'eng Teh-huai, Lo Jui-ch'ing, Ho Lung, Liu Shao-ch'i, Teng Hsiao-p'ing, and P'eng Chen were all in league with one another against the Mao line.

The differences over the Chinese response to the war in Vietnam had in all probability spread to other areas also. It is highly plausible that the real shock, and consequently a critical re-examination of Mao's external postures, came with the debacle in Indonesia. The tremors of the Indonesian political earthquake were felt far and wide; Mao's policy lay in ruins; even parties very close to Peking like the Japanese Communist Party were shaken up by the failure in Djakarta; the architect of that policy could not escape blame and an agonizing reprisal by the leaders in the Chinese Communist Party is indicated by available evidence. While the "powerholders taking the capitalist road" within the Communist Party displayed

---

[63]*Chieh-fang Chun-pao*, editorial circulated by *New China News Agency*, Peking, 16 August 1967.

[64]*New China News Agency*, Peking, 30 August 1967.

[65]*Ibid*.

disillusionment with the rigid Maoist stance in foreign relations, Mao stiffened in his determination to struggle for his ideas the world over. The cultural revolution made a perceptible impact on foreign policy and brought about a number of significant changes in Peking's foreign policy responses. The declaration of Peking that Mao was the leader of the world and that the thought of Mao Tse-tung must rule the four seas and the five continents and its meaning for China's foreign policy have been noted above. Some of the other important shifts can be briefly studied.

The sudden upsurge of xenophobia and unmistakable exhibition of anti-foreignism, particularly among the Red Guard students, is a phenomenon which has reminded many students of the Chinese field of earlier traditional manifestations of anti-foreignism in China. The Red Guards seemed not only to be protesting against certain "misdeeds" of the governments of some countries, but revealing an attitude of contempt and haughty disdain for other countries and peoples, and certainly for all canons of international behaviour and norms of conduct in foreign relations. Also, the range of their attack covered all the way from the Soviet Union to Britain. Such widely different countries as East Germany, Hungary, Kenya, Indonesia, Mongolia, Burma and India have all had a taste of what has come to be known as the "Red Guard treatment." It is questionable how far the entire body of the present dominant leadership in Peking is responsible for and endorses this state of near hysteria in relations with foreign countries, but it is unquestionable that the Red Guards have not just been acting on their own, that the element of spontaneity in the Chinese system is not significant, and that, therefore, a section of the leadership has contributed to the growth of this anti-foreign sentiment. Considering other developments in China and the attitudes of various leaders, it is tempting to identify this section of the leadership as Mao's wife (Chiang Ch'ing) and Ch'en Po-ta. The fact that while the Red Guards were ransacking and making a bonfire of the British legation, the security police were genuinely attempting to protect British life and property confirms the impression that the Red Guards were carrying out instructions from their headquarters and the police from theirs, and that the two headquarters were neither fully coordinated with each other, nor wholly united on China's attitude. At the same time, it is probable that the present phase of anti-foreignism will lose its virulent edge as the storm of the cultural revolution subsides and a more normal situation prevails.

The cultural revolution resulted in a sharp downward curve in the state of relations between China and the Soviet Union. The freezing point has long been crossed. Both officially and formally, the Soviet Union was declared a renegade and an outcast from the socialist community and Mao made it clear to the Communist world that simultaneous friendship with Moscow and Peking was unacceptable. (Only one reluctant exception, for obvious reasons, was made in the case of Vietnam.) The Chinese view of the Soviet Union was graphically described by a joint editorial of *Jen-min Jih-pao*, *Hung-ch'i* and *Chieh-fang Chun-pao*:[66] "The renegades Brezhnev, Kosygin and company now have the impudence to style themselves successors to the cause of the October Revolution and to engage in demagogy, flaunting the banner of 'commemorating' the 50th anniversary of the October Revolution. What a monstrous insult to the great Lenin, to the great October Revolution and to the great Soviet people. You renegades to the October Revolution, by what right do you commemorate the October Revolution? The only place for you is in the dock of history to be tried by the Marxist-Leninists and the hundreds of millions of revolutionary people all over the world!"

There was a violent anti-Soviet campaign in China during 1967 in which the Red Guards took a leading part. For nearly two weeks in February the Soviet Embassy was under siege by huge crowds of screaming, frenzied Red Guards, and diplomatic relations teetered on the brink of breakdown. Although the ultimate step was averted, the spirit of toleration had vanished, and Moscow and Peking resumed their polemical warfare with even greater venom. Since one of the objectives of the cultural revolution was to prevent the appearance in China of the phenomenon of Soviet revisionism, and to throw out all those who could be suspected of having caught the infection, a deterioration in Sino-Soviet relations was inevitable. At least during Mao's lifetime any improvement appears improbable.

There was also a perceptible change in the policy towards neighbouring countries. Peking's attitude had not only hardened but a reappraisal seemed to have taken place in the Maoist headquarters

[66] *Peking Review*, 10 November 1967.

about the need and utility of the continuation of a policy of sweet reasonableness towards Asian neighbours. Since the retreat from an assertive, forward foreign policy stance in 1960, China had carefully cultivated good neighbourly relations with many Asian countries, more especially its smaller neighbours. Peking had taken particular care to show that it could coexist with its neighbours and that if some neighbour did not get along with it, like India, the fault did not lie with China. Economic aid and cultural exchanges inevitably flowed from this policy.[67] Even as late as April 1966, Liu Shao-ch'i and his wife visited Afghanistan, Pakistan and Burma, and in Rangoon the two sides (Chinese and Burmese) were "glad to see that the Agreement on Economic and Technical Cooperation between China and Burma is being smoothly implemented, and that the technical personnel of the two countries have established good relations of cooperation between them." The Chinese side also "reaffirmed China's respect for the policy of peace and neutrality pursued by the Government of the Union of Burma in international affairs."[68] · By June 1967, however, the Burmese Government had become a "fascist," "reactionary," regime determined to oppose China and curry favour with U.S. imperialism.[69] After nearly two decades of lone struggle, ignored and slighted by the big Communist countries, the Burmese Communist Party suddenly gained recognition from Peking and the struggle there which had received no official note in China for all these years was declared to be a people's war.

Again, in the case of Nepal, the policy of friendship gradually withered away. In May 1966, an agreement was signed in Peking on "trade, intercourse and related questions between the Tibet Autonomous Region and Nepal,"[70] an extension of the agreement based on the "Five Principles"[71] signed by the two governments

[67]For a detailed discussion of China's policy towards and relations with Asian neighbours during this period, see V. P. Dutt: *China's Foreign Policy*, Asia Publishing House, Bombay, 1964, *China and the World*, Frederick A. Praeger, New York, 1966.

[68]Joint Communique of Liu Shao-ch'i and Ne Win, 19 April 1966. Text in *Peking Review*, 22 April 1966.

[69]Chinese Government's protest to the Burmese Government, *Peking Review*, 7 July 1967.

[70]*Peking Review*, 13 May 1966.

[71]The famous Five Principles of Peaceful Coexistence were: mutual respect

to convert the total sum of 160 million Indian rupees of economic aid provided in the October 1956 and March 1960 agreements into 12 million pounds sterling. The conversion was made at the gold standard value of the two currencies prior to India's rupee devaluation. But within months of this agreement, the cultural revolution caught up with Nepal also and some incidents in Khatmandu involving the use of Mao badges and Mao's photographs sparked off heated denunciations in Peking and angry statements by China's Foreign Ministry. Similarly, Prince Norodom Sihanouk of Cambodia felt the hot breath of the cultural revolution despite all the earlier *bonhomie* that had characterized Sino-Cambodian relations. In April 1966, Vice-Premier Li Hsien-nien had visited Cambodia and signed a fresh agreement on economic and cultural cooperation. He had praised Cambodia for proceeding "along the path of self-reliance, thus safeguarding its independence and sovereignty and assuring better development for its national construction."[72] But on 11 September 1967, Prince Sihanouk denounced Peking for promoting subversion in Cambodia, sending messages of greetings to banned parties and groups and interfering in the internal affairs of Nom Penh,[73] and he followed this up with the dismissal of two pro-Peking members of his government and a threat to break off relations with China unless Peking desisted from meddling in Cambodian internal politics. The breach was averted only because of Chou En-lai's personal appeal to the Cambodian ruler and an implied promise of correct behaviour in relations with Cambodia.

The relations with India, none-too-happy since 1959, continued at a level of high tension and the cultural revolution marked a further deterioration. India was now considered ripe for revolution and repeated calls were given to the Indian people to take up arms against the government. Student demonstrations and rioting in 1966 and other agitations were hailed as the beginning of the revolution in India. In 1965, "broad sections of the people protested

---

for each other's territorial integrity and sovereignty, non-aggression, non-interference in each other's internal affairs, equality and mutual benefit.

[72]*Peking Review*, 6 May 1966..

[73]Subsequently, Prince Sihanouk threatened that if China did not desist from meddling in Cambodia's internal affairs, the country would have to turn towards the U.S. for protection. *Hindustan Times*, 6 October 1967.

against the serious food scarcity and the intolerable sky-rocketing prices," but nevertheless these struggles were generally "confined to the field of economics." But, since the beginning of 1966, "the bloody suppression of the mass struggles by the troops and the police called out by the Congress government has aroused the revolutionary spirit of the people further." The demonstrations held by the Central Government Employees in the capital in July and the "current student movement which has spread to many towns and cities have raised a clear-cut slogan: 'Overthrow the Congress Government.'" India was "the home of the creed of 'non-violence.'" There, Peking asserted, the big landlords and the big bourgeoisie had, for many years, used "this narcotic to pulverize the people's revolutionary struggle." But, Peking was now confident, the Indian people had through their struggle come to understand the "deceptive nature" of "non-violence" and had "resorted to revolutionary violence more and more extensively to cope with counter-revolutionary violence." They were fighting the police either with bare hands or with sticks, stones, home-made grenades, and "other simple explosives." They "put up barricades in the streets to resist the brutal attacks of the reactionary authorities" and they "surround, smash and burn the buildings of the Indian National Congress and of the government as well as food stores, police vans, and police stations."[74]

Even the demonstration in Delhi over the agitation for the banning of cow-slaughter and the wave of violence that came in its wake was greeted by Peking as a great revolutionary phenomenon. "Although the direct cause of the New Delhi demonstration was the demand of the Hindus that the government ban the slaughter of cows which they consider 'sacred,' it was in fact an explosion of the Indian people's pent-up anger against the government and a part of the violent storm of popular opposition now sweeping the country," wrote a Peking weekly. It gleefully added that this was clear from the fact that "the angry crowd set fire to the buildings of All India Radio, the Transport Ministry, the Press Information Bureau, and other government departments, and attacked the residences of the President of the Congress Party, Kamaraj, and the Supply Minister, as well as the offices of the Power and Labour Ministers." In the face of

[74]*Peking Review*, 14 October 1946, p. 37.

this "popular opposition," the Indian Government resorted to the course common to all reactionaries: "armed repression." On this occasion "more than 500 people were killed or wounded" and Prime Minister Indira Gandhi "screamed that her government was determined to put down the opposition whatever the cost. This has further revealed the ferocious nature of the reactionary Congress Government."[75]

In this "surging wave of the Indian people's struggle" Peking found evidence of the correctness of the pet phrase of Mao that the political forces, in India like elsewhere in the world, were undergoing a "great upheaval, great division and great reorganization." Peking's analysis of the cause of this transformation in India is both revealing and noteworthy. In the view of Peking, "this is of course the inevitable result of the Congress Government's foreign policy of tailing after the United States, aligning with the Soviet Union and opposing China and of its reactionary domestic policy in the interests of the big landlords and the big bourgeoisie."[76] If India were not to "oppose China," it is fair to conclude from this, the complexion of the Indian government would change (as in the case of Pakistan). Significantly, the yardstick to judge and evaluate the foreign countries was their attitude towards China and the degree of their progressiveness was also determined by the measure of their friendship or hostility towards Peking.

The cultural revolution added another dimension to the relations between the two countries which touched a new low during this period. A rupture in diplomatic relations was narrowly averted as Peking proclaimed that the thought of Mao Tse-tung should be the guiding light for the people of India. On 12 June, the Chinese Government suddenly accused an Indian diplomat of espionage activities, stripped him of his diplomatic status, and asked him to appear before a people's court. Subsequently, on refusal to appear before a people's court, he was allowed to leave China immediately but was accompanied by hundreds of Red Guards to the Peking airport where he was humiliated, pushed about and manhandled, and again at Canton where he was paraded around in a truck and subjected to indignities. The incident had immediate and grave repercussions in Delhi where inflamed mobs attacked the Chinese

[75] *Peking Review*, 18 November 1966, p. 38.
[76] *Ibid.*, 14 October 1966.

embassy and beat up Chinese diplomats. The Government of India also, in retaliation, expelled some Chinese diplomats. The Red Guards in turn laid a siege to the Indian Embassy and hurled stones inside and broke window panes. For a while it appeared that the break was imminent and unavoidable, but gradually things cooled down.

Peking served notice, however, that the spread of the thought of Mao Tse-tung in India could not be stopped and that the "only way out for the Indian people is to rise in rebellion and struggle and, under the guidance of Marxism-Leninism, Mao Tse-tung's thought, use the gun to overthrow the reactionary ruling classes, drive out all imperialist gangsters and seize political power."[77] Peking confidently predicted that when the Indian people firmly grasped the mighty weapon of the thought of Mao Tse-tung, they would achieve still greater successes. Mao was the leader and his "thought" must be accepted as the present-day truth by the people of India, as also by the rest of the world.

Another noticeable change in the Asia policy of China in the current period was the changing role assigned to overseas Chinese communities. In the period between 1954 to 1958, Chou En-lai showed considerable anxiety to allay the fears of South-east Asian countries with sizable Chinese minorities and seemed to concede the principle of single nationality and to be ready to end the state of dual nationality. After a brief recourse to a hard policy in 1958-60, the Chinese reverted to the earlier policy in this regard, with a few exceptions, e. g., their attitudes towards Thailand and Malaysia. Even there, no active attempt, whatever the verbal fulminations, was made to involve the Chinese communities in a major way in Peking's politics. In the case of Malaya, Peking extended support and recognition to the Malayan National Liberation League and the armed struggle that it was claiming to be carrying on. Its chief representative P.V. Sarma was welcomed in Peking in early 1966 and assured of China's moral support.[78] Thailand, however, has come in for rougher treatment and more direct intervention. The proximity of frontiers with Thailand made a more active policy feasible and China has encouraged a movement of revolt by the Chinese minority on the frontier areas against the

[77]Article by Mi Chen in *Jen-min Jih-pao*, 2 June 1967.
[78]*Peking Review*, 21 January and 7 February 1966.

Thai government.

The Chinese communities were being gradually cast for a more interventionist role by the Maoists. The cultural revolution had had the effect of bringing forth demands in Peking that overseas Chinese align themselves with the "revolutionary, struggling" people and become more active in fomenting revolutions. The defiant wearing of Mao badges and other demonstrations of loyalty to Mao by pro-Peking Chinese in various countries of South-East Asia was symptomatic of the wind of change in Peking's policy. Red Guard posters criticizing Liao Ch'eng-chih, Chairman of the Central Commission for Overseas Chinese and Chairman of the Chinese Committee for Afro-Asian Solidarity, indicated the shift that was taking place in Peking. Interestingly, before 1960, Liao like Liu Shao-ch'i and others was also placed at the far left end of the political spectrum and was looked upon by outside observers as a militant nationalist. Liao was now under fire for being a rightist and for sacrificing the just struggle of the overseas Chinese communities. Supported by his "black boss" Liu Shao-ch'i, a Red Guard tabloid in Peking alleged, Liao advocated the "philosophy of survival" and enforced "capitulationism in overseas Chinese affairs abroad." He was accused of being afraid of political activities of the overseas Chinese lest these activities should irritate the local governments. Consequently, he ordered the suppression of "mass patriotic movements which had been under way abroad in an earth-shaking manner."[79]

At the time of the founding of New China, the overseas Chinese established many mass organizations to "educate and organize the broad revolutionary masses and carry out patriotic activities" but Liao later called for their dissolution so as not to arouse the suspicions of the local governments. He asked the overseas Chinese to "mind their own business," "to stick to their own posts" and "not to criticize the internal affairs of the local governments." In 1956, when Ngo Dinh Diem was "forcing overseas Chinese

[79]"Criticize and Repudiate Liao Ch'eng-chih's Revisionist Line of 'Three Capitulations and One Annihilation.' By the 'Long Cord in Hand' Fighting Team and 'Rebel to the End' Fighting Team of the Red Banner Corps of the Central Commission for Overseas Chinese Affairs," *P'i-Liao Chan-pao*, No. 4, 18 June 1967. *Survey of China Mainland Press*, Hong Kong, No. 4013, 1 September 1967.

in South Vietnam to become naturalized Vietnamese citizens,"
the "broad masses of overseas Chinese eagerly hoped that their
home government would support their struggle," and some overseas
Chinese "even came to our Embassy in X" expressing this wish,
but Liao was "unwilling to interfere with Ngo Dinh Diem's internal
affairs" and he dared not "mobilize the overseas Chinese to rise
in struggle." In 1957, using the "pretext" that some students of
overseas Chinese had dual nationality, the Indonesian "reactionaries"
(this was in Sukarno's time) forcibly took some Chinese schools
under their control and restricted the establishment of new schools
in some localities. The "revolutionary rebels" of his commission
insisted that Liao Ch'eng-chih was "the executioner assisting the
Indonesian reactionaries in strangling and ruining the culture and
education of overseas Chinese."

In 1959, the persecution of the Chinese was stepped up, according
to these Red Guards. But Liao did not "mobilize and organize the
overseas Chinese to wage mass self-defence struggles." On the
contrary, he put forward a plan for the withdrawal of 600,000
Chinese from Indonesia in one year; he even suggested calling
back three to five million overseas Chinese from various parts of
the world in the next seven or eight years. After the "September
30" incident in Indonesia, Liao was "scared by the white terror of
Indonesian fascist armymen." He strongly objected when the
overseas Chinese proposed to get organized and to protect themselves and wanted them to "sit down and wait for their death."
The "red rebels" declared that Liao Ch'eng-chih was "simply an
out-and-out rascal" and "deserved to be killed by one thousand
cuts." In order to "liberate overseas Chinese affairs, it is definitely
necessary to refute, overthrow, and discredit this counter-revolutionary revisionist."[80]

Of course, it does not follow that Peking would necessarily succeed
in making revolutionary heroes out of this all-class amorphous mass
of the overseas Chinese. A large number of them are traders, and
merchants and while they might feel a certain sense of pride in the
rise of China as a great power, they can hardly view their role as
carriers of the revolution with enthusiasm. Their urge is for protection against racial animosity, and for this, many of them might

[80] *Ibid.*

look up to Peking (or Formosa), but their objective will not be the creation of a system in which their own profession would be eliminated.

The general and gradual hardening of China's posture towards the world was thus quite apparent. Its intimate relationship with domestic developments was equally clear. China's conflict with many countries escalated; the cultural revolution brought new tensions in China's relations with many countries. But this should not lead us to the conclusion that China has now gone over to an adventurist line and that the old caution that characterized Peking's actions, as distinct from its verbal exercises, has been thrown to the winds. Peking continues to maintain considerable flexibility in its foreign policy and particularly after the recent curbing of the excesses of the Red Guards, some of the old sophistication has returned. All big countries have various options in dealing with small neighbours. They can extend the olive branch or the fist. They can dangle the carrot or wield the stick. And all big countries have alternated between the two approaches or a combination of them. Whether the neighbour will be met with a smile or a frown depends on various circumstances. In the case of Cambodia, to take only one instance, Chou En-lai was able to introduce a measure of moderation in China's stand and Peking decided to stay its hand. The caution that China continues to show in its response to the conflict in Vietnam is not unintentional. The fact that Peking is fully aware of the demands of national interests is corroborated by the state of China's relations with Pakistan. Despite all the fury of the cultural revolution and the calls for revolution to the peoples of other countries, the warmth and ostentation of friendship with Pakistan has not cooled a bit. Indeed, Peking has attempted to further strengthen the ties with Islamabad. Similar awareness of China's interests is evident in the case of relations with many other countries. The aberrations of the Red Guards notwithstanding, China is not intending to pursue an indiscriminate course of hostility and conflict with the world outside; it will pick and choose its adversaries and targets of attack.

CHAPTER FOUR

THE JANUARY REVOLUTION

THE ADOPTION OF the sixteen points as guidelines for the carrying on of the cultural revolution and the demands of the autumn farming season had brought about a slight pause in the storm in Peking. This led many observers to believe that the cultural revolution had spent itself and that more moderate forces led by Chou En-lai had gained control over the situation and would gradually bring about normalcy. The pause turned out to be a temporary respite and the cultural revolution proceeded with even greater violence, finally culminating in what has been generally referred to as the "January Revolution." The revolution gathered force in these few months and then exploded with a fury far surpassing the previous turbulent campaigns for which Peking was justly famous. Mao had given the call for great division, great turmoil, and great reorganization, but it is doubtful whether he foresaw the confusion and the disarray that it would cause. The Communist Party organization collapsed, authority withered, and the spectre of civil war hovered over the country.

The army, the students, the workers, the Party functionaries, the government administrators and, to a much lesser extent, the peasants were all drawn into the maelstrom. The leaders and the ranks were equally involved and affected. Thousands of party leaders and members were criticized, cast aside or made the target of public humiliation. Neither high nor low were spared. It was difficult, even for the Chinese, to know who stood where, who was a genuine revolutionary and who was not. Those who had tasted power were reluctant to part with it or share it with others, and various groups—even Red Guards—became locked in bitter internecine warfare. The old establishment fought with new contenders and the new contenders tried to exclude those who wanted to come in after them.

The violence and the ruthlessness of this struggle has been revealed by the Chinese themselves, particularly through wall newspapers.

How reliable is the information filtering through wall posters and wall newspapers is a question that has concerned students of the Chinese scene. Admittedly, there have been different kinds of wall posters and not all of them can be accepted as the authentic voice of the Maoist leadership. A certain discretion and caution is, therefore, necessary in accepting this course of information at its face value. What is not generally realized is that there is one kind of wall newspapers, particularly in Peking, which is almost official and, hence, fairly authentic. A number of Red Guard organizations in Peking, enjoying the sanction of the Maoist headquarters, were publishing printed newspapers pasted on the walls of Peking and the views expressed therein or events related therein were more trustworthy than unauthorized and hand-written posters. Among these were *Hung-wei Ping, Shou-tu Hung-wei Ping, Tung-fang Hung, Hung-se Tsao-fan Pao,* and a number of other tabloids published by officially recognized Red Guard organizations and these, obviously, carried the stamp of legitimacy. In analyzing the news conveyed through the wall posters, it is, therefore, necessary to weigh the source of publication. Equally, it is not legitimate to scoff at the entire range of information gathered from the wall posters and to refuse to accept as bona fide evidence even in those wall newspapers which carried official approval.

STRUGGLE WITHIN A STRUGGLE

With the return of Mao to Peking and the capture of the Party centre by the Maoists, it was inevitable that the struggle would become sharper and that the capital city would be the venue for the first battle. It has already been noted that Mao and his chief associates had taken recourse to the establishment of a new organization; the Red Guards were, to begin with, students on the rampage to weed out Mao's "enemies" from the Party and the Government. It has also been noted that, to give guidance to the cultural revolution, a Cultural Revolution Committee, headed by Ch'en Po-ta, was set up by the Party centre. Among its other important members were Chiang Ch'ing (wife of Mao) Wang Li, Ch'i Pen-yu, Chiang Ch'un-ch'iao, Kuan Feng, and Yao Wen-yuan. The Maoists soon discovered that the Red Guard student organizations in Peking were themselves shot through with bourgeois ideology and that the enemy (which subsequently, turned out to be the Head of State, Liu Shao-ch'i, and the Secretary-General of the Communist Party, Teng Hsiao-p'ing, and their followers) had penetrated these organizations too. A relentless struggle took place within the capital's Red Guard student organizations. In fact, this struggle had begun there even in the early phases of the cultural revolution and was so brutal that many committed suicide or otherwise met with their death.[1] The Capital's Red Guard Headquarters for institutes of higher education was found to have come under the influence of the forces that the Maoists were attacking, and had to be purged and reorganized. The Maoist leadership encouraged its supporters to. rebel against the Capital Higher Education General Headquarters; led by the Maoists in Peking Aeronautical Institute, together with their supporters in other colleges, a new Headquarters was organized in the teeth of sharp opposition from the old one and the conflict between the two persisted for a considerable period.[2]

The sharpness of this conflict was evident in other units and organizations in Peking as well. Kuan Feng, one of the members of the Cultural Revolution Committee, admitted in a talk to the Red Guards at the Institute of Geology that "a serious split exists now" but he ascribed it to the existence of two lines—the revolutionary and the reactionary—in the country.[3] The fluidity of the situation was evident from the attacks on the Cultural Revolution Committee (of the CC) itself which was held guilty of "instigating the masses to struggle against the masses" (something forbidden in the ground rules laid down by Mao in the Sixteen Points). (The real position was that the Maoists were permitted to rebel but the dissidents were not allowed to mobilize support.) The dissidents accused the

---

[1]This is borne out by many Red Guard pronouncements. See, for instance, "Record of the Discussions between Ch'i Pen-yu [Member of the Cultural Revolution Committee of the Central Committee] with the Leadership of the Original Capital Higher Education Red Guard General Headquarters," *Tung-fang Hung*, Peking, 20 December 1966.

[2]*Ibid.* (A similar account appears in the Fourth Announcement in the same issue.)

[3]*Wu-ch'an Chieh-chi Wen-hua Ta-ko-ming Yu-kuan Ts'ai-liao Pien-hui* (materials relating to the Great Proletarian Cultural Revolution), Canton, October 1966, Vol. II, pp. 31-3.

Cultural Revolution Group of "distrusting the masses" and "disbelieving in the self-liberation of the masses." A Maoist Red Guard newspaper bemoaned that "reactionary" posters had appeared on the streets of Peking "viciously attacking our great leader, Chairman Mao, and Deputy Chairman Lin." Simultaneously, the opposing group of Red Guards in the Peking Aeronautical Institute had "impatiently" come out with posters addressed to the Central Cultural Revolution Committee with "one enquiry," "two enquiries," "three enquiries," and "four enquiries."[4] Describing the critics in colourful language, another Red Guard mouthpiece said: "Recently, a bevy of flies dying of cold, flying and biting in confusion, and exerting their last struggle to survive, let out monstrous howls against the Cultural Revolution Committee of the Central Committee. Repeated howls will be of no avail, for ultimately the flies do not survive the winter."[5] Some of the Red Guards wanted to rebel so much that they had no use even for the Maoist Headquarters—the Cultural Revolution Committee. They said that they wanted to make revolution themselves and not have it guided by the Committee. Wall posters indicated that there was considerable criticism of Mao's wife, Chiang Chi'ng, who was the Vice-Chairman of the Cultural Revolution Committee, and Ch'en Po-ta had to defend her and her credentials as a leader in the cultural revolution. Ch'en said that it was he who had recommended her to the Communist Party and that she had done good work.

The struggle became so violent that the issue of who would control Peking hung in the balance. The opponents were denounced by the Maoists for intriguing to control the Red Guards. "They divided the Red Guards into three, six, and nine sections," complained the loyal Maoists. "They utilize the Red Guards to attack Red Guards." They schemed to choke the Red Guards to death in their cradle. They secretly set up "concentration camps," privately established jails, kidnapped opponents and inflicted "cruel punishments," and were comparable to "fascist Nazis."[6] In the fight for the capture of the broadcasting station of the capital, for instance,

[4]*Tung-fang Hung*, 17 December 1966.

[5]*Shou-tu Hung-wei Ping*, Peking, 11 December 1966.

[6]"Fifth order from the Headquarters of the Ta-Chuan Institute Red Guard Revolutionary Rebels of the Capital," *Shou-tu Hung-wei Ping*, 11 December 1966.

two iron doors, especially constructed (allegedly by the reactionaries) for the station, had been sealed and installed with an electric current and a pump for providing high voltage guns with water. There was a free fight with the use of iron clubs, kitchen knives, and hatchets.[7] Those who were involved in opposition to this group, on the other hand, accused the self-proclaimed Maoists of attacking the People's Liberation Army and described them as "rebels and roughnecks, robbers and bandits." They blamed the loyalists (a term used here for those who had the support of the Maoist Headquarters) for assaults on the Ministry of National Defence and for attacking factories, smashing machinery, and beating up workers. They criticized Ch'en Po-ta's speeches and complained that the Cultural Revolution Committee was adopting a partisan attitude in favour of some organizations and they reportedly even went to the extent saying that Mao's wife was pretending to be "left" but was actually "right." The loyalists, in turn, claimed that these people were also shouting, "long live Liu"[8] (obviously meaning Liu Shao-ch'i— clear evidence that the struggle was already revolving around Mao and Liu).

An indication of the desperate nature of the struggle was provided when the loyalist Red Guards held a mass rally on 4 December 1966 at Tien-an-men (Gate of the Heavenly Peace—China's Red Square), put up huge posters and gave the slogan: "Protect Chairman Mao." They swore to "guard Chairman Mao till death."[9] They claimed that with this massive demonstration they had dealt a fatal blow to the "capitalist reactionary line" and tilted the balance decisively in favour of Mao. The attack on 4 December was a marvel, they exulted. After this "great counter-attack," the city of Peking witnessed the "trend of attacking the capitalist reactionary line." Huge posters went up everywhere in the streets and alleys of Peking and propaganda cars fitted with loudspeakers sped along the main avenues blaring out "militant outcries." On 6 December, nearly one hundred thousand Red Guards from all over the country held a meeting at the Workers' Stadium in Peking to attack the "reactionary" line and later paraded in the streets of Peking to proclaim their determination to defend the "correct leadership of the

[7]*Hung-wei Ping*, Peking, 25 November 1966.
[8]*Tung-fang Hung*, 17 December 1966.
[9]*Shou-tu Hung-wei Ping*, 11 December 1966.

Cultural Revolution Committee."[10]

The struggle and the violence in Peking were also projected elsewhere in the country. Red Guards battled with Red Guards, as Party leaders at every level sought support for their position in a desperate bid for survival. To take a typical example: a Maoist leader in Peking, Chiang Chun-ch'iao, addressed Red Guards who had come to the capital from Fukien and comforted them because they had been "insulted and injured" in their own province. This showed, he said, that the cultural revolution was very necessary. If political power had not been in the hands of the Maoists, would they have been able to come to Peking to tell their hardships? He told them about the experience of the Red Guard students in Peking, of the Peking Aeronautical Institute, the Institute of Geology, the Peking Normal University, and the Tsinghua University, where the leftists were isolated, sometimes numbering only ten, and sometimes were even locked up. Top leaders had to intervene to get them released and rehabilitated.[11] From the reports it requires little ingenuity to imagine how intense the shake-up in various parts of China and how bewildering the confusion must have been.

The developing struggle was taking place at many levels: at the level of the top leadership and their moves among the ranks below, at the level of the provincial and local administration, at the level of the cadres under attack, and at the level of the Red Guard organizations that had proliferated all over the country. The various levels of these struggles sometimes dovetailed into each other, but quite often were independent of each other. Undoubtedly, the opposing forces at the summit were busy behind the lines to influence and manipulate the various groups which were locked in a fateful and extremely consequential battle. The Maoist headquarters was clearly making an all-out effort to control and direct the Red Guards. A similar effort on the part of those who knew by now that they were the real targets of the revolution must be presumed. Mao was gradually closing in the ring so that the attack could be concentrated on the "top person in authority taking the capitalist road" (Liu Shao-ch'i) and the man next to him in the hierarchy (Teng Hsiao-p'ing, Secretary-General of the Communist

[10]*Ibid.*
[11]*Wu-ch'an Chieh-chi   Wen-hua   Ta-ko-ming   Yu-kuan   Ts'ai-liao   Pien-hui*, Vol. III, pp. 16-8.

Party). As the autumn pause ended and the revolution once again acquired steam, evidence was accumulating that Mao's hidden enemy was his own intended successor, his lifetime "comrade-in-arms" and, besides him, the most powerful man in the Communist organization. It was unbelievable but nevertheless true that Mao had turned against the man who was not only one of his earliest followers and friends (it was in 1919 that Liu first joined Mao in his New People's Study Society) but who was hitherto regarded as his most faithful ideological spokesman and whom Mao had himself groomed as his successor.

FALL OF LIU SHAO-CH'I

An early indication of Liu's fall from grace was available in the discussion that one of the members of the Cultural Revolution Committee, Ch'i Pen-yu, had with the Red Guard students on 12 November 1966, in the course of which he was reported to have said that books "labelled as if they can teach you to be a better Communist are actually shot through with bourgeois ideology"[12]—an unmistakable reference to Liu Shao-ch'i's celebrated work, *How to be a Good Communist*. On 12 December,[13] the Red Guards dragged out for public humiliation P'eng Ch'en, Lo Jui-Ch'ing, Lu Ting-i, and other erstwhile high-ranking leaders, and shrieking crowds of Red Guards hurled at them accusations and abuses, spat at them, and subjected them to various other indignities. They were called Khrushchovs of China, a term which was eventually fixed on Liu Shao-ch'i. The first public attack on Liu Shao-ch'i by Red Guards (though it was not mentioned in the national newspapers) was made on 30 December by the Tsinghua University Red Guard, K'uai Ta-fu, who had already earned name by his leadership of the Maoist faction against heavy odds, having been declared a counter-revolutionary by the opposing group and even clamped into a prison but rescued and rehabilitated by Chou En-lai himself. In an article in a Red Guard newspaper, he said that both the revolution and the counter-revolution had someone in charge, a commander. The supreme commander of the "revolutionary camp" was Mao,

[12]See fn. 1.
[13]*Tung-fang Hung*, Peking, 17 December 1966. Photographs of this public humiliation were displayed in Peking on 16 January.

and that of the anti-revolutionary camp the "dark commander," Liu Shao-ch'i. "After more than six months of fierce struggle between the two lines, the people have clearly realized that the said headquarters is the dark bourgeois headquarters headed by Liu Shao-ch'i and Teng Hsiao-p'ing, and that the small handful of authoritarians in the Party following the capitalist road consists of Liu Shao-ch'i, Teng Hsiao-p'ing, Po I-po, Wang Jen-chung, Wang Kuang-mei, etc."[14]

K'uai Ta-fu, obviously writing under guidance from above,[15] accused Liu Shao-ch'i of having committed "countless heinous crimes" during the last twenty years. Since the Seventh Congress, it was now discovered, Liu had begun to "slip down the anti-Chairman Mao mud-hole and serve as the agent of the overthrown bourgeoisie." It was Liu Shao-ch'i, so went the accusation, who "openly advocated" at the Eighth Party Congress (1956) the theory of the subsiding of the class struggle and supplied the theoretical basis for the capitalist restoration. It was, again, he who "openly declared that we must learn from the capitalists," who "vigorously affirmed" the "revisionist viewpoint of the 20th Congress of the Soviet Communist Party," and who declared that intelligent men also existed in the "U. S. imperialist ruling clique, the sworn enemy of the people of the world." What was "even more abominable" was that Liu tried to erase the thought of Mao from the minds of the people. Liu was also condemned for the liberal concessions to the peasantry during 1960-62.

K'uai's attack on Liu's wife, Wang Kuang-mei, was equally vehement. On the eve of the Eleventh Plenum of the Central Committee, contrary to her usual practice, she made her appearance everywhere, put on an act before the public, persuasively extolled the work teams,[16] openly praised Liu Shao-ch'i, and willingly and tacitly approved the extreme reactionary slogan of "Long live Liu Shao-ch'i." She even objected to Mao's decision to withdraw the work teams. "Spreading poison everywhere," she made such statements as: "do not simplify," "perfection is impossible," "the work team has its achievements and defects," etc. "This was the Wang

---

[14]*Hung-wei Ping*, Peking, 30 December 1966.

[15]It would not be surprising if the article was actually written by a member of the Maoist headquarters.

[16]For the controversy over work teams, see Chapter Two.

Kuang-mei who went on a pleasure trip abroad wearing a gold necklace," sneered K'uai. There were even posters in the streets praising Wang Kuang-mei. In August 1966, she privately held "a round-table meeting to influence public opinion," provoked opposition between the "8.9 Association" and "8.8 Association" of Tsinghua and "attempted to split the students." She accused the "revolutionary people" as being rightists and created conflicts among the masses. She was the "principal pickpocket" o Tsinghua University.

Po I-po, the Economic Tsar of China,[17] was now described as the "cunning henchman" of Liu Shao-ch'i, who also "stretched his black claw into the University." Liu and his wife and Po also enlisted the good offices of Wang Jen-chung, the "big Pekinese dog," to carry out the Liu-Teng line under the name of the Central Cultural Revolution Committee. Wang Jen-chung was previously chief of the Hupeh Privincial Party Committee and a secretary of the Central-South Bureau of the Central Committee of the Chinese Communist Party,[18] and had been brought to Peking at the start of the cultural revolution in order to help, but had apparently now fallen a victim to it. He was accused of following a policy of "apparent obedience but secret resistance"; pretending to criticize the reactionary line, he "surreptitiously maintained a close contact with Wang Kuang-mei." But the real "back-stage black boss" of them all was Liu Shao-ch'i who was the "number one anti-revolutionary revisionist."[19]

It was only to be expected that powerful figures as these would move to protect their positions and mobilize support and that this would result in a ruthless struggle and sanguinary clashes. An aspect of this battle which has generally not received much notice is that, whereas Liu and his lieutenants emphasized the class origin of the Red Guards who could qualify for leadership, Maoists saw in this an attempt to frustrate Mao's plans and branded it as a

---

[17]An alternate member of the Politbureau since 1956, Po I-po was Vice-Premier, Chairman of the State Economic Commission, and Vice-Chairman of the State Planning Commission.

[18]Wang Jen-chung was a Long Marcher, an old Communist, and was concurrently Political Commissar of the Wuhan Military Region from 1963 onwards.

[19]K'uai Ta-fu, "Destroy the Liu-Teng Bourgeois Reactionary line and strive for new victories !" *Hung-wei Ping*, Peking, 30 December 1966,

"reactionary" philosophy. Liu Shao-ch'i and Teng Hsiao-p'ing were credited with propagating the view that "when the father is a hero, the son must be a brave man, and when the father is a reactionary, the son must be a rotten egg—this is basic." This was condemned as a reactionary, hereditary theory which was made use of by Liu and Teng to dampen the revolutionary zeal of many students whose class origin was not pure and who did not belong to either working class or poor peasant families or were not scions of Communist revolutionaries. Liu and Teng had got the "mistaken principle" adopted which relied only on students coming from the Five-Red categories and excluded those with "bad or general origin."[20]

For Mao the touchstone was not class origin but fidelity to Mao's thought; he wanted to broaden the ranks of the Red Guard students by including those whose parentage might not have been associated with the revolutionary classes, but who were his vociferous followers and who would do the job of cutting down his opponents for him— only those sons and daughters of the worker and poor peasant classes or of Communist Party members were welcome who would be his loyal "little generals" (a phrase much used by the Maoists to describe the Red Guard students). Liu and Teng, apparently, put more credence on the latter category of students, particularly children of Party members, who, it stands to reason, could also be expected to be more willing to listen to and abide by their opinions and positions.

The attack on Wang Jen-chung was highly significant because he was known to be a close protege of T'ao Chu, the powerful Communist leader in the south and First Secretary of the Central-South Bureau, and as in the case of Teng T'o, Wu Han, and many others, it was a definite pointer that the real object of attack was the higher "back-stage boss." T'ao Chu was the most influential Communist leader in Central-South China and had been called to Peking to guide the cultural revolution and he had brought Wang Jen-chung along with him. The denunciation of Wang clearly meant that the guns were being trained on T'ao Chu himself and it was only a question of time before T'ao would be exposed to public censure. The cultural revolution once again hurtled forward with

[20]*Shou-tu Hung-wei Chan-pao*, Editorial, Peking, 10 February 1967.

increasing speed and intensity. The Red Guards, actively encouraged and spurred on by the Maoist leadership, went on the offensive
against all known or suspected oppositionists among the Party and
government cadres. Big and small, high and low, all were smitten
down in an orgy of denunciations and dismissals and, by January of
the new year (1967), the tempest of the cultural revolution was
sweeping over much of China. The big guns fell, so did their proteges and followers and thousands of others drawn remorselessly into
the vortex. What a mighty fall it was for, Liu Shao-ch'i, Teng
Hsiao-p'ing, Ho Lung, T'ao Chu, Lo Jui-ch'ing, P'eng Chen, Lu
Ting-i, Po I-po, and Li Wei-han !

A WORD OF CAUTION BUT A FLOOD OF REVOLUTIONARY APPEALS

Inevitably, the ferment created by the Red Guards had led to large-
scale conflict and disturbance. A number of people were involved
in the game of mutual denunciations and the Maoist leadership had
shown some awareness of the problems arising from it, and exhortations to the Red Guards to limit this offensive to as few persons as
was necessary were combined with cheers for the work done by them
on behalf of Mao. Through their chief theoretical organ, the
Hung-ch'i (Red Flag), they advised their youthful supporters to
concentrate on the enemies and desist from over-diversification of the
attack. An editorial in September 1966 reminded the Red Guards
of Lin Piao's instructions that they must distinguish between enemies
and friends, pay attention to "uniting with the majority," and they
must follow the decision that the main target of attack were "those
in power who have wormed their way into the Party and are taking
the capitalist road." A distinction should be made between those
who merely followed the leaders in pursuing the "bougeois reactionary line" and those who were the instigators and initiators of the line,
and in any case mass quarrels and fights were not permissible.[21]
A subsequent editorial in November repeated the theme and
stressed that those who put forward the wrong line should be dis-
tinguished from those who had put it into effect, and those who
had done so consciously from those who did it unwittingly; the
serious errors should be treated differently from minor ones. The

[21]*Hung-ch'i*, No. 12, 1966.

Maoist leadership seemed to hold out one last chance to the purveyors of the "reactionary bourgeois line" to rehabilitate themselves if they made a public confession and showed willingness to come back to the correct line of Mao. The conditions were: they must "openly admit to the masses that they have put the wrong line into effect, seriously redress the wrong done to the revolutionary masses who have been described as 'counter-revolutionaries,' 'anti-Party elements,' 'rightists,' 'phoney left-wingers but genuine right-wingers,' openly retrieve their character and support the revolutionary action of the revolutionary masses."[22] This command to appear in sackcloth and ashes for all the world to see seemed to have been directed as much to the higher echelons of the leadership as to the lower-ranking cadres.

These were, however, half-hearted attempts to keep the situation well in hand, for Mao had no intention to bridle the Red Guards and restrict the upsurge created by them at this time. The disturbances being created by the "revolutionary rebels" were not yet taken seriously and it was perhaps hoped that the situation would remain under control. Therefore, the call for discrimination in fighting the enemies was drowned by louder and more insistent calls for pressing ahead with the revolution and exposing all the monsters and demons. "There can be no construction without destruction," *Hung-ch'i* said explicitly, and, therefore, the mass struggle must go on. The bourgeois reactionary line must be thoroughly repudiated and the "power-holders" in the Party taking the capitalist road must be overthrown.[23] In a New Year editorial this ideological mouthpiece of the Maoists served notice that in 1967 "China's Great Proletarian Cultural Revolution will continue to develop" in line with the experience of contemporary Chinese history that "all cultural revolution movements began with students' movements sparking and merging into workers' and peasants' movements." The cultural revolution "must go from the offices, schools and cultural circles to the factories and mines and the rural areas so that all positions are captured by Mao Tse-tung's thought. Any argument against the carrying out of a large-scale proletarian cultural revolution in factories and mines and the rural areas is incorrect." The editorial urged the revolutionary rebels to carry the cultural

[22]*Ibid.*, editorial, No. 14, 1966.
[23]*Ibid.*, No. 13, 1966.

revolution to its logical conclusion and promised that 1967 would be a year of all-round development for the revolution.[24]

The movement led by the Red Guards had developed a momentum of its own and a few words of caution were not going to halt the storm. The revolution now swept over the country like a hurricane, shaking the foundations of the system and involving the country in such turmoil and conflict the like of which had not been witnessed in China ever since the founding of the new regime in 1949. Even before the New Year editorial of *Hung-ch'i* officially sanctioned the spread of the revolution to workers and peasants, the Red Guard students had gone to the factories and fields to agitate the workers and peasants and to stir them into action against Party authorities and all others who were believed to be resisting Mao's policies. From early November, the "young soldiers of revolution," organizations of revolutionary teachers and students such as "Red Flag" of Peking Aeronautical Institute, "East is Red" of the Institute of Geology and "Chinkangshan Red Guards" of Tsinghua University took the rounds of factories, "charging forward to fulfil the tasks of struggle, criticism, and reform," according to Red Guard wall posters.[25]

This was a reversal of the earlier decision in September that the Red Guards would stay away from the factories and fields leaving the workers and peasants to carry out their own revolution without affecting production. Apparently, the cultural revolution had failed to take off in the factories and fields, and a push from outside was needed. The proletariat had not responded too enthusiastically to the proletarian cultural revolution and the youngsters from the universities and schools had to be mobilized to activate it. But this was also the beginning of trouble on a much larger scale. The industrial enterprises were more generally affected than the peasantry. The welcome received by the youthful propagators of Mao's thought was not exactly warm and at many places sanguinary clashes took place between the workers and Red Guard students. "Some people" who were not "informed of the truth" proceeded to defend and protect the factories.

For instance, the happenings in the First Lathe Factory in Peking were significant. The Red Guards from the Institute of Mechanical

[24]*Ibid.*, No. 1, 1967.
[25]*Hung-se Tsao-fan Pao*, Peking, Inaugural Issue, 26 December 1966.

Engineering were unceremoniously thrown out over the factory walls by the workers. But these students "kept on fighting" and finally entered the factory. In another instance, at the Peking Internal Combustion Factory, the Red Guards from the Agricultural Engineering Institute were driven out of the factory and for more than ten days they were "left outside in the bitter cold, receiving no food from the factory authorities." In a more serious incident at the Kuang-hua Lumber Factory, a thousand workers repeatedly attacked the Red Guards from the Peking Aeronautical Institute and were "instigated" to "harass" the State Council Office and even struck work for three days.[26] The Chao-yang Watch and Clock Factory was similarly shut down. The workers seemed to resent the intrusion and interference by students and their struggle against factory authorities. These instances were multiplied as the movement spread from Peking to other areas in the country. Violence flared up in various parts of the country.

Not only did the Red Guards from the universities and schools clash with workers in factories and industrial enterprises, there was mounting trouble among various groups of workers themselves. The account given by the Maoists of what transpired at the Peking No. 1 Cotton Mill was typical of the events in many parts of the country. The Cultural Revolution Preparatory Committee of the mill, established in place of the earlier Party Committee, was accused of peddling the bourgeois reactionary line when 151 members of the "Thought of Mao Tse-tung Red Guards" and the "Tung-fang Hung Militant Red Guards"—two organizations which apparently enjoyed the backing of the Red Guard headquarters in the capital— were branded as "counter-revolutionaries" by the rival Red Guard organization owing allegiance to the Preparatory Committee. According to the version of the Maoist-supported organizations, the opposing Red Guard groups sealed their offices and set up private jails to try "comrades who held different opinions." Over five hundred members of this group mercilessly beat up the "true Maoists," "tortured" many of them and "even humiliated some of the women comrades." The end was still not in sight and "the struggle was still very cruel."[27] Similar reports poured in from other factories and mines.

[26]*Ibid.*
[27]*Shou-tu Hung-wei Ping*, No. 12, 26 November 1966.

The Red Guards also stormed various Ministries and governmental organizations in the capital as well as in the provinces. In Peking, the Minister in the Ministry of Geology, Tsou Chia-yu, fled rather early in the struggle and could not be traced for ten days despite the clamours of the Red Guards and the wrathful denunciation by a member of the Central Cultural Revolution Committee, Kuan Feng, who was "mad" at the minister for deserting his post.[28] The minister's daughter was also alleged to have mobilized support for her father and collected a group of people to revile the "Tung-fang Hung" Red Guards of the Geological Institute, who were spear-heading the attack on Tsou. From November to January, the attack on the ministries and governmental organizations became all-pervasive causing uncontrollable confusion and disruption. Ministries of Petroleum, Railways, Agriculture, and a host of others were subjected to *gheraos* and the leading personnel exposed to public accusation and criticism. Even the Ministries of Foreign Affairs and Public Security could not escape the wrath of the Red Guards.

The Minister for Petroleum, Yu Ch'iu-li, and his deputy K'ang Shih-en were described as the leaders of the reactionary Liu-Teng (Liu Shao-ch'i and Teng Hsiao-p'ing) line in the petroleum industry and in the western part of Peking. Lieutenant-General Yu ch'iu-li, who started life as a guard attendant of Jen Pi-shih, was in the Long March and had held various ranks as Political Commissar to PLA units before being inducted into the Ministry of Petroleum. K'ang Shih-en had joined the Eighth Route Army in 1937 as a student and had been long associated with the petroleum industry in various capacities in Communist China. With the Maoist Red Guards shouting for their blood Yu and K'ang, with their backs to the wall, organized counter-resistance and set up the "Monkey Soldier" Red Guards from among the children of cadres, the daughter of Yu being one of its active members. This team took up the cudgels for the Party leaders in their petroleum system and a sharp struggle ensued. The Maoists alleged that when the revolutionary rebels of Petroleum Plant No. 1 came to the capital to "expose the crimes of K'ang Shih-en and others before the Central Committee," they were made the victim of "cruel persecution" by the supporters of Yu and

[28]Kuan Feng's speech at the Round-Table Conference at the Institute of Geology. (See fn. 3.)

K'ang and were compelled to return home. The same fate awaited the "15 revolutionary faculty members and students" of Liaoning University and the Northeast Industrial College when they came to Peking to proffer charges against the leadership in the Ministry of Petroleum. Yu and K'ang instructed Jen Ch'eng-yu, the director of the Political Department of the Ministry of Petroleum, to suppress the petitioners and force them to go back. Subsequently, Yu Ch'iu-li took refuge in the Northeast but eventually had to return to Peking and face his accusers.[29]

The Railway Minister, Lu Cheng-ts'ao, received particularly severe denunciation from the Maoist Red Guards. Former Commander Lu was a graduate of the Northeast Military Academy (1922); he joined the Communist Party in 1937 and was Commander of the Central Hopei Military Area. He later commanded various other military regions under the Communists and was a member of Communist China's top level military consultative organization, the National Defence Council as well as of the Central Committee of the Party. He paid for his close links with Lo Jui-ch'ing, the disgraced Chief of Staff. Variously described as "reactionary rascal," "Lu the Baldy," "despotic emperor Chin Shih of modern times." Lu was accused of having compared the Maoist leadership to "AhQ,"[30] which could not tolerate any mention of its weaknesses.[31] He sided with the "rightists" in 1962 (when China was facing a serious economic crisis) and had the temerity to "directly praise the Soviet revisionists." He was reported to have said that Pavlov of the USSR did not support the Soviet system even on his death-bed but the Soviets still conferred many medals on him. The moral being that "as long as a person was good at some speciality, we must give him encouragement and support." His other crime was that he believed that, whereas class struggle was "the great truth," "we must also see the small truths concerning food and clothing and education" and that "politics in command must be combined with material incentives." His biggest and most unforgivable crime was that he could not or would not read Mao's books.[32]

[29]*Chin-chun Pao*, Peking, 1 April 1967.
[30]"AhQ" was the celebrated half-idiotic character in Lu Hsun's classic by the same title.
[31]*Hung T'ieh-tao*, Peking, 11 February 1967.
[32]*Ibid.*

Marshal Ch'en Yi, the Foreign Minister, also came in for considerable mauling at the hands of the Red Guards. It is reported that he was also dragged out and made to face crowds of accusing Red Guards but he has so far escaped official description as a counter-revolutionary revisionist. The criticism against him mounted in the third phase of the cultural revolution.[33]

STRUGGLE AT FOUR LEVELS

The same story was repeated in the provinces and in the towns and the countryside of China. The Party and government leadership was generally under heavy attack by the Mao-backed Red Guards organizations. The fat was in the fire and the sweep of the revolution became so broad as to endanger the governmental and political cohesion of the country. Almost every Party, government, industrial, and educational unit was the scene of sharp, often violent, conflicts, with the previous authorities defending themselves from the sledgehammer-like attacks of the opponents and various groups making a strong bid for rebellion and power. Red Guard organizations sprang up among the workers and government employees and various other units and institutions and even in some suburban communes near the big cities. They all marshalled their strength to fight to carry out the revolution, according to their own lights and, not less significantly, to wrest power from others. It is important to note that the struggle was now under way at least at four levels, sometimes interlocked and sometimes independent of each other.

First, and quite obviously, there was the duel at the summit between Mao and Liu Shao-ch'i. This struggle involved the leadership, and the shifting nature of the power structure at the top was an indication of the fierceness and ruthlessness of the battle. Liu Shao-ch'i, Teng Hsiao-p'ing, and P'eng Chen constituted the trinity of power in the previous scheme of things. They were now displaced, derided, and disgraced. For a while, T'ao Chu had jumped many notches in the new power structure but was soon enough sent hurtling downwards. Lin Piao was named Mao's successor, and Chou En-lai, now number three in the hierarchy (Mao included), with maintaining a precarious perch at the top. Besides them arose

[33]See next chapter.

new contestants dominating the power structure—Mao's wife Chiang Ch'ing, Ch'en Po-ta, K'ang Sheng, and their supporters Wang Li, Hsieh Fu-chih, Chiang Chun-ch'iao, Ch'i Pen-yu, Kuan Fang, and Yao Wen-yuan. Some of this latter group were hardly national figures until suddenly drawn near the base of power. Barring Ch'en Po-ta, K'ang Sheng, and Hsieh Fu-chih, none of them was even a member of the Central Committee of the Communist Party, nor did any of these figure in the previous secretariat of the Central Committee.

This war at the top led to the struggle at the second level. Not only did the giants fall but all their nominees and followers were also hounded out. Since the chiefs themselves were thrown out for being disloyal to the Chief of Chiefs, it was inevitable that suspicion would fall on their proteges and close associates both at Peking and in the provinces. The leadership which had now been thrown out of the Party Centre had held power tightly for many years. They were believed to be the successors of Mao. They were entrenched in the Party and government positions. They were now being picked up one by one and were fighting for their lives. At the same time, since the struggle against the Party and bureaucratic power-holders was developing into a general assault by the Red Guards on the leadership, the Party cadres and the government functionaries, every leader and Party cadre whether managing a factory or in charge of an institution or government unit was put on the defensive, fighting off the attacks on him and deeply embroiled in the commotion of the cultural revolution. It was the fusion of the struggle at these two levels that made the situation so explosive.

Last, but not least, were the developing feuds among the Red Guards themselves. Thousands of such organizations had mushroomed across the country as rivals and bidders of power against the old establishment. Some of them were accused by the Maoists of having been infiltrated by the followers of the "bourgeois reactionary Liu-Teng Line," some were suspected of being "left" in appearance but "right" in point of fact, while many more were engaged in a plain struggle for power. This infighting among the Red Guards, as we shall see, became the principal feature of the cultural revolution in the subsequent period.

The revolution of Mao moved from the universities and schools to Party organizations, industrial enterprises, factories, mines, government units, transport and communications system, and so on, with such lightning rapidity that the entire structure cracked and creaked, and all but came crashing down.   Besides Peking, a number of provinces and big cities were seething with struggle, discord, and confusion.   Provinces and cities outside the capital became the new centres of struggle for the seizure of power and counter-resistance. Surprisingly, Shanghai which was Mao's base before the Eleventh Plenum and which was, therefore, believed to be a Mao stronghold gave early evidence of having once again come under the influence of the "revisionists" and a serious arena of conflict between the two lines.   Besides Shanghai, the struggle was also serious in the provinces of Fukien, Shansi, Shensi, Shantung, Kiangsi, Kwangtung, Kweichow, Chinghai, Anhwei, Szechuan, Sinkiang, Inner Mongolia, and, reportedly, Tibet.

TROUBLE IN THE PROVINCES

The developments in Shanghai were not only surprising but symptomatic of what was going on in other parts of the country too.   Mao had made Shanghai his base before he was certain of controlling the situation in Peking, and Shanghai was, therefore, considered a "pocket borough" of the Maoists.   But as soon as Mao left, it appears that the "revisionists" raised their heads again and continued to rule the roost in the Shanghai Municipal Party Committee —or may be that the "power-holders" there were hedging in the implementation of the Mao line, notwithstanding verbal support, and that Mao was acutely dissatisfied with the Shanghai Party leadership.   Word must have passed on to Mao's men in Shanghai through Yao Wen-yuan and, in December 1966, the Red Guards mounted an all-out attack on the real or fancied opponents.   They attacked the Municipal Party Committee leadership; they stormed other State organizations; they went to the factories; and they even involved peasants of the suburban communes.   They in turn were attacked by opposing groups and organizations.   It was a nasty fight in which both sides used all available means. Water and electric supplies were cut off, transport was disrupted, and port operations were suspended as rival groups of workers, students, and peasants clashed.[34]

[34]Peking Radio, Home Service, 16 January 1967.

A new accusation came to be levelled by the Maoists against their opponents—that of "economism." It was alleged that a handful of power-holders in the Shanghai Municipal Party Committee "whipped up a gust of ill wind" and used material incentives to "corrupt and soften up" workers in order to shift the general orientation of the struggle. They issued supplementary wages and promised promotions to win the support of the workers and "instigated them to ask for wages and amenities and leave their posts of production."[35] Whether all these accusations were true, there is hardly any way of assessing, but, whatever the means employed (and in such a "life and death" struggle, means were the least important consideration), the workers were divided in their loyalties and the struggle among various groups was bloody. As a result, trains did not run for many days and did not run on time for many more days; there was a break in the water and electric supply, there was no loading at the docks for days and production halted at many places. The inland water transport system also broke down for some time with many workers deserting their boats. Half the boats of the sixth shipping team of the Shanghai Municipal Inland Waterway Transport Company were left at anchor. The movement of coal, iron, and agricultural subsidiary products between urban and rural areas was disorganized and the supply of raw materials to Shanghai factories was disrupted.[36]

The peasantry on the outskirts of Shanghai were also affected. The Maoist supporters among the rural accounting and finance personnel in the suburban communes reported that "a few rotten eggs" in the Party had "stirred up the evil wind of economism" in the communes and "inflicted damage on collective economy and production." At this time of the year, the communes were busy settling the year-end distribution of income and produce and the "rotten eggs" used the opportunity to win support by increasing distribution and inducing the "hoodwinked masses" to agitate for State loans and, if these were not forthcoming, to rebel on the pattern established by the cultural revolution. In some places all the reserves accumulated over the past years were released for distribution. Some "ignorant commune members" went away to "exchange revolutionary experience" (that was like giving a taste of

[35]*Ibid.* (Quoted in *New China News Agency*, Peking, 19 January 1967.)
[36]Shanghai Radio, Regional Service, 13 January 1967.

their own medicine to the Maoists), leaving their posts of production and severely upsetting the year-end agricultural production and the marketing of vegetables, "with adverse effect on the livelihood of the city and neighbouring towns."[37] Since the Maoists controlled all the media of propaganda, it was difficult to say with any confidence who used what nefarious means. It is quite plausible that, taking advantage of the confusion of the cultural revolution, the peasants helped themselves to a larger share of the income than they were otherwise entitled to and slashed the State's share and the reserves they were expected to lay aside.

"Economism" became a much used—and much abused—word henceforth and for months to come the Maoists belaboured their opponents for using this trick to snare and delude the masses and erode their revolutionary enthusiasm. Economism was officially described as a philosophy which "advocates that the proletariat struggle only for a small increase in wages and welfare benefits, that the proletariat concerns itself with the temporary interests of the individual but not with the far-reaching and basic interests of the proletariat as a whole, and that the proletariat should not pursue political struggles for the realization of socialism and Communism." It was bad even under the capitalist system, for it limited the struggle of the proletariat to wage increases and reform, but under the socialist system it was "even more reactionary." "It is the tool of capitalism for counter-revolutionary restoration." The "modern revisionists," represented by Khrushchov, "have been lending all efforts in propagating and promoting economism. They have nullified class and class struggle in a socialist society, and denied the necessity of proletarian dictatorship. They have advertised materialistic stimuli and advocated putting bank-notes in command. They have vigorously seduced people to pursue the economic interests of the individual, and put capitalist ideas on a rampage to destroy the socialist system and lead the Soviet Union on the road of capitalist restoration."[38]

It is highly unlikely that any of the dissidents in the Communist Party really stood for the kind of policies that this denunciation implied. More probably, it was a question of proportion and priorities. During the period of economic difficulties, Mao him-

[37]*Ibid.*, 14 January 1967.
[38]*Jen-min Jih-pao*, 16 January 1967.

self had agreed to the restoration of the primacy of material incentives
and possibly his so-called opponents favoured continuing with such
policies. It is also significant that despite all this belabouring of
the opposition in regard to "putting bank-notes in command," there
was no real attempt to replace the existing system of remuneration
based on the principle of "each according to his work" and "more
for more (and better) work" with anything like what was experi-
mented with in the first flush of enthusiasm on the establishment of
the communes in 1958.

The first decisive blows for victory were struck by the "revolutionary rebels" of Mao on 4 January when they announced the
seizure of *Wen-hui Pao* and on 7 January when they ordered
the Shanghai branch of the People's Bank of China to freeze payments until the Central Government issued the appropriate instructions.[39] On 9 January, they issued a public notice accusing the
power-holders in the Shanghai Party Committee of various crimes
against socialism and expressing their determination to fight for
Mao's line and smash the plots of the reactionaries. They also took
over control of various enterprises and institutions, including the
Shanghai Railway Station and the Shanghai Railway Bureau.
That there were more powerful back-stage backers was evident
from the alacrity with which on 11 January a message of greetings
to the Shanghai Workers' Revolutionary Rebel Headquarters and
31 other "revolutionary mass organizations" was sent by Peking
in the name of the Central Committee, the State Council, the Military
Control Commission of Party's Central Committee, and the Cultural
Revolution Committee.

The message backed the "urgent notice" of 9 January and declared
the "rebels" in Shanghai to be "models in studying and applying
Chairman Mao's works in a living way." It commended them for
"exposing the schemes of the bourgeois reactionary line's new
counter-attack" and "launching a forceful counter-offensive" and
extolled them for setting "a brilliant example for the working class
and all labouring people and revolutionary masses throughout the
country." It called upon the Party, the government, the army,
and the people to take concerted action and "beat back the new
counter-attack of the bourgeois reactionary line."[40] The trouble in

[39] *New China News Agency*, Peking, 19 January 1967.
[40] *Ibid.*, 11 January 1967.

Shanghai has continued for a long time and has not yet ended.

Reports from Shansi also spoke of violent clashes between the royalists and the loyalists. (The present authors refer to the groups under attack by the Maoist-backed revolutionary rebels as "royalists"—a term often used by the Maoists—and the latter groups as "loyalists.") On 13 January, the Revolutionary Rebel General Headquarters of Shansi, which had been set up by twenty-five revolutionary rebel organizations, announced the seizure of power from the Party and government organs of the Shansi Provincial Party Committee and Provincial People's Council and the T'aiyuan Municipal Party Committee and the Municipal People's Council. This was preceded, and followed, by large-scale fighting between the Red Guards and the workers supporting the "power-holders" under attack. "Tens of thousands of workers," according to the Maoists themselves, were provoked to besiege and attack the revolutionary rebels. Many workers went away to other places to exchange revolutionary experience. Work stopped in many enterprises and production suffered and "terrifying communications accidents" took place. Large quantities of firearms, ammunition, and "black material"—that is, dossiers on the local Maoists—were also reportedly seized. The loyalists accused the royalists of setting up a secret intelligence service, installing clandestine listening devices, and grouping the "revolutionary organizations" into three categories, listing their leading members in an attempt to harm them soon. Large numbers of houses, buildings, cars, and funds were used in this local warfare and money poured out in thousands of yuan.[41] The Revolutionary Rebel Headquarters announced the assumption of all power and the freezing of funds and their use only under their own authorization. They also described those who opposed Mao and Lin Piao or the Cultural Revolution Committee and those who sabotaged production as counter-revolutionaries to be punished accordingly. All mass organizations and individuals were forbidden to make "illegal use" of firearms and ammunition and to reveal State secrets.

In Shensi, too, the Red Guards and the workers clashed in the last ten days of December 1966, and the demon of economism bared its ugly face. Since all the media of mass communication, pro-

[41] *New China News Agency*, T'aiyuan, 25 January 1967; Peking Radio, 24 January 1967.

paganda, and dissemination of information were under the control of the Maoists, it was their opponents—rightly or otherwise—who were blamed for all the misdeeds, though it is fair to assume, reading between the lines, that both sides used all available means to strike the other down. The "Party office-holders taking the capitalist road" in Sian tried to suppress the revolution by making "an about-turn of 180 degrees" and attacking the real revolutionaries in the name of criticizing the bourgeois reactionary line. "Taking advantage of the legal right of the revolutionary masses to set up revolutionary organizations," according to the Maoists, they "continued to exploit the misled revolutionary comrades and revolutionary staff and workers to set up a number of organizations to protect themselves and to put up stubborn resistance to the revolutionary rebels."[42] Many workers were sent away to Peking in the name of making revolution and a big strike was caused. The royalists apparently established a rival Sian Workers and Peasants Headquarters which was roundly condemned as reactionary by the Maoists and for inciting the workers to go on a strike for nearly half a month. Their organizations were also criticized for "loyally executing the bourgeois reactionary line of the North-West Bureau, the Provincial CCP Committee, and the Sian Municipal CCP Committee."[43]

A similar report came from Foochow in Fukien province that a large number of workers were incited to leave their posts of production and go to Peking, thereby undermining production.[44] The power-holders, "taking advantage of their leading positions," encouraged workers to demand higher wages and better benefits under threat of a strike. As a result, there were power stoppages, suspension of production, and strikes in a number of units. The loyalists warned the royalists: "You are only allowed to behave obediently and you are not permitted to speak and act as you please. Otherwise, suppression by force will be applied."[45] A rally of the loyalist Red Guards and workers on 11 January appealed to all

[42]Open letter to the people of Sian city from revolutionary rebels of Sian area factories and hospitals of the PLA General Rear Services Department. (*New China News Agency*, Sian, 18 January 1967.)

[43]*Sian Regional Service*, 19 January 1967.

[44]*New China News Agency*, Foochow, 12 January 1967.

[45]*Foochow Regional Service*, 12 January 1967.

concerned to return to their posts of production and promised to reexamine the "revisionist" aspects of the wage system but put it off till victory had been achieved in the cultural revolution. The rally announced the dismissal from all positions within and outside the Party of Yang Shou-wen, deputy director of the Planning Committee of Foochow Municipality, on the charge that he violated State regulations by issuing additional funds for capital construction and increasing workers' wages without authorization in order to sabotage the cultural revolution. Yang Shou-wen, along with Yang Nu-yuan, deputy director of the Bureau of the Chemical Industry of Foochow Municipality, and a number of other leading cadres were dragged out on the rostrum amidst a lot of shouting and denunciation.[46] Significantly, there was as yet no formal seizure of power and no establishment of a provisional revolutionary committee. The Maoists did not feel strong enough yet to do so, and, instead, by holding out veiled threats hoped to change the policies of Fukien Provincial and Municipal CCP Committees whose "responsible comrades" were present at the rally to listen to the criticisms and exposures. Meanwhile, struggle continued in various Party, government, administrative, economic and other units, and in factories and suburban communes.

Many leaflets criticizing Ch'en Po-ta and the Central Cultural Revolution Committee appeared in Foochow also and a number of people were arrested at the instance of the Maoists for distributing such "black" leaflets. *Fuchien Jih-pao*, which was the mouthpiece of the Maoists, accused "certain responsible personnel" within the Provincial Party Committee of being behind this attack on the Cultural Revolution Committee and called such people "our mortal enemies." Only the Left was allowed to rebel, it warned, and the Right was not permitted to "emancipate itself." Its call was: "Put to death those who resist, without fear of consequences, and try according to law those who do not resist."[47]

The same story of "economism" came from Chekiang where the peasantry seemed to have been involved on a larger scale than had been usual in the cultural revolution. Inevitably, the "handful of power-holders taking the capitalist road" were blamed for all the "misdeeds" of the peasantry. Armed conflicts took place and many peasants left farm production to join the revolution in the

[46]*Ibid.*   [47]*Ibid.*, 22 January 1967.

cities—no doubt all because of the "provocation of the power-holders." The peasants—or at least a section of them—rebelled against the State's requisitioning of the extra grain output and asked for higher prices for such purchases of the surplus. Conditions of a free market developed in the countryside. The "power-holders" were accused of privately distributing accumulation funds, public welfare funds, and collective reserve grain of the production brigades and teams.[48]

The Party Committee of Shaohsing county, for instance, was held responsible for paying supplementary wages, raising allowances, increasing incentives, and making so-called back payments to commune members engaged in capital construction. The amount of funds "wasted" by the "handful in authority" by the end of the year 1964, was stated to total nearly 600,000 yuan. The situation got so critical that the "revolutionary cadres" of the Shaohsing County People's Bank stepped forward to refuse payment of one million yuan because "it was not in line with State regulations."[49] More serious was the case of Kaihua County Party Committee. The "handful" there went so far as to approve the reallocation of 620,000 yuan of the so-called resettlement funds.[50]

An urgent notice issued on 20 January by twenty revolutionary rebel organizations, including the Revolutionary Rebel United General Headquarters of Chekiang province, called on the peasantry to crush counter-revolutionary economism in the countryside at this time of the year-end final accounting and distribution in response to Chairman Mao's "great call" to "grasp revolution and promote production" and to "prepare for war and for the time of scarcity." While berating economism, the notice of the Maoists was careful in calling for the correct handling of the three-way relationship between the State, the collective, and the commune members. It promised dire punishment for those who in the name of destroying the "four old things" robbed the people of property, committed graft and theft, forcibly took over houses that belonged to the collective and "bullied and oppressed the masses." It announced the freezing of all public funds of the communes and called on all cadres to stick to their posts and do a better job of farm production.[51]

[48]New China News Agency, Hangchow, 31 January 1967.
[49]Ibid., 20 January 1967.   [50]See fn. 47.
[51]New China News Agency, Hangchow, 21 January 1967,

As at many other places, railway transport in Hangchow (Che-kiang) was in a state of confusion and the operation of railway lines, signals, and communications had been disrupted. On 14 January, the "revolutionary rebel workers" of the Hangchow Rail-way Branch Bureau announced that they had wrested power back from the "handful of persons in authority in the Party taking the capitalist road" and had restored railway transport. They claimed that trains running on the Shanghai-Hangchow and Hsiao-shah Ning-po lines had resumed their regular schedules and that by 17 January the number of freight trains loaded in three days showed a 100 per cent increase compared with the first ten days of January. In order to make up for the shortage of crew members, some of whom had deserted their posts of work, the revolutionary rebels "voluntarily worked extra hours to enable the trains to leave on time." Despite these claims of victory, reports continued to pour in about clashes and quarrels between different groups of workers and students.

In Kiangsi also Mao's revolutionary rebels opened fire against the Kiangsi Provincial CCP Committee where as usual "a handful" were resisting the "proletarian revolutionary line represented by Chairman Mao" and "savagely suppressing the revolutionary masses." This handful had provoked many "bloody incidents," committing "towering crimes," and still seemed to be unwilling to admit their crimes and "bow heads before the masses." They incited the Workers' Red Militia Detachment and Peasants' Red Army (or Peasants' Red Militia Detachment)—organizations set up by the "power-holders" in the Party—to "besiege and attack" the revolutionary rebels and as in other places they were accused of practising "counter-revolutionary economism" and of distributing the funds of the communes in order to sabotage collective economy. The Red Guards were beaten up at a workers' club by members of the Workers' Red Militia Detachment and the Peasants' Red Militia Detachment and similar incidents were reported elsewhere. The injured Red Guards from various localities were brought to Nanch'-ang and "comfort teams" were organized by various Red Guard organizations in Nanch'ang as a token of concern for their injured comrades.

On 22 January, the Maoists of the Revolutionary Rebel Corpse of the Provincial CCP Committee Office held a rally in Nanch'ang dragging out "with extreme anger" the "ring leaders" in the Party leadership who had been suppressing the cultural revolution and the revolutionary rebels.   The participants in the rally were "highly indignant"; the sound of slogans rose continuously, and the speeches were "extremely pungent."   They pledged to overthrow completely the handful of Party office-holders who were taking the capitalist path.[52] They also took over *Kiangsi Daily* while blaming the Party "die-hards" for paying 10,000 yuan to more than 100 workers of the printing house for printing the paper and instigating them to go to Peking to voice complaints.[53]   Similar seizure of the leadership of the Kiangsi Provincial Higher People's Court from the hands of the office-holders who had taken the "capitalist road" was brought off, and the Red Guards announced that a "brand new, revolutionary Kiangsi Provincial Higher People's Court has appeared."   The leadership of the Court—"an important tool for the dictatorship of the proletariat"—was now "for ever in the hands of the proletarian revolutionary rebels" and the Court would play its "proper part in resolutely supporting the revolutionary struggle of the revolutionary rebels, resolutely defending the revolutionary rebels and strengthening dictatorship over the enemy."[54]

In the province of Chinghai, too, the Provincial Communist Party leadership was the target of attack by the local Red Guards who accused the "handful" taking the "capitalist road" resorting to various devices in suppressing the revolutionaries and clinging to power.   They (the "power-holders") first adopted the strategem of making the masses fight among themselves while they themselves were, as a famous Chinese proverb goes, "sitting on top of the mountain to watch the tigers fight."   In Sining and Minho, they repeatedly created "serious incidents" and disregarded Mao's instructions that no one must incite the masses to fight among themselves.   They used, according to the catalogue of crimes listed against them by the Maoists, "double-dealing tactics," overt and covert, to control the mass organizations of workers and students to safeguard their position.   They instigated "some workers and peasants" to encircle the revolutionary rebels and to harass the liaison stations and headquarters of eleven revolutionary mass

[52]*Nanch'ang Regional Service*, 22, 23, and 24 January 1967.
[53]*New China News Agency*, Nanch'ang, 22 January 1967.
[54]*Nanch'ang Regional Service*, 24 January 1967.

organizations. They next resorted to the sabotage of production and at their instigation "thousands of workers and peasants"
abandoned their work-posts. They made available funds and transport facilities to provoke fighting among the masses and "directly
sabotaged agricultural and industrial production, interrupted communications and transport, and undermined finance." The charge
of economism was inevitably laid at the door of the "power-
holders" who used "cash and material incentives" to "deceive the
revolutionary masses into compliance." They gave economic
benefits as a bait to induce a large number of peasants to come to
Sining from other areas in an attempt to incite one group of people
against another. The "last device" of the "power-holders" under
attack was that when they found the situation unfavourable
to them, they began to wave the red flag of criticizing the
"bourgeois reac- tionary line" in order to cover up their own
bourgeois line.[55]

In the southwest in Kweichow also the battle had already been
joined between the Maoist revolutionary rebels and their supposed
enemies—the usual "handful" in the Kweichow Provincial Party
Committee and the "handful" in various Party and government
units in the province. From June to December 1966, a series
of clashes took place between the two sides, and the Maoists
complained that the "power-holders" had "frenziedly suppressed"
the revolutionaries and falsely accused thousands of them of being
"counter-revolutionaries" and that they had used "the machinery
of the dictatorship" for exercising "brutal dictatorship" over the
rebels, arrested many Red Guards, set up private prisons, and tortured many of them. The duration and scope of this brutal conflict
was stated to be unparalleled during the cultural revolution. The
"power-holders" were also blamed for organizing "royalist organizations," such as the workers' disciplinary teams and the workers'
pioneering crops to "oppose the revolutionaries, carry out struggle
by coercion, cause incidents, undermine production, and sabotage
the great proletarian cultural revolution."[56]

"Several tens of thousands" of members of twenty-two revolutionary rebel organizations held a rally in Kweiyang (capital of

[55]Text of the message of the Red Guard organizations to the people of Chinghai Province. (*New China News Agency*, Sining, 17 January 1967.)

[56]*New China News Agency*, Kweiyang, 31 January 1967.

Kweichow) on 12 January to pledge support for Peking's call to oppose economism. The rally adopted "an urgent order to the people of Kweichow" to stay at their places of work and boost production, to persuade and mobilize those who had gone to Peking and other places to air complaints and "establish contacts" to come back and make revolution at home, and to appeal to those who had left the province due to factional struggles to return to their original posts. It also directed the provincial Party organization to recover all the "vast amounts" of expenses granted for travelling to other places to make complaints and contacts from the office-holders who issued them but agreed that the recovery might be made in instalments. It also announced the freezing of the "bank accounts of all offices, bodies and enterprises"—only the "masses' bank accounts" were exempt from this order.[57]

On 25 January, the General Command Headquarters of Proletarian Revolutionary Rebels of Kweichow announced the seizure of power from the Party and government organizations of Kweichow and Kweiyang municipalities, denouncing the Provincial Party Committee leaders for having followed a policy of suppressing the revolutionaries and living a decadent life like princes in an independent kingdom. They issued a four-point manifesto with a call for all power to the revolutionary rebels, threatening prosecution of those who resist, "grasping revolution and stimulating production," resolutely combating economism and strengthening the "dictatorship of the proletariat." Anyone who "opposes Chairman Mao, Vice-Chairman Lin Piao, and the Cultural Revolution Committee of the Party Central Committee is to be arrested immediately and prosecuted as a counter-revolutionary." Anyone guilty of sabotaging production was to be prosecuted and anyone directing "the spearhead against the People's Liberation Army," using weapons and ammunition or divulging secret information, was to be called to account. The notice ordered all personnel to resume production, restore communications, "liquidate all mobile capital," and take sanctions against speculation.[58]

The cultural revolution and the attendant conflict was also beginning to spread in Kwangtung, Szechuan, Inner Mongolia, and Sin-

[57]*Kweiyang Regional Service*, 13 January 1967.
[58]See fn. 56.

kiang. The situation became much more explosive subsequently
and all through 1967 there were grave incidents, breakdown of
authority, transport chaos, and violent clashes in these areas. In
Canton, the "revolutionary rebel" organizations were already
complaining in January that the usual "handful" in the Party
apparatus in Kwangtung was resorting to "economism" and instigating the worker-peasant masses to fight with weapons in its plot to
bring about struggles of workers and peasants against students and
students against students. This "handful" was not only "callous"
about the reception of the Red Guards from outside who had come
to exchange revolutionary experiences, but also doled out large sums
to workers as material incentives and for the purpose of making
contacts elsewhere[59] (a rather contradictory charge in view of the
fact that the Red Guards were roaming all over the country to
exchange "revolutionary experiences"). The revolutionary rebel
organizations "ordered" the Party office-holders to immediately
resume work—implying that they were not on their seats earlier—
and "face the masses" (meaning the "revolutionary rebels") and
accept their supervision. The office-holders were also warned
against attempting to obstruct the Red Guard students from going
to the factories and spreading the revolution there. The "rebels"
accused some of the "royalist organizations" of committing assault,
robbery, theft, wrecking vehicles of the revolutionary rebels, "un-
bridled distribution of reactionary leaflets and robbing the people's
armed forces," and ordered the Public Security Departments to
exercise dictatorship over such people.[60] The trouble in Canton
had, however, just begun and the struggle became much sharper
in the ensuing months. The Central-South Bureau of the Central
Committee and the Kwangtung Provincial CCP Committee had
been dominated by T'ao Chu and his men and with his fall from
grace and the opening of the attack against his proteges, the Central-
South region became aflame.

Similarly, in Chungking, the struggle against the South-West
Bureau of the Central Committee and the Provincial and Municipal
Party Committees was developing into a fierce conflict which has
yet to be fully resolved. The revolutionary rebels in Chungking
were already accusing regional and the local Party leadership of

[59]Canton Radio, City Service, 16 January 1967.
[60]*Ibid.*

creating "white terror" and carrying out "fascist dictatorship" in South-West China. They claimed that many revolutionary rebels had been purged, beaten and jailed and promised that in 1967 they would carry out the struggle in an all-round manner and achieve a decisive victory.[61] The Szechuan developments were characteristic of many other places—the developing struggle between the Party leaders and cadres and their organizations at various levels and those of the Red Guards and revolutionary rebels, for the Party functionaries were not only fighting desperately to save their skins but also claimed to be no less revolutionary than the "rebels."

While the conflict was spreading to various provinces of China and becoming increasingly serious, events in Peking, too, indicated a deterioration in the situation. The clashes between the workers and the students and among the students and the beginning of the campaign against Liu Shao-ch'i, Teng Hsiao-p'ing, and many other ministers and ministries have already been noted. A revamping of the Propaganda Department of the Central Committee in January was further evidence of a fierce struggle at the top. T'ao Chu who had suddenly risen to be number four in the Communist hierarchy was also struck down and removed from his position as Head of the Propaganda Department. In his place came Wang Li, a relatively obscure leader until recently, who was also now acting as First Secretary of the Peking Party Committee. *Jen-min Jih-pao* (People's Daily) also had a new editor, and Wu Leng-hsi was replaced by Tang Ping-chu who was at the same time a member of the army cultural revolution group, indicating that there would be stricter control over propaganda.[62]

This was accompanied by a surprise reorganization of the army cultural revolution group and the appointment of Mao's wife Chiang Ch'ing as an adviser to the new group. This shake-up in the army group suggested that even though the army by and large continued to side with Mao, all was not well there; and that in view of the impending call on the army to shoulder heavier responsibilities in carrying on the cultural revolution, Mao felt the need of

---

[61]"Seizure of Power by the Proletariat is Justified," "August 15" Combat Regiment of Chungking University Red Guard Corpse of Chungking Red Guard Revolutionary Rebel Headquarters, *New China News Agency*, Peking, 1 February 1967.

[62]*Tanjug* (English), 13 January 1967.

tightening the grip over the army. That Mao was meeting with some resistance even within the army was clear from the official statements. For instance, one radio broadcast meant for internal consumption mentioned the exposure of "some senior and junior personnel within the army" who "stubbornly clung to the bourgeois reactionary line." The report said that these people then suddenly made "a 180-degree about-turn," giving the appearance of being leftists and shouting high-sounding slogans and hitting hard at the "dead tigers" in order to "fool the masses and raise their political capital." There was a purge in an Air Force academy where persons in authority were taking the capitalist road and persisting in the bourgeois-reactionary line. It was even alleged that, there also, the power-holders resorted to "economism" to "win over the masses by promising them material benefits."[63]

Writing immediately after the reorganization of the army cultural revolution group, *Chieh-fang Chun-pao* (Liberation Army Daily) explained editorially that this reorganization was "a result of the struggle in our Army between the two lines." It was necessary to "break through much resistance" which came primarily from "the handful of people who have wormed their way into the Army," and the paper cautioned that even now "persons in charge of some units" had a very poor understanding of their tasks and were receptive to the "bourgeois reactionary line." The army paper made it clear that "the guns" must be "in the hands of those loyal to Chairman Mao" and that the presence of "revisionists" in the army was particularly dangerous. The army was responsible for defending the country and, therefore, "not a trace of vacillation can be permitted under the pretext of the special conditions of the Army." The cultural revolution could be "in danger of collapsing halfway," unless the army stood "firmly and conscientiously" on the side of Mao. Admitting that the Left (the Maoist revolutionary rebels) had committed some mistakes, the paper nevertheless called on the army men to stand by the leftists unwervingly and not make a fuss over their mistakes and scold and criticize them arbitrarily.[64]

It was symptomatic of the confusion in Peking and its consequences that the Party Central Committee issued a directive on 11 January, calling for the immediate arrest of persons who opposed Mao and

[63]Peking Radio, Home Service, 17 January 1967.
[64]*Chieh-fang Chun-pao*, editorial, 14 January 1967.

Lin Piao or put up posters against them, and stricter punishment against all violators of law and order. Those representing the so-called bourgeois-reactionary line had already officially qualified as breakers of the law, as people who provoked incidents and disturbed peace. The directive also called for punishment to those who used material incentives or "economic bribery" in the struggle and induced workers to demand higher wages and higher grades for wage determination.[65] Additionally, the directive revealed some anxiety on the part of the Maoist leadership about the growing state of lawlessness and the increasing frequency of incidents of larceny, pillage, murder, and disruption of transport.

The disruption had spread from transport to trade. The unified control over finances that Peking had hitherto exercised broke down. The expenditure of money lost its sanctity. Work piled up in offices with no one certain who was in charge and no one prepared to assume responsibility. Harbours cluttered up with unloaded ships and goods waiting to be loaded. Foreign queries went unanswered and foreign trade was in the doldrums.

The anarchy in the field of finance and trade was particularly a matter of concern requiring urgent action by the Red Guards. A rally of nearly a 100,000 "revolutionary rebel fighters in finance and trade," attended among others by Chou En-lai and Li Hsien-nien, was organized with the objective of mobilizing Maoist forces in this field and halting further deterioration. The rally declared null and void decisions made during the movement concerning the revision of wages, increase of allowances, advancement of welfare cash awards and subsidies to cadres, workers, and students "given indiscriminately for exchanging experiences," and other allowances that did not conform to regulations, and called for the refund of such payments. It also enjoined upon the Red Guards to turn in materials and funds confiscated by the Red Guards in their abolition of the "four olds," including anything that might have been privately distributed among them.[66]

The rally declared it the duty of all revolutionary rebels throughout the country to assist the PLA and the public security departments entrusted with the security of national banks and warned that "subversive elements" inciting the masses to besiege the banks and

[65]*Tanjug* (English), 17 January 1967.
[66]*New China News Agency*, Peking, 21 January 1967.

forcibly draw money would be treated as counter-revolutionaries. It directed the revolutionary rebels in the foreign trade departments in the interests of protecting China's international prestige to take immediate action to coordinate urgent measures with the "revolutionary people of the departments concerned," to resolve the existing problems arising from "harbour stagnation" so as to "guarantee the timely unloading of imported goods and strict implementation of contracts signed with foreigners." They must also "clear up all the cables and correspondence from abroad that have accumulated, answer them promptly, grasp firmly the delivery of exported goods and the ordering of imported goods, and strive to fulfil or over-fulfil the national foreign trade plan for 1967."[67]

The gravity of the situation was also noticeable from the reassurance of the Maoist leadership to their followers that they would be protected against any attempt by the opposing group or groups at equalizing the scores subsequently if they managed to recover their position after the movement had spent its fury. Reportedly—by the Maoists—those people who were the targets of the Red Guards and revolutionary rebels had held out the threat that they would settle accounts with their accusers at a later date when they got a chance to reassume their power. They were alleged to have said to the Maoist denunciators: "Now is the time to lure snakes out of their holes. When all the snakes are out, they will be exterminated." They also expressed their confidence that they would regain their positions in the final stage of the movement and threatened the Maoist rebels that it was premature to conclude who was right and who was wrong and that the Red Guards could do whatever they wanted to make trouble, for "they are exposing themselves, so we can settle accounts with them in the future."[68] *Jen-min Jih-pao* assured the Maoist revolutionary rebels that the dream of the dissidents to come back to power would not be allowed to be realized and that the radiance of Mao's thought would sweep away all monsters.

The reports from the provinces and from Peking clearly signified a grave turn in the cultural revolution. The country was heading towards large-scale confusion, clashes, and chaos. The revolution had got out of hand; it had got derailed. Mao's design which

[67] *Ibid.*
[68] "Settling Accounts After the Autumn," *Jen-min Jih-pao*, 16 January 1967.

had worked very satisfactorily until December became blurred and fell to pieces. Mao had hoped to regain control of the Party through the organization of the Red Guards and he had evidently counted upon the creation of a purer, more revolutionary organization which at his behest would keep the revolutionary momentum going. Both the expectations had been belied. The Party machinery lay in ruins but there was nothing very much left to control, and it would be a painfully slow process to reconstruct it and clothe it with the previous respectability and authority. The Red Guards' simultaneous offensive against authority at all levels, in the Centre and provinces as well as in various units and organizations, sparked off a general struggle—almost a free-for-all—which proved to be uncontrollable. No one knew who was or was not a "power-holder taking the capitalist road," who was or was not loyal to the thought of Mao. Since every person in any responsible position from a cadre in a small organization to the "top person in authority" felt threatened, the resistance that Mao encountered had not been anticipated and Mao's plan went away.

What must have been a harder pill to swallow was the revelation that the new revolutionary organizations were no purer than the Party and the erstwhile mass organizations, now practically disbanded. They were subject to the same bourgeois diseases and all too soon were fighting for power and position. The new phenomenon that was just beginning to manifest itself—that of factional fighting among the Maoist revolutionary rebels—became the dominant feature of the struggle during the rest of the last year. Mao had not bargained for that either.

It was plain that the confusion within the country had reached a point where it posed a threat to law and order and cohesion of the country. The revolutionary rebels had not been able to seize power in quick swoops except in a few places; elsewhere it promised to be a long drawn-out struggle which would do incalculable harm to the unity and stability of the country. As the Maoists themselves admitted, the revolutionary rebels constituted a tiny minority and had not yet won over the majority to their side. The Red Guards' general assault on authority and against Party and government cadres indiscriminately resulted both in the disruption of administration, and fierce resistance by the cadres under attack. The success of the Red Guards could no longer be taken for granted. Moreover, the Red Guards had started quarrelling among themselves. An additional factor to reckon with was the approaching busy spring farming season and the need to concentrate attention on harvesting and sowing in time. Also, production in factories and farms was being adversely affected. What happened in Shanghai, where much of the rural population left the farms and flocked to the cities to demand more material benefits, was true of many other places too.[69] Unless production could be quickly restored to normal, the consequences could be disastrous. The economic confusion had to be ended even more urgently than the political and administrative confusion.

Mao had to act swiftly to save the situation before it led to a complete collapse of authority and total confusion. He had to abandon his grand design and devise a new strategy in response to the new situation. He had to call the army in to end the confusion, help the Leftists to seize control, re-establish law and order and normal functioning of the administration, and to prevent further disruption in production. At the same time, he evolved the new strategy aimed at narrowing the conflict, isolating the chief enemies, softening the struggle against the majority of cadres and attempting to draw them on to the side of the Maoists through the adoption of a dual policy of dangling the carrot and wielding the stick. The Damocles' sword of dismissal, public exposure, and humiliation was hanging over their heads, but now the carrot of reinstatement in power and rehabilitation of position was also dangled should they give full-throated support to the cultural revolution and the Maoist line and demarcate themselves from the chief enemies of the Maoists.

The army was called upon to enter the foray and, reversing his earlier decision that the army should not interfere in the cultural revolution, Mao now asked the army to intervene decisively and to come to the succour of the Leftists. The appeal was made probably on 18 January, although the usual dates mentioned are 21 January and 23 January.[70] The Maoist mouthpiece in the army, *Chieh-fang Chun-pao*, came out with two successive editorials on 25 January and 26 January spelling out the tasks of the army in the

---

[69] *Wen-hui Pao*, Shanghai, editorial, 20 January 1967.
[70] See, for example, a report by the Political Department of the Kweichow Provincial Military Command in *Jen-min Jih-pao*, 12 April 1967.

new situation in the light of Mao's directive. In its editorial of 25 January, the paper said that "in this great struggle," the army "must firmly stand on the side of the proletarian revolutionaries" and "the People's Liberation Army must firmly support and assist them, for this is a vital call from our great leader Chairman Mao. We must follow Chairman Mao's instructions and enthusiastically, unequivocally, and whole-heartedly support the proletarian revolutionary rebels in rising to seize power. Even though they may be just a minority temporarily, we must support them without the slightest hesitation."

The paper made it clear that "in the new situation in the present great proletarian cultural revolution, it is not possible for the PLA to refrain from intervening." It warned those people who were using "no-intervention as a pretext to suppress the masses in reality" that this was "absolutely impermissible. The so-called non-intervention is false." The question was not whether or not to intervene but which side to stand on. "It was a question of whether to support the proletarian revolutionaries or to support the conservative-minded people or even the Rightists."[71]

The second editorial repeated Mao's call and gave instances commending the prompt action by some PLA units in responding to Mao's instruction and supporting the Leftists. It said that, at the crucial moment in which the cultural revolution had entered the stage of seizure of power, "our great leader Chairman Mao issued a militant call to the whole army that the PLA should give active support to the broad masses of the Left groups. The commanders and fighters must resolutely support and most warmly respond to this call." As an instance, the paper mentioned for particular praise the quick action taken by "commanders and fighters of a certain PLA unit in Harbin" in taking the lead and setting an example. At a critical moment when the "revolutionary Leftists" were "encircled by the reactionary organization of the so-called 'Army of the Disabled and Demobilized Soldiers' they took immediate action upon receiving the order to encircle these people and force the handful of reactionary elements of this organization to surrender. This action has greatly deflated the arrogance of the

[71]"The Chinese PLA Firmly Backs the Proletarian Revolutionaries," *Chieh-fang Chun-pao*, editorial, 25 January 1967, circulated by *New China News Agency*, 25 January 1967,

Rightists and greatly boosted the morale of the Leftists. This is really heartening news."[72]

This intrusion of the army into the struggle became more and more prominent in the months to come and, finally, it was essentially the army which was keeping the wheels of administration and production moving: the army came to be in charge of the country. The other arm of the new strategy evolved by Mao under the compulsion of conditions of disintegration was to whip up unity among the revolutionary rebels as well as with a large number of cadres. Mao gave instruction for a new call for the formation of a grand alliance of "revolutionary students, workers and cadres," which with the help of the "revolutionary army" would seize power from the small group of reactionaries.[73] Mao was now keen to circumscribe the conflict and to limit the firing range of the Red Guards—to Liu Shao-ch'i and those who were identifiably associated with him, and a small group of incorrigible dissidents. All other cadres, high or low, who were prepared to proclaim their allegiance to Mao and the "revolutionary line" could be welcomed back to the fold and rehabilitated. This was necessary in order to avert a collapse of the administration and to prevent large-scale civil conflict threatened by the indiscriminate attack by the Red Guards on all those who had any position or responsibility. The call from Peking for a grand alliance became more and more insistent in the coming months but it did not prove to be as easy a task as Mao had perhaps hoped.[74]

The kind of alliance that the Maoists in Peking had in mind is well illustrated by what happened in Heilungkiang in northeast China. On 31 January, the revolutionary rebels held a mass rally in Harbin, the capital of Heilungkiang, where they duly took an oath of loyalty to Mao and proclaimed the seizure of power from the Heilungkiang Provincial Party Committee. Setting the pattern for other areas they announced the formation of a Provincial Revolutionary Committee of Red Rebels which was declared to have taken over "all power of the Party and the government and the financial and cultural power of Heilungkiang Provincial Committee

---

[72]"Fully Support the Proletarian Revolutionaries with Actual Deeds," *Chieh-fang Chun-pao*, editorial, 26 January 1967.

[73]See, for instance, *Jen-min Jih-pao*, editorial, 22 January 1967.

[74]For details, see next chapter.

and Provincial People's Council."[75]   The rally called for the suppression of the "extremely small number of principal ringleaders and criminals of such counter-revolutionary organizations as the 'Red Flag Army,' 'Combat Preparedness Army,' and 'Jung-fu Chun' (Army of the Demobilized Soldiers), and such royalist organizations as 'August 8 Corpse' and 'Red Militia Detachments.'"

But the odd though highly significant development was that among the participants in the new revolutionary committee were the First Secretary of the Northeast Bureau of the Central Committee, Sung Jen-ch'iung, and the First Secretary of the Heilungkiang Provincial Party Committee, P'an Fu-sheng, both of whom addressed the rally, denounced the "power-holders" in the Party taking the capitalist road, admitted their errors, promised to rectify them, to read Mao's thought more penetratingly and to act according to Mao's instructions and shouted: "Long Live Chairman Mao!" The rally in its public declaration called upon all "responsible comrades at all levels to unite with the revolutionary rebels in the struggle to seize power. Cadres who had committed ordinary mistakes must work well, stick to their posts and discharge their duties properly under the supervision of the revolutionary masses."[76] The rally's declaration also underlined the need for equal attention to revolution and production.   The army officers in the region also joined the rally and the new revolutionary committee.

This "experience" of Heilungkiang in seizing power was highly lauded by the Maoists in Peking. *Jen-min Jih-pao* commended the experience of the Heilungkiang revolutionary rebels as "fairly comprehensive" and "successful" and worth study and emulation by "revolutionaries" in other parts of the country.   The most prominent feature of this experience was that the "revolutionaries" had united with the "senior leading members of the provincial Party Committee who followed Chairman Mao's correct line and senior leading members of the People's Liberation Army to form a three-way alliance to seize power."   The "Left forces" within the units where power was to be seized made common cause with the "middle forces" and struck against only the "most stubborn reactionary forces."   This "three-way combination" of representatives of the Maoist revolutionary rebels, representatives of the PLA,

[75] *New China News Agency*, Harbin, 1 February 1967.
[76] *Ibid.*

and "revolutionary leading cadres" in the Party and government organizations, declared the paper, was "of extreme importance in the current struggle" to seize power. [77]

In fact, the paper warned that so long as this problem (of the Red Guards making way in the new power structure for the army-men and the cadres) was not "properly solved," the Maoist Red Guards could not really seize power, nor could they consolidate it even if they managed to seize it. The leadership could not be provided by the Red Guards alone. The support of the army was crucial in suppressing the "counter-revolutionaries" and swiftly defeating "the class enemy's conspiratorial activities to counter the seizure of power." No less vital was the support of the large majority of cadres. They were "politically more mature" and had "greater ability in organizational work." Mao was indirectly admitting that the administration could hardly run and production proceed normally without the participation of those who had acquired the necessary skills and experience. "The seizure and control of power will be greatly facilitated by their (the cadres) becoming a part of the nucleus of the leadership of the 'three-way alliance,' " the paper put it rather euphemistically. "Therefore, sufficient importance must be attached to the role played by long-tempered revolutionary cadres in the struggle to seize power."[78] It was now blandly announced for the benefit of the Red Guards that the over-whelming majority of cadres were revolutionary and were loyal to the thought of Mao Tse-tung.

Mao's retreat in the revolution was evident and was to continue for much of the rest of the year. He was finally forced to fall back upon the guns of the army to enable his supporters to wrest power and to maintain it. He was also compelled to order the return to power of the cadre who wielded power before. Mao's primary concern henceforward was to put the brakes on the developing conflict between the Red Guards, and the cadres and among the Red Guards themselves. His chief anxiety was to prevent the eruption of a civil conflict which, even though not challenging his position, would leave the country weakened, exhausted, and rent asunder in the violent explosions. The return of the cadres was necessary to limit the conflict and to provide for continuity of

[77] *Jen-min Jih-pao*, editorial, 10 February 1968.
[78] *Ibid.*

administration and utilization of managerial skills. The principal slogan of the Maoist headquarters in the subsequent months was the formation of a "three-way alliance" of the "revolutionary rebels," "revolutionary cadres," and the People's Liberation Army. Mao hoped this would provide the panacea for the troubles among his youthful storm-troopers and end the dislocation of administration and production. But, it was easier to fan the flames of "rebellion" but far less easy to control them and limit their intensity.

The army was called in to restore order and help the Maoists to power. The Chinese press carried a spate of reports about declarations of loyalty by the army commanders and units and about army intervention at various places in favour of the Leftists. Reportedly, "commanders and fighters" of the naval and air forces and of army units in Peking, Nanking, Foochow, Kunming, Shenyang, Wuhan, Tsinan, and other areas held meetings and put up wall posters in response to the editorial of *Chieh-fang Chun-pao*, and army men in Kwangchow, Chengtu, Lanchow, Sinkiang, Inner Mongolia, and Tibet, "enthusiastically acclaimed the great alliance of the revolutionary rebels" and vowed to stand on the side of Mao Tse-tung and the Left.[79]   In Harbin the army crushed the attempts of the Army of the Demobilized Soldiers (Jung-fu Chun), declared to be a counter-revolutionary organization, to create trouble for the Red Guards.[80]   In Hofei (Anhwei province) in compliance with Mao's call the army units stationed there kept guard at a mass rally of the revolutionary rebels called to "criticize, refute, and struggle against those in power in the Party who follow the capitalist path."[81]   Even in Shansi, where the seizure of power by the revolutionary rebels had been announced on 13 January, the power struggle was substantially decided by the support to the Maoists of the army units there. The army paraded in the capital city of T'aiyuan and held demonstrations in support of the Leftists.[82]

The dragging of the army into the politics of the cultural revolution created many problems, not the least for the army itself. A theoretical, abstract pronouncement of fidelity to Mao was one thing, but

[79] *New China News Agency*, Peking, 26 and 28 January 1967.

[80] *Kuang-ming Jih-pao*, 31 January 1967.

[81] *New China News Agency*, Hofei, 27 January 1967; *Chieh-fang Chun-pao*, editorial, 27 January 1967.

[82] *New China News Agency*, Peking, 28 January 1967.

active intervention to put one group of contenders to power was quite another kettle of fish. When the onus of responsibility for the restoration of order and maintenance of the production lines was placed on the army, it had to concern itself with not only the problem of the power of the Red Guards but also of administration. Which group was a purer Maoist organization, which rival faction was genuinely Leftist, which contending clique should be supported —all these problems baffled the army and involved it in frequent trouble with the Red Guards.[83]

Mao's need for containing the conflict and narrowing the canvas continued to grow and the approaching farming season in February made it imperative to attempt a pause and consolidate the position. Grain was as important as politics and the demands of agricultural production could not be sacrificed at the altar of revolution—this much Mao had realized from the experience of the big leap. Every effort was made by Peking to concentrate attention on the busy agricultural season and to prevent disruption of agricultural production. The month of February saw a slight pause but the genie that Mao had let loose could not be easily bottled up again, the divisive forces that were mutually embattling showed no sign of melting away and many of the problems that had arisen along with the rise of the Red Guards multiplied and grew to life-size proportions subsequently.

[83]For details see next chapter.

CHAPTER FIVE

THE FLOODTIDE

THE RECOURSE to the army and the appeal for the return of the cadres made a material difference to the situation in the cultural revolution, but the process that Mao had set going in 1966 could not be stemmed. The dykes once having been lifted could only result in a floodtide and it required a great deal of effort and time to control the surging waters and recover the losses. Thus the principal features of the situation in the subsequent period were: continued Red Guard assault on a number of important personages and ministries, the outbreak of violence on a large scale in many parts of the country, the growing factional fighting among the Red Guards, the reluctance of the cadres to assume responsibility, the rise of powerful military commanders, and the expanding role of the army in controlling the chaotic situation, the growing concern of the army to maintain order, stability and production, and the consequent conflict with the Red Guards in many places, and last but not least, the continuing efforts of Mao to end the violence and bring about unity among the warring factions which pushed him further down the alley of retreat and compromise. All these currents, cross-currents, and undercurrents were flowing simultaneously and impinging on each other.

ATTACK ON LEADERS

Mao's main concern now was to focus the struggle on Liu Shao-ch'i and a few other top leaders, and those who were still stubbornly supporting him. Liu had proved to be a tough adversary and, despite half-hearted confessions about his inadequate grasp of the thought of Mao Tse-tung, and having followed a "bourgeois reactionary" line, had stood his ground and had become a symbolic whipping boy of the Maoists. The entire ferocity of the Red Guard storm was sought to bear upon the "top person in authority taking the capitalist road." The concentration of the attack on Liu was intended to serve a dual purpose. It was expected to break the resistance of Liu and serve as a warning signal to others and, hopefully, it might narrow down the expanding conflict at the lower levels and take the heat off from the factional struggles in different parts of the country.

While, therefore, Mao took recourse to the army and retreated all along the line in regard to the implementation of his policies and the attack on the cadre, the campaign against Liu Shao-ch'i and some other leaders like Teng Hsiao-p'ing, T'ao Chu, P'eng Chen, and P'eng Teh-huai was stepped up. The national press as well as the Red Guard newspapers published article after article to denounce them as inveterate reactionaries and implacable foes of Mao Tse-tung. Liu Shao-ch'i was compared to Khrushchov and portrayed as the repository of all bourgeois evils, a political speculator who had decided way back in the twenties that he would achieve fame and get on the top of the world through the Communist Party, and an old-time opponent of Mao who opposed Mao at every step and peddled the revisionist line all through his life. (How he could have survived as the number one man under Mao, had this really been so, passes comprehension.)

The indictment of Liu was an across-the-board indictment; its sweep ranged from personal foibles to political ambitions, to his activities in the Party, in economic policy planning, in the fields of arts and literature, to his past opinions and present attitudes. The burden of this indictment can be summed up as follows: Liu Shao-ch'i joined the Communist Party in order to achieve fame, but was not as a true revolutionary; indeed he was a capitalist agent in the Party. He denied the class line of Mao at every historic stage. In 1935, he praised the Kuomintang and Chiang Kai-shek (at a time when the Communists were plugging for a united front with Chiang against Japanese aggression), and again in 1944, he spread illusions about the coming era of peace and democracy, instead of preaching class struggle (as Mao was presumed to be doing).[1] In 1949, after the establishment of the new regime, when the Communist Party had adopted a policy of mixed economy at least during the first

[1] Articles in *Kuang-ming Jih-pao*, 25 and 29 April 1967.

phase, Liu allegedly welcomed capitalist exploitation of the workers and went around visiting the capitalists and encouraging them to exploit the workers![2] "As recently as 10 years ago," he maintained that the landlord and the bourgeois class had been eliminated and that the "main contradiction" between the bourgeois and the proletariat had been resolved.[3]

Within the Party, Liu was accused of having built his own empire and encouraging "slavishness." He said that the minority must abide by the majority and he advocated "blind and absolute obedience in the sphere of organization."[4] Mao's contention is that truth may be with the minority (as in the present cultural revolution) and that the ultimate yardstick was whether there was obedience to the thought of Mao Tse-tung. "Usurping the name of the Party, China's Khrushchov distorts the Party's organizational discipline into the discipline of the bourgeois royalists.... Ours is the democracy under the dictatorship of the proletariat and democracy under the guidance of the great thought of Mao Tse-tung."[5] His book *How to be a Good Communist*, particularly the revised edition published in 1962, at a time when the "Soviet revisionists" and "reactionaries" all over the world were "maligning" China and gloating over its "temporary difficulties," was bitterly denounced for its criticism of "left opportunism," "excessive struggle within the Party" and "dogmatism" which was viewed as a disguised attack against "the great leader of the Chinese people, Chairman Mao,"[6] and for preaching "self-cultivation" instead of selfless devotion to the revolution, using quotations from Mencius rather than Mao Tse-tung.

In the sphere of economic policies, the charge-sheet against Liu was somewhat contradictory, but the gist of it was that Liu and his group wanted to carry the process of reorganization both in agriculture and industry still further which in Mao's view would have pushed China's economy down the road of capitalist restoration. The failures in agriculture and industry in 1959 and 1960 had compelled even Mao to acquiesce in changes calculated to assure the

[2]Article in *Jen-min Jih-pao*, 15 April 1967.
[3]*Ibid.*, 6 May 1967.
[4]*Ibid.*, 6 April 1967.
[5]*Kuang-ming Jih-pao*, 29 April 1967.
[6]Speech by Nieh Yuan-tzu at a mass rally of the Congress of the Red Guards in Peking on 3 April, *New China News Agency*, Peking, 6 April 1967.

peasantry of reasonable remuneration according to the quantity and quality of work and a small measure of freedom to retain the income from household occupations or from the agricultural produce, or poultry, from their tiny plots—small "freedoms" intended to provide some incentives to the peasant to increase production. Suitable changes with the same view had also been made in agricultural organization with the decentralization of authority of management and operation of field-work and distribution of income from the commune to the production teams, roughly equivalent to a village. A recurring charge against Liu and his friends was that they wanted to scuttle the collective organization, encourage a contract system of fixation of output quotas for each peasant household, leaving it free to enjoy some returns from the surplus as well as from the produce of their private small-scale occupations, and relax the rigid organizational control over agriculture.

A further accusation against the "Liuists" was that they conspired to bring about changes in the organizational patterns of industries in order to limit party and political intervention, promote independent and efficient operation of various industrial enterprises, and relate this to the cost-profit factor in order to ensure their efficient as well as remunerative functioning.[7] This was castigated as the creation of trusts (or corporations) to run industries—with the ultimate and ulterior objective of restoring capitalism in China. Many of these charges against Liu seem to be wild and far-fetched, but it is probable that, surveying the ruins of the big leap and the commune movement, Liu and his associates were inclined to loosen the tight grip over the functioning of agricultural farms and industrial enterprises and encourage local initiative, believing that the Party had best confine itself to the formulation of policies, broad targets, and overall supervision, leaving the day-to-day operation under the care of technically and organizationally skilled managers and peasants.

Another frequent criticism that has suddenly been levelled in the wake of the cultural revolution is that during the 1930's when Liu was supervising underground work in the Kuomintang areas, he prompted many high-ranking Communists captured by the Kuomin-

[7]"The Plot of the Top Ambitionist to Operate Trusts on a Large Scale Must be Thoroughly Exposed," *Kuang-ming Jih-pao*, 9 May 1967.

tang to offer confessions, make abject apologies, and thus secure their release on the promise to abstain from any such activities in the future. This was now condemned as a violation of revolutionary dignity and an evidence of Liu's slavish mentality and his ulterior loyalty to the bourgeois reactionary line. The possibility of a few such cases cannot be ruled out, but whether Liu can be fairly blamed for having taken recourse to such means is doubtful, and what is still more doubtful is that Mao had not at least condoned the action at the time, considering that Liu's stock remained high with Mao until a few years ago.

Apart from the scathing attack on Liu Shao-ch'i, and similar attacks on other fallen leaders like Teng Hsiao-p'ing, T'ao Chu, P'eng Teh-huai, and P'eng Chen, many other high and medium-ranking leaders of the Party and the government also came within the range of Red Guard cross-fire. In some cases the denunciation followed the disgrace and virtual expulsion from office, while in others, the leaders survived the Red Guard onslaught. To take a few prominent instances, An Tzu-wen, chief of the Organization Department of the CCP Central Committee, and Wu Hsiu-ch'uan, member of the Central Committee of the Party and a Deputy Foreign Minister, met the same fate, as their "back-stage boss," Liu Shao-ch'i; both Ch'en Yi and Li Hsien-nien, Minister of Finance, encountered heavy weather but were saved by Chou En-lai. More and more hidden enemies seemed to be discovered as the cultural revolution rumbled on.

As in the case of many other leading Communist functionaries, like P'eng Chen, An Tzu-wen was also accused of having established an "independent kingdom" in the Central Committee's Organization Department which was "controlled for over twenty years by counter-revolutionary revisionist An Tzu-wen." An was called a "big renegade," an "old anti-Communist hand," and an "inveterate intriguer." He was an "important member" of the "counter-revolutionary revisionist group of P'eng, Lo, and Yang." Together they collected "capitulationists and renegades, formed groups for private ends and schemed to usurp the leadership of the Party, the Army, and the Government."[8] Not unexpectedly, An was found

---

[8]"Pursue the Desperate Foe," *Chui-chiung K'ou*, Peking, No. 4, 20 May 1967; *Survey of China Mainland Press*, Hong Kong, No. 3970, 29 June 1967.

to have no respect for Mao but a great deal of esteem for P'eng Chen. "P'eng Chen," An was reported to have said, "has ability of a high degree. His style of work is good. He sees far and stands high." And during the preparations for the Eighth National Congress of the Party he even had the audacity to submit a list of candidates for the Politbureau in which he included the "big renegade" Po I-po but left out Lin Piao. It has not been stated whether he submitted the list to Mao or to Liu Shao-ch'i or to the Central Committee. If this accusation is not fabricated (as it could very well have been), it reveals a picture of factional struggles within the Party leadership even before the divergencies developed over the big leap attempt.

Mao's anger against An Tzu-wen appears to date back at least to 1962. That year, Mao, according to the Red Guard version, said both orally and in writing that the CC's Organization Department had never made reports to the Central Committee and that it had become an independent kingdom. An was annoyed with the criticism and suppressed it from the lower levels. He had made common cause with P'eng Chen, Lu Ting-i, and Yang K'un-shan and even Lo Jui-ch'ing and "planted many time-bombs in various departments in all parts of the country." They had their supporters appointed secretaries of regional bureaus of the Party and directors and vice-directors of central Party organs, thus "usurping the leadership powers of these organs." When Lo Jui-ch'ing was criticized in March 1966, P'eng Chen had An Tzu-wen included in the seven-man group in charge of criticism of Lo. Because of An's efforts, this group declared Lo's problem to be only a "reflection of bourgeois thinking in the Party" and he was still called a "comrade"; there was no mention, the Maoists complained of Lo's "ignominious history and wavering in the past."[9]

Another ranking Communist functionary whose past history of "wavering" was now raked up was Wu Hsiu-ch'uan who came to prominence abroad when he represented New China by special invitation at the United Nations in 1950 and delivered stinging statements against the United States. He was also subsequently China's ambassador to Yugoslavia (May 1955—September 1958). Significantly, Wu was denounced for friendship with Yugoslav and Soviet revisionists. His past history of links with the Soviet Union

[9] *Ibid.*

was recalled, starting from 1931 when he returned from the Soviet Union and when the Soviet-returned group led by Wang Ming was in power in the Party. Wu not only toed the "left opportunist" line but also acted as a loyal interpreter for the German representative of the Third International, Li-teh (Richter)—a "big renegade." Even at the Tsunyi conference in January 1935 (which finally and indisputably established the leadership of Mao), Wu, a "rotten egg," faithfully interpreted Richter's reports and speeches which obviously were at variance with Mao's line.[10]

The Maoists contended that Wu remained an agent of the Soviet Union and a revisionist. In 1960, he attended a conference of the Warsaw Pact countries and heard Khrushchov openly abusing Mao but kept the incident to himself and did not breathe a word to Peking about it. It was also revealed that during his tenure in Yugoslavia, when the Yugoslav Communists published their draft programme in 1958, Wu sent a cable from Belgrade suggesting that China send a mission to the forthcoming Yugoslav Communist Party's Congress. (This draft programme sparked off a furious campaign against the Yugoslav Communists in the Chinese press.) Wu was also accused of maintaining "improper relations" with Tito. This charge of national betrayal and treachery was made against other disgraced leaders like P'eng Teh-huai, too, who was alleged to have maintained "improper relations" with the Soviets. The differences within the Chinese Party over the fall of Khrushchov and its meaning are now apparent from the accusation against Wu that he spread illusions about the new Soviet leadership after Khrushchov stepped down. Wu asserted that the emergence of the new leadership marked the beginning of fundamental reforms and that it would be possible to win over the new leadership "after seven or eight years of struggle."

The factional and personal struggles within the Party have often been revealed in a flash during the cultural revolution—and although one-sided, the material released during this movement has illuminated many dark corners and provided new perspectives about the story of the last few years. The element of personal struggle not only between Liu and Mao but also among other leaders is unmistakably present. Just as An Tzu-wen was alleged to have been

---

[10]"Irrefutable Evidence of the Crime of Wu Hsiu-ch'uan's Betrayal of the Party and the Country," *Hung-wei Chan-pao*, Peking, 13 April 1967.

working against Lin Piao at the instigation of some others, Wu was also accused of slandering K'ang Sheng and "stirring up a gust of evil wind" against the Cultural Revolution Committee and K'ang Sheng. Allegedly, Wu had said that K'ang Sheng should not represent the Cultural Revolution Committee and that the Revolutionary Rebel General Headquarters of Peking (an organization condemned by the Maoists as having sunk into the quagmire of revisionism) was really backed up by Wang Li who in turn was being prompted by K'ang Sheng. This was obviously an attempt, though unsuccessful, to involve K'ang Sheng in the struggle against the revisionists. The role of K'ang Sheng, however, is a little mysterious. He was a member of the original five-member committee appointed by the Party high command to conduct the cultural revolution, of which P'eng Chen was the chief at that time. This group produced a report—probably in February 1966—which was later denounced as the black February outline of the counter-revolutionary revisionists. But K'ang Sheng was exonerated and it was explained in his defence that he was not a party to it. It is possible that Mao had kept him in the group as his agent to silently watch and report on the group and its activities.

Not unexpectedly, Wu was condemned as a collaborator of P'eng Chen who, the Red Guard denunciation said, had opposed Lin Piao even in 1945. Wu was now condemned as a "sworn partner" and an "able fighter for opposing Supreme Commander Lin." From this and other Red Guard writings of this time it appears that there was a personal struggle for power between Lin Piao and P'eng Chen for a long time, and that Lin Piao must have played an active role in the ouster of P'eng. The indirect resistance to Mao's line might have been one reason but another important factor in the fall of P'eng Chen could have been the personal animosity and struggle for power between the two.

Inevitably, among the catalogue of Wu's crimes was the ridicule of the big leap and the lack of loyalty and respect for Mao. In a speech in 1962, he was alleged to have attributed China's economic difficulties to natural calamities, on the one hand, and to the fact that "a great many people want to be Chairman Mao's good pupils," on the other.[11] This crime of *lese majeste*, it has already been noted,

[11]*Ibid.*

was laid at the door of practically all the prominent Communists now under attack. To take another instance of this period, Wang Ping-chang,[12] Minister in the Seventh Ministry of Machine Building, was belaboured for exhibiting such disrespect, of which two examples were cited. In the spring of 1965, a director of the political cadres' department in the Ministry attended a conference in Peking whose members were received in audience by Mao. Returning to the ministry, the director reported to Wang that he had been "greatly inspired and educated" by Mao's reception. Wang's sardonic comment was: how could you have been "educated" when you saw Mao for the first time in your life? In 1968, Liu and Teng approved a "black document" of the Communist Youth League Central Committee to be used for indoctrination purposes, which provided for the study of "Marxism-Leninism and Mao Tse-tung's works" but did not explicitly mention the words "Mao Tse-tung's thought." This was held as a deliberate affront to Mao by the "revisionists." Wang also ordered utilization of these materials for institutes under his Ministry.[13]

Indeed, as the Red Guard denouncement itself put it, "in the last analysis the most serious of his (Wang's) crimes was that he sold himself to the Liu-Teng black headquarters," opposed Mao and vilified the "invincible thought of Mao Tse-tung."[14]

Among other Party stalwarts who came under Red Guard fire were Marshal Ch'en Yi, the Foreign Minister, and Li Hsien-nien, the Minister for Finance, both members of the Politbureau. Ch'en Yi was even said to have been dragged out by the Red Guards but he held his ground and was not prepared to wear the "hat" of counter-revolutionary revisionism, as the Chinese saying goes. Reportedly, Ch'en Yi and Li Hsien-nien were protected by Chou En-lai.

Against Ch'en Yi, apart from the usual charges of "rabid opposi-

[12]Lieutenant General Wang Ping-chang, a native of Hunan, was a graduate of the Red Army College in Moscow. He was Vice-Commander of the Air Force, a post he retained when he became Minister in the Seventh Ministry of Machine Building in July 1965.

[13]Tsao-fan Yu-li, 1 May 1967. A tabloid published by the Propaganda Services Department of "916" Revolutionary Rebel Corps of the Seventh Ministry of Machine Building, Peking.

[14]Ibid.

tion" to Mao ("Speaking about fixed notions, the thought of Mao
Tse-tung is just one fixed notion. This Mao Tse-tung's thought is
downright Chinese stuff; let us not take it abroad," Ch'en Yi was
alleged to have said), the Red Guards were worked up because he
criticized their manner of functioning as "unreasonable mobs" and
was bold enough to reject the accusation of counter-revolutionary
revisionism against veteran Communists. He dared the "rebels"
to continue the struggle against him but warned them that he would
also put up posters against them and made it plain that the question
of who was revolutionary and who was not had not been settled.
He—how dare he?—described many of the Red Guard charges
against Liu Shao-ch'i as fabrications and, significantly, added that,
four or five years ago, Liu had not opposed Mao. He himself
was not afraid of tragic misfortunes: he had been a revolutionary
for 40 years, he said, and would fight at the risk of his life. He had
not expected that things would come to such a pass. But he was
unreconciled and unrepentant and was ready to face the consequences.[15]

Li Hsien-nien, Finance Minister and high-ranking Party leader,
also had to face prolonged hostility of the Red Guards whose chief
complaint against him was that he encouraged indiscriminate attacks
against the bulk of the cadres and internecine warfare among the
masses in the Ministry of Finance, with the result that nearly
90 per cent of all the cadres in the Ministry became subject to attack,
while Li extended the umbrella of protection to a few chosen ones.[16]
These were the ones that should have been held accountable before
the Red Guards, but Li turned the rebels against one another and
made no distinction between the upper and the lower stratum of
cadres. One of Mao's directives in this movement was to concentrate on the upper echelons of the cadres and to go easy on the lower
ones because it was the higher ones who were greater obstacles in
the spread of Mao's thought and who had formed groups and cliques
around important Party leaders—the lower ones would in any case
fall in line once the decisions were handed down to them.

Even Marshal Nieh Jung-chen did not escape severe criticism by
the Red Guards. Marshal Nieh, a native of Szechuan, joined the

[15] *Hung-wei Chan-pao*, 13 April 1967.
[16] *Pei-ching Kung-she*, 12 April 1967.

Communist Youth Corps in France in 1922 and the Chinese Communist Party in 1923, participated in the Long March and was one of the important military leaders of Communist China. He was also a Vice-Premier in the Peking Government and Chairman of the National Scientific-Technical Commission, a high-powered body entrusted with the development of modern technology, including nuclear technology. The Red Guards criticized Nieh for shielding counter-revolutionary revisionists like Wang Ping-chang.[17] The tone and tenor of the criticism of Nieh contrasted rather interestingly with that used for the others. The Red Guards hedged from directly dubbing Nieh as a counter-revolutionary revisionist. They still called him a "comrade" and said that their aim in "bombarding" him was to "save" him so that he allied himself firmly with the Mao line. They were "aware" that the Central Cultural Revolution Committee had "high esteem" for him. But the Red Guards were not satisfied with his criticism of the "Liu-Teng bourgeois line" in the scientific research programme. They suspected that he had deliberately given General Lo Jui-ch'ing over to the "conservative" faction for criticism (so that the denunciation would be lighter) and had provided protection to Wang Ping-chang whom the Red Guards described as "a landlord and bourgeois representative— a homosexual criminal and a big rascal."[18]

The criticism of Ch'en Yi, Li Hsien-nien, and Nieh Jung-chen and the variation in the kind and quality of criticism raises the question— who prompted the Red Guards in the campaign against these leaders who had not yet officially fallen from grace? It would be rather naive to believe that these were spontaneous outpourings with no hidden, directing hand behind them. Just as the Red Guards accused many Party functionaries of acting at the behest of some back-stage bosses, it was equally true that they too had higher links and were supplied with materials for attacking veteran Party leaders. Quite possibly, in the factional struggle at the top, some persons in the Maoist headquarters had inspired these criticisms and managed these campaigns. These criticisms were known to have exasperated Chou En-lai who repeatedly told the Red Guards to leave these leaders alone and not to direct the spearhead of their attack against them.

[17]*Tsao-fan Yu-li*, Peking, 28 May 1967.
[18]*Ibid.*

While this cut-throat struggle at the top continued, a more violent struggle at the lower levels threatened to tear the country apart. The year 1967 was marked by three major trends: (1) the violent explosion involving Red Guards in a sanguinary struggle across the country against the Party and government cadres and more alarmingly among themselves resulting in economic and administrative dislocation and political chaos as well as dramatic instances of local army defiance as in Wuhan, Chungking, and Sinkiang; (2) the desperate measures adopted by Mao and his associates in the ruling elite to restore order and stability and contain the violent conflicts among the Red Guards by readmitting the large majority of Party and government personnel into the power structure, by slowing down on economic changes and retaining the previous economic organizational structure with its emphasis on material incentives and a piece-rate wage system and by—reluctantly or otherwise—vastly increasing the power and authority of local army commanders who were often inclined to spike the activities of the Red Guards and whose first concern seemed to be not revolution but stability and continuity, particularly of the production machine; (3) the rule of the army in major areas of the country and the emergence of a new, delicate regional power structure dominated by the army and in which the old cadres reappeared, though with diminished authority and near fatal loss of face and a badly bruised self-confidence, while the influence and power of the Red Guards also slumped proportionately.

VIOLENCE GRIPS THE COUNTRY

The fighting and feuding had already become apparent in December and January and has been partially noted in the previous chapter. Mao's wife and her chief associate in directing the cultural revolution, Ch'en Po-ta, reportedly warned the Red Guards at a forum on 27 December 1966 against "a growing tendency towards anarchism"[19]—a word much used to describe the situation later. Ch'en Po-ta even advised the students not to take over the administration of their schools and universities, but to learn from the military

[19]Minutes compiled by K'uai Ta-fu and Ch'en Yu-yen of Tsinghua University and put up in wall posters on 31 December 1966.

training of the PLA. Of course, this was the time when the Maoist leadership was more concerned with pushing the revolution and the struggle against the highly placed opponents was the order of the day. Mao's wife also urged the students to step up the battle against Liu Shao-ch'i whose "true face," she said, she discovered in 1964 when she listened to a seven-hour "Khrushchov-style" speech made by Liu. She added that Wang Kuang-mei was a "dishonest person" and that she (Chiang Ch'ing) supported those who would seize her. The Red Guards were promised that the materials relating to the criticism of Liu would be made available to them for use in the developing campaign against him.

Whatever constraints the demands of spring farming might have imposed on the momentum of the revolution in China, they were both short-lived and insufficient to prevent the accumulating blow-up. The developments of the last one year had a logic of their own and it was not possible to create tailor-made situations to suit the wishes of Mao. The events of December and January (1967) had a snow-balling effect and inevitably led to mutual denunciation and violence. The revolution degenerated into factional squabbles, the breaking of heads, and a gradually rising level of violence and bloodshed. The Red Guard statements are replete with accounts of such violence and fighting. Various Red Guard organizations competed for power and were locked in a mighty struggle, each trying to establish its own supremacy and to elbow out the others. It was natural that they would use the most convenient means available to them to discredit their rivals and that was to call them revision-ists and anti-Maoists. Each claimed to be a more loyal, more thorough and purer follower of Mao and threw suspicion on the other's sincerity and commitment. In this struggle for power at lower levels, Red Guards engaged Red Guards, and very often they even engaged the local army personnel, and thousands of Party and government workers engaged the Red Guards, and everyone seemed to engage everyone else in a fierce battle for survival.

The Red Guard literature is full of such dramatic events often describing the happening in great detail and, therefore, the evidence of such a struggle is massive and incontrovertible, although the mutual mud-slinging and the labelling may not be accurate. There is no need here to reproduce all those accounts, but a few graphic ones may be mentioned.

Take, for instance, the most favourite and applauded Red Guard organizations of the capital—the "Politics and Law Commune" of the Peking Institute of Politics and Law and the "Tung-fang Hung" (East Wind) of Peking Institute of Mining— which were particularly assiduous in carrying out the behests of Mao's headquarters and weeding out those regarded as enemies and political unreliables. But hardly had the new year (1967) dawned when the two were at loggerheads. The Politics and Law Commune seized control over the Public Security Bureau of the capital but apparently excluded the Tung-fang-hung Red Guards of the Mining Institute from this take-over. This enraged the latter group and a three-way struggle developed, for the security bureau personnel and the policemen resented the violent intrusion of the outsiders. The Red Guards of the Mining Institute besieged the security bureau's branch office at Shihchingkuan and snatched away the hat-badges of the policemen. There followed a violent clash with the Red Guards of the Politics and Law Commune and many people were injured in the fighting and taken to the hospital. The army had to be alerted and the sub-bureau was handed over to the Peking Garrison Headquarters.[20]

The Maoist headquarters called a meeting of the representatives of the three organizations on 1 February at the assembly hall of the Peking Municipal Public Security Bureau for a doze of admonition and advice and for softening their internal struggle and bringing about renewed unity. The meeting was addressed by Vice-Premier Hsieh Fu-chih who had stepped into the former Mayor P'eng Chen's shoes and Ch'i Pen-yu, influential Left-wing member of the Cultural Revolution Committee. Making the main speech Ch'i Pen-yu said that both the Politics and Law Commune and the Tung-fang-hung of the Mining Institute were revolutionary organizations and had performed meritorious service in defence of Mao's leadership and line. "Now those two revolutionary organizations fight each other at the Public Security Bureau. They are members of the same family but they do not recognize each other." Members of one group were fighting those of the other, causing bloodshed. It had come to the Peking municipality as a great shock. Even Premier

---

[20]Hsieh Fu Tsung-li, *Ch'i Pen-yu T'ung-chih Chiang-kuan* (speeches of Vice-Premier Hsieh and Comrade Ch'i Pen-yu), Peking, 2 February 1967.

Chou En-lai, he said, was shocked. He advised them to visit their wounded comrades and comfort them and pleaded with them to come together and fight the common enemy. It was Liu Shao-ch'i and his supporters who had to be pulled down; they must not start pulling down one another.

Ch'i Pen-yu said that Mao had just drawn up the two great policies that the army must join the foray and support the leftists and that the leftists must conduct the class struggle against the enemy and not against one another (the policy of "three-way alliance," in other words). It was wrong to believe that the army should stay away; the army must intervene. Revealing the differences even within the army over this, he said that Liu Chih-chien had opposed the intervention of the army and had been criticized by Mao. In order to resolve the factional troubles, the leadership was planning to form a wider Peking Commune including all the various Red Guard organizations but during the interim period, Ch'i Pen-yu indicated that the Security Bureau might be put under the charge of the army.[21]

Or take this report from Shantung by a Red Guard student of the Shantung Normal College who belonged to a group established for the express purpose of exchanging revolutionary experience with workers and other groups and organizations. In Shantung there were already two rival organizations in existence: the Shantung Workers' Revolutionary Rebel Association with supporters in the Shantung University and the Shantung Workers' Rebel General Command with associates in the Shantung Normal College. On the night of 25 January, the first group mobilized a large number of people, attacked the branch offices of the latter organization and rounded up their supporters in six trucks. According to this account, dozens of people "entered our quarters, destroying things in the building and turning the whole place into shambles. Apart from grabbing two telephone sets, they removed reams of paper and our suitcases, smashing all the locks of desks and cabinets and emptying the drawers and shelves of all the files and documents."[22] They kicked and manhandled their opponents and took them to a

[21]*Ibid.*

[22]"Supreme Directive," issued on 26 January 1967, entitled: A strong protest against the fast atrocities of a small handful of persons of the Shantung Revolutionary Rebel Association—an account of arrests made by these people.

suburban village, detaining some people and turning others loose at a far away place from the city of Tsinan (the capital of Shantung).

If one multiplies such incidents a thousand times—and reports in the Red Guard wall posters and newspapers came from all parts of China—one can visualize the dangerous situation that was developing with the rising tide of violence and factional fighting sweeping across the country. In many cases the incidents were far more serious and there were prolonged and bloody struggles, unprecedented since the establishment of the Communist regime. However, before we take note of some of these dramatic developments, a word of caution is needed in assessing and evaluating the impact of these events. Generally speaking, it appears that the fighting and the disruption was more conspicuous and spectacular in the cities and towns and suburban villages, but that the countryside remote and distant from the centres of trouble was considerably less affected and less subject to the depredations of the Red Guard groups and their opponents. The suburban villages in many places were, however, the scene of bitter clashes as rival groups mobilized their support among the peasantry who also, in numerous cases, took the opportunity of flocking into the cities, joining the spree and sometimes demanding more concessions and higher wages.

Canton, to take another instance, was a battle ground between competing groups for many long months and even the army was drawn into the struggle. In Canton, one group styling itself as the Red Flag and the other one generally referred to as the East Wind, fought long and pitched battles and employed every possible means to seize power. The first group was accused of bringing about a sham seizure and of secret alliance with the "power-holders" within the Kwangtung Provincial Communist Party led by Chao Tse-yang, the first secretary. Around these two were clustered smaller Red Guard groups in various organizations, one particularly controversial organization, the August One Combat Corps, which claimed to be an exceptionally active Maoist group, was declared a counter-revolutionary organization, and still later was reported to have been exonerated—probably by Peking.

In their struggle for power, these groups "ransacked houses, seized people, insulted others, enforced physical punishment, even tied up people, making them kneel down and subjected the masses to merciless beating." What was worse, the army itself became divided and, according to a public notice of the Canton Military Region, a "small number of people with ulterior motives" incited some "ignorant elements," even using the names of members of the Central Military Affairs Committee in order to point the spearhead of the struggle against the army." It appears that on the night of 7 February (1967), a group of students of the military academies and schools, and Red Guards of art and literature groups attacked units and departments of the Canton Military Garrison, took control of "a number of organs" and barracks, and made "unreasonable demands" and even intimidated the leadership cadres and seized some military personnel and took them away. The attempt seemed to make some of the military leaders the target of struggle. The incident was obviously serious and the Central Committee's Military Control Committee in Peking acting with great alacrity and in two successive orders the following day declared the happenings an internal matter of the army and forbade local "revolutionary organizations" and "revolutionary teachers and students" from intervening. The second order issued on the evening of 8 February admitted that those who had taken part in the seizure and demonstrations had not yet withdrawn from the area and once again enjoined upon them to do so immediately. They were told that if they had any problems, they could telephone Peking or send representatives to settle them. The Canton Military Command in its order of 8 February warned all those who were inciting the people to continue attacks on the military leadership that the army "will resolutely take all necessary measures in accordance with the orders of the Supreme Commander."[24]

Various revolutionary rebel organizations dutifully echoed the Peking orders and the August One Combat Corps also issued a resounding proclamation denouncing the assault on the Canton Garrison, but apparently all this was a part of the complicated and somewhat confusing game of factional struggles raging in Kwangtung, and shortly afterwards, on 1 March the August One Combat Corps was labelled as a counter-revolutionary organization by an

[24] *Ibid.*

order of the Canton Military District of the Chinese People's Liberation Army. The branded organization was accused of engaging in armed struggle, employing terrorist tactics, wearing false uniforms to pose as military personnel, defaming the PLA, passing on military secrets to agents in Hong Kong as well as information regarding the situation in the cultural revolution, stealing money and property, maltreating and insulting women, and so on and so forth.

This apparently firm action and the denouncement of some of the rival organizations did not indicate a decisiveness of the cultural revolution or the location of the true and the false Maoists, but was only a manifestation of the fierce internal struggle among the various groups which continued to escalate and seriously disturb peace in this border province. The infighting became more intense in the subsequent months and various reports mentioned pitched battles among rival organizations, disruption of transport, and even public hangings by the lamp-posts.

In fact, even the ubiquitous August One Combat Corps seemed to have survived the February ordeal and continued to be involved in the factional fighting, and the attacks against the Canton military leadership did not cease. An idea of the highly confusing and complicated nature of this struggle can be obtained from one Red Guard report as late as August 1967.[25] This spoke of fresh violence in the months of July and August involving the use of automatic rifles, light and heavy machine-guns and artillery and the "assassination of revolutionary rebels." This group claimed that on the one side were ranged (truly Maoist!) organizations like the Kunglien (Workers' United Headquarters), Red Flag Workers, the August One Combat Corps, the Red Flag Poor and Lower Middle Peasants, Canton Railway General Headquarters, the Red Headquarters of State Organs, Red Guard Headquarters, the Third Headquarters, and the New First Headquarters (the old First Headquarters obviously being in the enemy camp). On the other side were (no doubt "conservatives" and "capitalist roaders"!) the District-Headquarters, the Red Headquarters, Ch'un-lei, the Talien Tse-tsung, the Association of suburban Poor Peasants, the

[25]"The Current Situation in Canton and Our Policy," *Hung-ssu Pao-tung*, Canton, 22 August 1967 (a tabloid published by the Central-South Institute of Forestry, Canton Red Guard Headquarters).

Doctrine Guards, and the "revisionist" First Headquarters. It was also admitted that standing between them were a "considerable number of masses" who just stood aside and took no position.

Even according to this partisan account of one of the groups, the fighting was ruthless and bloody. On 20 August, "many revolutionary comrades fell into the blood pool; many revolutionary path-finders were kidnapped and thrown into the cells of the District Headquarters and Doctrine Guards where they were savagely tortured.... The beautiful, prosperous city of Canton was engulfed by white terror."[26] The "capitalist roaders" were also stated to have mobilized the suburban peasants to besiege the city and a section of them was now "emotionally opposed to the revolutionary rebels." The result of it all in the words of these Red Guards was: "Production in many factories has shown a notable drop. Some factories have come to a standstill. The railways are paralysed, the port is paralysed, and highway transport is gravely affected. Chaos reigns in communications in the city. There is acute shortage of commodity supplies, particularly necessaries of livelihood." This account also admitted that this group, too, was arming itself for "self-defence." It justified its appeal to its supporters to "quickly arm themselves" by the need to maintain "social order" and "to overwhelm the conservative forces in the military aspect."

Even more significantly, these Red Guard groups continued to shoot darted arrows at the military leadership in Canton and darkly hint about the usurpation of the army leadership by the revisionists and capitalist-roaders. There were particularly scathing attacks against "Canton's T'an Chen-lin" by this group of Red Guards. Canton's T'an was accused of being a sworn partner of T'ao Chu and was described as a "stray dog," a "household slave" of T'ao Chu and, of course, chiefly responsible for the violent incidents and the policy of forcible suppression of these groups,[27] which might be an indication that the Canton struggle had also become involved in the struggle at Peking where a fierce personal and group struggle was being unfolded leading to strange alliances and permutations and combinations. The Red Guards clashed against one another and

[26]*Ibid.*
[27]"On Military Coups in the Great Cultural Revolution," *Hung-ssu Pao-tung*, 22 August 1967.

split over power and influence but some times they were like mario-
nettes being managed from behind and their fighting was a reflection
of the more devious, the more unpredictable and, therefore, less
clearly comprehensible, but nonetheless more vital and more vicious,
feuding at the top. The reference to "Canton's T'an" is to none
else than Huang Yung-sheng, who was a close follower of Lin
Piao and at this time was Commander of the Canton Military
District. It may be recalled that T'an Chen-lin was an old
Communist military leader. He took part in the famous Autumn
Harvest Uprising led by Mao in 1927, was commander of the Third
Field Army Group in 1946, became a member of the Politbureau in
1956, Vice-Premier and Vice-Chairman of the State Planning
Commission from October 1962, and had now become a casualty
of the cultural revolution.

What happened in Canton was not untypical of what was happening in the rest of China, particularly in the towns and cities. The
army, too, was getting deeply involved, sometimes confused about
who was genuinely Left and who was not, sometimes using heavy-
handed measures to maintain order and stability, and sometimes
swirled away in the currents and cross-currents rocking Peking.
The struggle was sharper at some places and less sharp at others
but the pot was boiling everywhere. Kwangtung apart, a number
of other border provinces also witnessed large-scale trouble, among
them Inner Mongolia, Sinkiang, and Tibet, and provinces like
Szechuan and Hupeh (specially Wuhan) were for a long time in the
limelight. Information is necessarily sketchy about the exact shape
of things but certain general remarks can be confidently made from
the information revealed by Peking and the Red Guards.

In Inner Mongolia, a sharp battle had begun to develop in the
"January Revolution" and it was evident that a chief target of the
struggle was no less a person than Ulanfu,[28] a veteran Mongol

[28]Ulanfu joined the Communist Youth Corps in 1924 and the Chinese
Communist Party in 1925, studied at the Sun Yat-sen University in Moscow and
was a Yenan veteran. He has been Vice-Premier of Communist China, member
of the National Defence Council, and Chairman of the Inner Mongolian Autonomous People's Committee. He was made a full General and was conferred
the Order of Liberation, first Class, in 1955. He was a member of the Central
Committee of the Communist Party and an alternate member of the Politbureau
since 1956.

Communist leader and until recently Peking's main Party representative and spokesman for this sensitive area, who was now held guilty of pandering to "petty nationalism" of the Mongolian race on this side of China's border, of stirring up anti-Han[29] sentiments and of making common cause with local nationalists and "reactionaries." (It needs no omniscience to visualize Peking's constant concern and worry over the situation in this province where the overwhelming majority of the population has ethnic and emotional ties with their brethren across the frontier in Outer Mongolia). The Maoists viewed with suspicion most of the local cadres and non-Han leaders. As they did for many other provinces, the Peking Red Guard Headquarters sent a contingent to Huehot also to stroke the fires of the cultural revolution. Their opponents organized themselves into the Red Guard Army and the Revolutionary Fighters, who further appealed to their own followers for "unity against the outsiders," and as in many other places the two sides fought long and pitched battles. The Peking contingent of the Red Guards reported a grim picture of armed struggle, innumerable casualties, and scores of persons missing. They alleged that the local garrison command was siding with the reactionaries and had thrown a blanket of "white terror" over the city, with ten motor vehicles mounted with machine-guns patrolling the city day and night.[30]

In two emergency telegrams to Mao, Lin Piao, Chou En-lai, the Military Affairs Committee, and the Cultural Revolution Committee, the loyalists appealed for immediate and urgent aid. They informed Peking that as a protest against the suppression and violence, sixty-nine of them had gone on an indefinite hunger-strike which had already lasted for over 52 hours and could result in fatal consequences. They besought immediate assistance and asked for the punishment of the leading personnel of the Inner Mongolian Military District and a take-over by the Military Control Committee.[31]

It was Peking's task, particularly Chou En-lai's to provide succour

[29]The dominant nationality in China is the Han nationality. The minority nationalities constitute about 6 per cent of the total population and are particularly concentrated in Sinkiang, Inner Mongolia, Manchuria, Tibet, Szechuan, Yunnan, Kwangsi, and Kwangtung.

[30]*Yu-t'ien Feng-lei*, Peking, 10 February 1967, published by the National Posts and Telegraph System, Revolutionary Rebel General Headquarters.

[31]*Ibid.*

to the aggrieved Red Guards and also to keep the situation in hand and prevent a bigger explosion. While the campaign against Ulanfu continued, Peking's moves were directed towards maintaining watchful relations with the army command and towards limiting local conflict. In line with its policy of enlarging the ranks of the "rebels," particularly by compromising with the cadres and the military leaders, Peking apparently chose to play the balancing role of not abandoning the leftists but at the same time not driving the cadres and military leaders into a corner. Gradually, with the backward turn that Peking had to adopt, the leftists were criticized for making too many enemies and for promoting anarchist trends. The official propaganda now called upon the clashing groups to read Mao's works and resolve the differences. An editorial in *Inner Mongolian Daily*, on 14 September, criticized the "mistaken ideas" of the "rebels" which were jeopardizing the formation of "the revolutionary grand alliance." The instructions: persist in forming an alliance and oppose splits.[32]

Developments in Sinkiang have been shrouded in mystery. But this much is known that the restlessness of a national minority was not the only headache for Peking whose problems were further bedevilled by the assertion of authority and autonomy by the local military boss, General Wang En-mao.[33] The Red Guards made initial attempts to develop the movement there but were put down with a decisiveness and thoroughness unmatched elsewhere. The General made it clear that he would stand no nonsense and that at least in his realm there must be no breakdown, no disruption, and no free-for-all. So far, Mao had chosen to make his peace with the recalcitrant but determined General—obviously in view of the highly sensitive location of the province and its unique strategic importance as China's major nuclear and missile base and testing ground. Perhaps the same considerations had moved the General

[32]Inner Mongolian Regional Service, *Huehot*, 23 September 1967.

[33]Lieutenant General Wang En-mao, a native of Kiangsi, has been associated with the Chinese revolution almost since 1927. He has also had a prolonged spell of work in Sinkiang which apparently enabled him to consolidate his position in the province. He was Political Commissar of the First Field Army in 1949, Secretary of CCP Sinkiang Sub-Bureau in 1952 as well as Political Commissar of the Sinkiang Military Area in the same year, and Commander of the Sinkiang Military Area from 1956. He is also a member of the Central Committee of the Chinese Communist Party.

in taking such a firm stand and it might be inappropriate
to label him as "anti-Maoist" as such or to ascribe to him political
ambitions of a secessionist nature.   However, the case of Wang
En-mao does point to the general phenomenon of the recurring
problem in Chinese history of powerful military leaders eroding
central authority and compelling the central government to seek
compromises and to attempt to balance various forces and personalities with or against one another.

About Tibet, information has been even scantier and there are
more question marks than answers.   Undoubtedly, according to
Peking's accounts, the cultural revolution extended its grip to this
turbulent, outlying area and there were clashes and struggles among
Red Guards and their opponents.   At one time the target of the
Red Guard struggle seemed to be the local military commander
and vice-chairman of the Preparatory Committee for the Autonomous Region of Tibet, Lieutenant-General Chang Kuo-hua,[34]
who was at one time believed to have got the axe.   Soon enough he
emerged as the military commander of the southwest where a more
consequential and bitter struggle had been under way during most
of 1967.   Szechuan turned out to be one of the worst trouble spots
putting up the most stubborn resistance to a Maoist take-over.

Many of the elements in the present upheaval discerned earlier
coalesced in Szechuan to produce a highly volatile and explosive
situation—rival organizations of "revolutionary rebels" flying at
each other's throats, the resistance put up by the cadres in authority
in self-defence and, on top of it all, the attempt by the provincial
Party and military chief to maintain his power and authority.   It
was only after months and months of agonizing struggle, verging
on civil warfare, that the First Secretary of the Southwest Bureau of
the Central Committee, Li Ching-ch'uan,[35] was humbled and brought

[34]Chang Kuo-hua, Commander of the Honan-Kiangsu-Anhwei Army (of
the Chinese Communists) in 1947, has also had a firm base of authority in Tibet.
He was in Peking's delegation to negotiate with the Tibetans the "Agreement
on Measures for Peaceful Liberation of Tibet" in 1951, and led the PLA units
into Tibet the same year.   He has been Commander of the Tibet Military
Area since 1952, one of the secretaries of the CCP Tibet Work Committee and
a Deputy from Tibet to the National People's Congress in Peking.   He is also a
member of the National Defence Council.

[35]Li Ching-ch'uan was an old-timer in the Communist Party.   He has been a
member of the Politbureau since 1958.   Graduating from the "Resist-Japan

to heel by the Maoists.   But even this seems to have been brought off by substituting in his place a person who was no doubt powerful but did not exactly enjoy the reputation of being a staunch Maoist during the cultural revolution, General Chang Kuo-hua who had experienced much Red Guard hostile activity in Tibet.

In Szechuan it was a long, hot day for the Maoists whose principal and primary adversary for many months was Li Ching-ch'uan who had formed around him his own Red Guard organizations confronting those from Peking and their local supporters.   The two sides turned on each other and during the months of April and July there were repeated clashes and bloodshed.   A loyalist despatch from Chungking in April published by the Peking Red Guards carries an angry denunciation of "counter-revolutionary restoration from top to bottom" in the Chungking area and the "towering crimes" of a handful of Party power-holders in the Southwest Bureau and the Chungking Municipal Party Committee opposing Mao and the Central Committee. They had brought about a "sham seizure" of power and created "white terror" to suppress the "revolutionary masses."   One organization particularly mentioned for condemnation was the August 15 Fighting Corps of Chungking University which was playing the "inglorious role" of an ally of Party power-holders led by Li Ching-ch'uan.[36]   A subsequent Peking report in May sharply denounced Li Ching-ch'uan for the "bloody suppression of proletarian revolutionaries" in Chengtu. It was alleged by the Peking Red Guards that on 6 May an "extremely serious counter-revolutionary incident" took place in Chengtu, when the Industrial Army, a "royalist organization" controlled by Li, carried out violent suppression and there ensued a "shocking,

---

College," he became Political Commissar of the Regiment of Guards, First Front Army, 1931.   Since the founding of the new regime in China, he had had ample opportunity to establish his power in Szechuan.   He was made Chairman of the Chengtu Military Control Committee in 1950, Political Commissar of the Southwest Military Region in the same year, Chairman of the West Szechuan Administrative Office also in the same year, Chairman of the Szechuan People's Government in 1952, First Secretary of the CCP Szechuan Provincial Party in 1956 and finally First Secretary of the Southwest Bureau of the Central Committee in 1961.

[36]"A Report to the Revolutionary Masses of the Capital by a Representative of the Chungking-bound Fighting Corps of Universities and Colleges in the Capital," *Hung-yen Chan-pao*, Peking, No. 1, 15 April 1967.

bloody tragedy" in Chengtu. The rival organizations involved were Chengtu Workers Revolutionary Rebel Corps and "Szechuan University's August 26." The Peking Red Guards expressed "painful sorrow" for the "martyrs" of Chengtu and pledged to fight with Li Ching-ch'uan to death and until the "Great South-west" was "liberated."[37]

Li was finally worsted, but throughout most of 1967 the factional fighting of the Red Guards, threatening to get out of hand any time, remained a major source of worry to Mao. In analyzing the com-plicated nature of developments in the cultural revolution, it has been observed above that, generally speaking, when the Red Guards were pursuing and hounding important leaders and functionaries, they were obviously prompted by more powerful personages in the top leadership. However, as the situation developed after December 1966, not only did the Red Guard assaults on the cadres lead to a general deterioration of the political situation but the Red Guards also fell upon one another and were increasingly involved in a convulsive movement whose primary aim was to seize and hold power for their own group and to deny others a share. Mutually suspicious or jealous, they tried to secure for themselves a dominat-ing position to the exclusion of others and in order to establish their own hegemony they took to the splitting of heads and fighting it out. A number of instances of this infighting have been cited above, but no attempt is made here—nor is this necessary—to provide an exhaustive coverage of these occurrences. Red Guard literature is replete with such cases and the general phenomenon is well known.

In fact, the crux of the problem was stated most pithily by a Maoist mouthpiece in Shanghai, *Wen-hui Pao*. As late as 14 September 1967, it said in an editorial that much of the trouble could be traced to the ambition of various Red Guard organizations to become the "nucleus" (of power) and ascribed it to the "factional nature of the petty bourgeoisie." The paper lamented that "each one [Red Guard organization] wants to be the nucleus" and that "as a result, a state of disintegration has come about."[38] This candid acknowledgement

---

[37]Statement by the Standing Committee of the Peking Municipal Congress of Workers," *Pei-ching Kung-jen*, 17 May 1967.

[38]*Wen-hui Pao*, Shanghai, Editorial, 14 September 1967.

of the source of trouble and the resulting damage should be regarded
as one of the crucial factors determining Maoist strategy in this
period.

REVOLUTION IN REVERSE GEAR

The beginning of the retreat from the extremist frenzy of the cultural revolution with the intervention of the army has already been
noted in the previous chapter. In the new phase, Mao's "great
strategic plan," to which constant references were made in articles
and wall newspapers during 1967, rested on two legs: the orders
to the army to move in and bring about leftist victory as well as
stability, and the orders to the followers to establish a "three-in-one"
alliance of revolutionary rebels, the revolutionary cadres, and the
army. The appeal to the army and the appeal for unity were
designed to end the growing political and administrative instability
and to save the movement that Mao had launched. The increasing
level of violence in the country and the attendant confusion and
dislocation which made the need for unity more insistent, but
equally more difficult to extract more and more concessions from
Mao, and brought the revolution almost to a grinding halt. Not
only the conflict with the cadres had to be contained but the fratricidal
warfare among the Red Guards had also to be ended. New problems and new difficulties continued to rise resulting in apparently
paradoxical and inexplicable twists and turns of tactics.

Mao called the army in to pull the Red Guard chestnuts out of the
fire. He hoped it would put the leftists in command and establish
order and unity. But once having taken charge, the army's task
necessarily extended beyond a concern for the position of the leftists
and revolved a great deal around keeping the wheels of administration and production moving. The local situation was often confusing. There were generally a medley of noisy, competing Red
Guard organizations. Too often they pressed their claims so
clamorously as to create conditions bordering on breakdown of
authority and leading to the stoppage of work. It was too great a
strain on the prescience of the army to sift the grain from the chaff,
pick out the truly revolutionary ones and install them in the seat
of power. Not only could it err in choosing between the conflicting
claims of the "revolutionary rebels," but it occasionally found itself

annoyingly involved in their politics. Often it was easier and safer to restrain all of them—sometimes just to put down the Red Guards and get on with the job of keeping the country going. In any case, the army had its own job to do and was not over-solicitous about the advice and guidance of the "rebels." Inevitably, at many places as soon as the army was called out, friction marred the relations between the army and sections of the Red Guards, and the relations between the local army units and the "revolutionary rebels" were not conspicuously harmonious. The Red Guards, who thought the world was theirs, appeared to resent the intrusion of the army and at some places vented their anger at the local command.

Mao's strategy, therefore, went through three distinct stages in which he tried to alternate between the need for army control and its implications with attempts to keep intact the prestige and influence of the leftists and to promote happier relations between the two. The first and foremost need, however, was to establish fully the authority of the army to avert a breakdown. So the first slogan given in January (1967) was to support the army. The Red Guards were told to cooperate with the army and abide by its instructions and actions, and to desist from either carrying the cultural revolution into the army from outside or to start a struggle against it. The army was to conduct its own cultural revolution in its own way and according to the requirements of the situation.

An eight-point order to the army issued on 28 January 1967 by the Military Control Commission and personally approved by Mao, while calling on the army to intervene in the cultural revolution and to support the "genuine proletarian cultural revolutionaries," authorized it to adopt "measures of dictatorship" against "organizations and elements proved counter-revolutionary based on concrete evidence." If attacks had been made against the military organs, they should be investigated if instigated by counter-revolutionaries, but may be closed if the leftists had been involved. But the order forbade any further attacks against the military organs and also sternly prohibited any "attacks on or contacts with the war preparedness system and the intelligence security system." "It is forbidden," the order laid down, "to request or loot source materials that are not related to the cultural revolution. Materials that are related to the cultural revolution should be temporarily sealed and stored to await proper handling."

The cultural revolution within the army units should conform to the requirements of the situation as well as the demands of reasoning and moderation. The military order warned against struggle by force, seizing people within the army units without proper authorization and compelling them to wear dunce hats and black placards, or parading them through the streets and making them kneel down, etc. It also called upon all teachers and students from the military academies, army litterateurs and art groups, and workers of hospitals and military factories who had moved out to "exchange revolutionary experience" to return to their localities and base units to carry out the struggle there and not to "loiter about in Peking and other places."[39]

When the army took over, despite all the political indoctrination and steeling in the thought of Mao Tse-tung, it saw as its function not merely to decide which querulous Red Guard unit was right or wrong, but essentially, to restore order, authority, and normalcy. This had nothing to do with the Army's theoretical loyalty to Mao which was not questioned. By and large, the army stood for stability, discipline, and continuity of the production lines as well as for the maintenance of the interests of the peasantry with whom it had intimate relationship. At times the soldiers were genuinely baffled about the choice of the "genuine proletarian revolutionaries"; at times, on the other hand, they were not particularly soft towards the revolutionary rebels disturbing peace in the area. Although the army had to be given a free hand to control the potentially chaotic situation resulting from the "January revolution," its strong-arm measures against the Red Guards at many places were a matter of obvious concern to the Maoist headquarters. On 6 April, fresh instructions were issued in which a new slogan "cherish the masses" was given to the army.[40] The "masses," of course, meant the Red Guard supporters of Mao.

The main aim of the 10-point order of 6 April was to restrain the army from excessive curbing of the "revolutionary rebels" so that their authority over the people was not fatally undermined. An editorial of Chieh-fang Chun-pao (Liberation Army Daily) explaining the purport of the instructions to the army stressed that

[39]The order went up on the walls of Peking on 29 January 1967.
[40]See Chiang Ch'ing's speech at the inaugural rally of the new Peking Municipal Revolutionary Committee, Jen-min th-pao, 21 April 1967.

the PLA should "grasp the main orientation of the struggle" which was directed at "the handful of power-holders in the Party taking the capitalist road" and so "under no circumstances should the PLA turn against the revolutionary masses." The soldiers were cautioned that the power-holders were trying to confuse them by "exaggerating the mistakes" of the Red Guards. The "revolutionary rebels" were a "new force" and, therefore, could not be expected to be flawless, but they were otherwise all right. The army should show patience with them and help them attain unity.[41]

Peking was, however, equally anxious that the PLA's control be maintained effectively and was constrained to do a considerable measure of tight-rope walking, now exhorting the "rebels" to support the army, now appealing to the army to cherish the "rebels." Chiang Ch'ing, for instance, in a major speech at a rally to mark the formation of the new Peking Municipal Revolutionary Committee told the Red Guards that it was in order to write posters and to send them to anyone in the PLA about whom they were critical, or to report the matter to the higher authorities, not excluding the Central Committee, but hastened to add that "under no circumstances should we direct the spearhead of the struggle against the PLA." The purpose of the eight-point order of 28 January was to call upon the people to rally behind the army; the "main point" of the ten-point order issued on 6 April was that the PLA "should correctly deal with the masses and cherish the people." She was quick to emphasize that the one should not be used against the other and, significantly, the ten-point order must not be used to violate the eight-point order. The reason for this, she admitted, was: "We put forth this question because, on the one hand, we fear that comrades may make mistakes and, on the other hand, bad elements may make use of the ten-point order. Therefore, we now emphatically put forth the call of supporting the PLA and cherishing the people."[42]

The same theme was developed a month later by *Jen-min Jih-pao* (People's Daily) clearly under the impact of the attempt by sections of the Red Guards to rely on the ten-point order to even their scores with those army leaders and units which had tried to put them down. The editorial warned the Red Guards that, with-

---

[41]*Chieh-fang Chun-pao*, editorial reproduced in *Jen-min Jih-pao*, 10 April 1967.
[42]See fn. 40.

out the PLA's support, victory in the cultural revolution was impossible. "Precisely because we have the PLA, which is loyal to Chairman Mao and his proletarian revolutionary line, as staunch backer, we were able to launch the world-shaking great proletarian cultural revolution." It reminded the "rebels"; "without the PLA, it would be impossible to carry out the great proletarian cultural revolution." It was, therefore, entirely incorrect to use the ten-point order to supercede the earlier eight-point order.[43] The fears of Mao's wife and other Maoist spokesmen were rooted in the realities of China's situation, and the frictions between the "revolutionary rebels" and the local army units, and the commanders continued to create problems for the leadership.

THE RETURN OF THE CADRE

Besides moving in the army, Mao had to alter his revolutionary scheme and bring the cadre back to the gravity of power. The Red Guards could not fill the gap of experienced administrators, managers, technicians and bureaucrats. The administration had to be run on a reasonable level of efficiency, the factories had to be managed with a certain degree of competence and expertise; the momentum of the country—the government, the economy, the system—had to be maintained. Who would provide the leadership, the guidance to plants and enterprises, the direction to communes, the managerial skills, the administrative drive? Those who had acquired all this experience could not be bundled out except at the peril of administrative and economic disorganization. More importantly, the Red Guards pressed so hard—and almost indiscriminately—on the cadres in the first phase of the revolution, leaving little option to them but to struggle for their survival and to hit back, that the conflict enlarged to unmanagable proportions. All authority was breaking down and the withdrawal of the cadre threatened to bring the administrative and economic machinery to a grinding halt. It was necessary to narrow the conflict, stop the general conflagration, focus the struggle against a smaller number of people, bring the largest number of cadres back to their jobs, and make continued use of their experience and skills so that the

[43] *Jen-min Jih-pao*, editorial, 12 May 1967.

disruption and the threatened bigger breakdown could be avoided and the movement forward maintained.

The appeal to the cadre to return and make common cause with the revolutionary rebels has been partially noted in the preceding chapter. This became a recurring refrain henceforth in Maoist pronouncements and proclamations. Throughout 1967, Peking stressed the need and the importance of including the cadre in the "three-way-alliance" advocated by Mao in order to cope with the situation resulting from the January revolution. The invitation addressed to the cadres used the double-edged weapon of threat and blandishment, the stick and the carrot. If they did not line up with the Maoists, they would be discarded and would end up in the company of counter-revolutionaries. But if they proclaimed their loyalty to the revolutionary line of Mao Tse-tung, they would be back in power and could win fresh laurels. The admonition to the "revolutionary rebels" reminded them that by and large the cadres were good and loyal, besides being experienced and indispensable.

The decision of the Central Committee of the Chinese Communist Party in August 1966 had categorized the cadres according to the nature and degree of their "mistakes" in following the "bourgeois reactionary" line, but the stress at the time was on struggle and, therefore, few distinctions were made between cadres of different categories. In the new situation, the emphasis turned on using the cadres and differentiating the large majority from a small number of die-hards. Even those who had committed "serious mistakes" could rectify themselves and return to the fold by recognizing their errors and promising to reform themselves. The choice before the cadres was the threat of mass denunciation and dismissal or the prospect of re-inclusion in the power elite if only they acknowledged that they had erred in the past and promised to abide by Maoist instructions in future.[44] What was imperative was that they dissociated themselves from the "top Party person in authority" and a "handful" allied to him and his line. Even the "leading cadres" were given the chance for rehabilitation if they just made

---

[44] See, for instance, an article entitled "Observe them, Help them and Unite with them—Thoughts on taking the Mass Line in Educating and Uniting with the Cadres," *Jen-min Jih-pao*, 26 April, 1967.

the necessary propitiation.[45] Admit that you had made mistakes and declare your determination to be loyal to Mao—that was the cadres' road back to power.

Having first allowed a general assault on the cadres by the Red Guards, Peking had the rather embarrassing task of persuading them that that had not been really the objective and that they should make peace with the cadres. An earlier statement of Mao (made in 1964) was recalled and commended to the "revolutionary rebels" for their edification and guidance. Mao had then said: "The great majority of the cadres are good or comparatively good." The official line now was that "this wise thesis" of Chairman Mao was "a correct evaluation of the basic situation of cadres which is universally applicable to all areas and units" and that the "proletarian revolutionaries must have faith in this evaluation."[46] They must "encourage" the cadres to "rise in revolution" and welcome them back in their midst.

The blame for the indiscriminate attack on the cadre was now laid at the door of the "bourgeois rightists" who had deflected the struggle by hitting hard at a large number of people in order to save a small number. This was actually an error, "leftist" in form but "rightist" in essence. In any case, the importance that Mao gave to the cadre question in order to control the situation was evident from the injunction to the Red Guards that the attitude towards the cadres provided the "key" to the outcome of the upheaval in China, for it was urged, persistence in the posture of hostility would be driving "millions" to the enemy's side.[47] An article in *Jen-min Jih-pao* in August 1967, while calling upon the Red Guards to "boldly use" the cadres, frankly acknowledged that without the support of the cadres for Mao's cause, "success cannot be achieved." The Red Guards were "immature," they could not wield power. Power would be lost if the cadres could not be won over.[48] Even those who had made "serious mistakes" of line must be given the

---

[45]As an illustration of this dual tactic of offering a bait and threatening with the axe, see a despatch entitled "Shantung Cadres Oppose Bourgeois Reactionary Line," *New China News Agency*, Peking, 18 April 1967.

[46]Commentator's article in *Jen-min Jih-pao*, 18 April 1967.

[47]"Resolutely Act on Chairman Mao's Instructions and Correctly Treat Cadres who have Erred," *Jen-min Jih-pao*, 11 August 1967.

[48]"Boldly Use the Revolutionary Cadres Well," *ibid.*, 18 August 1967.

opportunity to reform and join the ranks of the Maoists.

All these exhortations were necessary even half a year after Mao had issued the first instructions on the change of course because the actual process of uniting the Red Guards and the cadres did not have a smooth sailing. The cadres, having been made to grovel in the dust, were reluctant to assume responsibility; some were afraid and some highly piqued, but all were smarting under the impact of the blows delivered at their position and prestige by the "revolutionary rebels." They had to be coaxed, cajoled, and bludgeoned into reassuming responsibility for running the affairs of the State. For their part, the Red Guards, too, were averse to seeing the return of the cadres and sharing power with them. At many places they continued to deride the cadres either for their "mistakes" of the past in following the "bourgeois reactionary line" or for their attempt to jump on the band wagon after it had already started rolling on, in other words, accusing them of being "Johnies-come-lately." That is why persistent efforts had to be made to educate the Red Guards on the paramount need for conciliating the cadres. As an official report put it, one particular obstacle which stood in the way of the Red Guards uniting with the majority of cadres was an "obsession with sentiments such as personal affection or grievances, gain or loss in the midst of struggle and to use these personal sentiments to determine, whether or not, a certain cadre should be united with and liberated."[49] The Red Guards' disdain for the cadres and their disinclination to share power could not be easily overcome.

CURBING THE RED GUARDS AND THE STRUGGLE BY FORCE

As noted earlier, in the situation arising in the wake of the developments in December-January 1966-67, Mao suddenly faced a very serious problem of internecine warfare among the Red Guards, which compelled him to alter his plans and withdraw many steps backwards in order to limit the conflict. Many instances of such infighting have been previously noted and the evidence for this is massive and incontrovertible. Some of the steps taken to curb this struggle may be noted. One of the first requirements was to get

[49]*New China News Agency*, Peking, 10 August 1967.

the Red Guard students back to the schools and universities. This was necessary to defuse the conflict between them and other sections of the people, particularly in cases where they were agitating and "exchanging revolutionary experience" with other units and areas, and to scale down the level of violence gripping the country. In early March, a circular issued in the name of the Central Committee asked all those "revolutionary teachers and students" who had left for factories, villages and other areas to return to their institutions by 20 March. In order not to dampen their enthusiasm, they were told that they should continue to carry on the revolution in their own institutions and were advised to establish provisional organs of power there through an alliance with "revolutionary teachers, revolutionary students, and revolutionary cadres."[50]

It did not prove to be an easy task to persuade the roving ambassadors of the cultural revolution to come back and another circular was issued on 20 April jointly by the Central Committee, the State Council, the Military Control Committee, and the Cultural Revolution Committee banning travel to other places to establish revolutionary ties. This was reinforced by another order of the new Peking Municipal Revolutionary Committee on 14 May. It called upon all the "revolutionary masses" who had gone to other parts of the country to immediately return to Peking and those who were in Peking from other places to get back to their own units and warned that the Central Committee's order must be strictly enforced.[51]

At the same time, Peking decided to put the Red Guard students through a period of military and political training by the PLA. Clearly, the objective was to instil a greater sense of discipline among the youthful "rebels" and to control the situation by putting them under the charge of the army. The Central Committee's instructions of 14 March, asking the teachers and students to return to their class-rooms, laid down that they would receive "short term military and political training." Later, it was stated that Mao had himself "instructed the PLA to give military and political training to universities, secondary schools, and higher forms of primary schools, stage by stage, and group by group." Mao had said that it was "an excellent idea to send army cadres to train revolutionary teachers and students. There is a tremendous difference between

[50]*Hsin Pei-ta*, Peking, 14 March 1967.
[51]*Pei-ching Kung-jen*, 17 May 1967.

those who have such training and those who have not."[52] Thus, the universities and the schools were put under the tutelage of the army. An editorial in *Chieh-fang Chun-pao*, two months after the first circular, written obviously in response to the deteriorating situation, called upon the army to "resolutely fulfil the glorious task of training revolutionary teachers and students."[53] The same day, *Jen-min Jih-pao*, in its editorial, commended such training and claimed that it was being conducted "under the attentive direction of our great leader Chairman Mao." The purpose of such training was apparent from this official advice to the army that both the "organizations of the left which had made mistakes" and the "ordinary people in conservative organizations" should be "treated correctly" and that they should not be "excluded and discriminated against."[54]

The concern of the Maoist headquarters for disciplining the Red Guards which is patent from these orders and pronouncements and other exhortations could only grow with the rising crescendo of Red Guard warfare and violence. There were repeated calls by Peking and through the mouths of faithful spokesmen to establish and respect "revolutionary authority" and to unite for the common cause. The baby should not be thrown along with the bath-tub water and it was not all authority which was to be repudiated but only "bourgeois authority." Although the "power-holders" were blamed for the spread of the notion of "exclude all and overthrow all indiscriminately," the Maoist statements made it clear that their chief anxiety was the "anarchism" being displayed by the Red Guards.[55] This is how an authoritative statement described the activities of at least a section of the Red Guards:

> ... some people relax the demands on themselves, advocate ultra-democracy and blur the line between the extensive democracy under the dictatorship of the proletariat and the liberalism of the bourgeoisie. They do whatever they like, going from place to place to cause trouble without principle. This makes the friends

[52]*Chieh-fang Chun-pao*, editorial, 16 May 1967.
[53]*Ibid*.
[54]*Jen-min Jih-pao*, editorial, 16 May 1967.
[55]Jen Li-hsin, "Anarchism is a Penalty for Opportunist Sins," *Jen-min Jih-pao*, 11 May 1967.

grieve but the enemies happy. It must be pointed out that this is a current of anarchist ideas. If this current is allowed to overflow unchecked, we shall become loose in unity and organization, passive in work, divergent in opinions, and the revolutionary ranks will split. A small split is a serious mistake, and a big split is a crime.... Anarchism is the opposite of our view. It aims at overthrowing "all" authority, saying nonsensically that the power-holders are problematic, that all responsible persons should stand aside.... It must be pointed out emphatically: This is an anarchist idea that is "left" in form but right in essence.... They want to sabotage the establishment of the three-way-alliance provisional organs of power that are revolutionary and representative and have proletarian revolutionary authority.[56]

The situation, however, continued to deteriorate and became so critical that Peking was constrained to issue an urgent and direct appeal to its supporters to "immediately curb struggle by force." In a high-level editorial, *Jen-min Jih-pao* complained and confessed that "of late a gust of sinister wind of struggle by force has appeared in some areas between units and between mass organizations." It frankly acknowledged that this had "interfered with the great orientation of the struggle.... affected and wrecked production, upset the orderly process of revolution, destroyed State property and threatened security in the lives of the people." This sinister wind must be checked, the official paper warned and called for strict implementation of the 16-point decision of the Central Committee of August 1966 and conduct the struggle through reason and not by coercion.[57]

The violence and factional fighting had swept Peking as well as other cities and towns, and it was revealed that Mao had "personally approved and made public" a circular order by the Peking Municipal Revolutionary Committee directing the Red Guards to desist from struggling by force and beating up people, smashing things, looting, confiscating private property, and making unauthorized arrests. No violation of labour discipline or law was to be permitted. No work stoppage was to be allowed. No destruction of State property

[56]"Vigorously Establish the Revolutionary Discipline and Revolutionary Authority of the Proletariat," *Kuang-ming Jih-pao*, 8 May 1967.
[57]*Jen-min Jih-pao*, editorial, 22 May 1967.

was to be tolerated. Once again it strictly ordered all those who were roving about in Peking and elsewhere to get back to their original places of work or study. Significantly, the order warned that the "Peking garrison forces of the People's Liberation Army and representatives of the armed forces have the authority to deal with the question of struggle through coercion and force" and "all departments concerned must comply and disobedience must not be allowed."[58]

There can, thus, be no possible doubt about the serious and widespread nature of the conflict. This series of measures spread over many months bear clear testimony to it. That it continued to harass the Maoist leadership in the coming months was evident from an order issued jointly on 5 September by the Central Committee, the State Council, Military Affairs Committee, and the Cultural Revolution Committee forbidding seizure of arms, equipment, and other military supplies from the PLA. The order warned the people: "The PLA and the arms, equipment and material supplies of all descriptions in its possession are inviolable. No outsiders are allowed to enter and occupy PLA command centres." It plainly told all the mass organizations and individuals that "irrespective of their affiliations" (that is, no matter how left and loyal they were), they were forbidden to seize arms, ammunition, or other military supplies from the PLA and the arsenals, military stores and defence enterprises, or to intercept such arms and supplies being carried in trains, trucks or ships. The arms and equipment already seized must all be put under seal and stored and a time-limit set for their return. Equally significantly, the order strictly prohibited the PLA and its allied institutes and schools from handing over without specific central authorization, any arms, ammunition, vehicles or other military supplies to any organization or individual.[59]

To maintain a delicate balance between curbing the Red Guard excesses and fratricidal warfare, and still keeping their enthusiasm at a high pitch, between establishing the authority and supremacy of the PLA and yet restraining it from putting down too heavily the Red Guard struggles, and between securing the cooperation and

---

[58]*Ibid.*
[59]*Chung-fa*, Peking, No. 288, 1967.

utilization of the experience and skills of the cadres and at the same time ensuring their surrender and loyalty to Mao's line, taxed and continues to tax the ingenuity of Mao and his close associates at the top and provides at least a partial explanation for the various turns and shifts in their policies and moves.

THE WUHAN EPISODE

The defiance of Peking by the military command of the Wuhan Military Region was undoubtedly one of the most daring and dramatic episodes in the cultural revolution, indeed in the entire period of Chinese Communist rule over the mainland. The exact sequence of events and the role of various individuals involved will not be known to the outside world until Peking chooses to reveal the secrets of the Forbidden Palace, but a reasonably accurate picture can be gleaned from the information provided by official statements and Red Guard materials. What shook the country and made headlines all over the world was the arrest and subsequent release, under mysterious conditions in July, of Hsieh Fu-chih, Vice-Premier and alternate member of the Politbureau and concurrently chief of the cultural revolution group in the army, and Wang Li, member of the Cultural Revolution Committee and editor of *Hung-ch'i* (Red Flag), who had apparently gone to Wuhan on a mission of resolving the critical situation that had arisen there, as a result of prolonged factional fighting.

Clearly, there was a back-drop to the scenario as it was unfolded in July. For over six months, rival organizations competed and fought for supremacy and the evidence suggests that their struggle grew more intense and sanguinary involving the army and the regional Party leadership. On one side were the Peking-based Wuhan Liaison Centre of the Tung-fang-hung General Command of the Peking Mining and Industrial College and the South-bound Revolutionary Rebel Brigade of the Capital and their local supporters, mostly among students and steel workers, who had banded themselves together under the omnibus designation of the General Command of Wuhan Proletarian Revolutionary Group. Opposing them were the "One Million Brave Soldiers" drawn largely from factory workers, shop assistants, government personnel, and militiamen. They were probably supported by the Party organization led by Wang Ko-wen, secretary of the Wuhan Party Committee, and Hsin Pu, deputy director of the CCP Propaganda Department. They also secured the support of Chen Tsai-tao and Chung Han-hua, Commander and Political Commissar respectively of the military region. It has also been alleged by the Maoists that behind all this support for the "conservative" organizations was the hidden hand of Wang Jen-chung, the disgraced Party boss of the region who until recently held a commanding position in the area.

Many heads were broken and much blood was shed in this conflict and when the going became too rough for the loyalist organizations, who had influential supporters in Peking, an appeal was made to the Maoist headquarters in Peking for relief. It was at this stage that Hsieh Fu-chih and Wang Li were sent to Wuhan on 14 July to save the truly "leftist" organizations and resolve the conflict. When their sympathies came to be known and they suggested action which was tantamount to the branding of the organizations favoured to the local Party and army command as counter-revolutionary and to implied criticism of the military leadership, they were arrested and, according to one report, beaten up. This action sent tremors of shock throughout the country, and Peking had to act swiftly. What exactly happened is not quite clear. Some reports said that Mao threatened immediate and severe military action to crush this insubordination and that air force units were despatched to the area to take control. According to another report Chou En-lai himself flew to Wuhan to bring around the rebellious army chiefs. In any case, Hsieh and Wang were released and were accorded a hero's welcome on arrival back at Peking. What was still more significant was that Mao decided to tread rather gingerly in dealing with this defiance by the local army command. While Ch'en Tsai-tao was denounced, not only was a distinction sought to be made between the handful of leaders and the rank and file, but even the culprits were treated comparatively lightly and given an opportunity to express regret, to reform themselves and rejoin the "revolutionary ranks." This was in line with Mao's efforts throughout this period to maintain the unity and cohesion of the army and to make concessions if necessary to achieve this objective, for the army was needed to keep control over the situation.

THE COUNT-DOWN

Mao had initially hoped for a quick dissolution of the old authority and an equally rapid reorganization of new authority through the formation of revolutionary committees which could take over from the existing local and provincial organs of power.   This was not to be, and the road towards the achievement of this goal proved to be painfully long and tortuous.   The count-down was still not very impressive.   In a speech at a mass rally at the Chinese Academy of Sciences on 26 May, Chou En-lai admitted that thus far only six provinces and cities had been able to pull together a "grand alliance" (that is, committees embracing Red Guards, "revolutionary cadres," and the local PLA command): Shanghai, Kwaichow, Shansi, Heilungkiang, Shantung, and Peking.   But he counselled patience and particularly appealed to the Red Guards to "refrain from fighting, smashing, looting, dragging people out, kidnapping, and raiding."   They must not act like the "September 16" faction in the Seventh Ministry of Machine Building in the matter of seizure of power.   As Chou put it, the "September 16" group and the "September 15" faction in the same Ministry had equal strength but "if you don't recognize them, they will hit you, but you can't re-cognize them just because you are afraid of being hit."[60]   Incidentally, Chou also revealed that since August 1966 he had taken over both the Academy and the State Scientific and Technological Commission as its previous leadership had been guilty of belonging to the "black gang of revisionists."

Mao's time-table had been upset and his earlier grand design had misfired.   He had to make quick changes in his strategy although there was a long way to go before order could be fully restored and new power organized in various provinces and cities.   It was apparently his hope that with the assistance of the army and the stress on keeping the cadre with the "revolutionary rebels" in the new alignment of power, the process of forming revolutionary committees all over the country as the new centres of power would be facilitated and speeded up.   Change-consolidation-change has been the favourite tactics of Mao, although this time the type of consolidation that he had to order was radically different from what he had earlier envisaged.

[60]*K'o-chi Chan-pao*, Peking, 2 June 1967.

CHAPTER SIX

AFTER THE ACT

SOME OF THE PRINCIPAL developments and trends in the cultural revolution have been analysed in the previous chapters which were written between 1966 and 67. No attempt has been made to change them, although some more information is now available and certainly many other things have happened late in 1967 and 1968 which will be discussed in this chapter. In our view, the story remains substantially intact and these authors see no reason to alter their views in the light of subsequent developments.

MAO TOURS THE COUNTRY

The flood tide of revolutionary violence and upheaval in the wake of the January revolution has been noted in the last chapter. The Red Guard students, the workers and sections of the peasantry fragmented into myriads of groups fought among themselves and against one another. With all their efforts to instil some discipline into the Red Guard factions and increasing recourse to army control, confusion prevailed and violence continued to erupt at various places, and it took nearly all of 1968 to restore relative normalcy. The so-called January revolution had opened the dykes and the flood waters were all over the place. The Red Guards, once having tasted blood, would not easily throw in the towel and at least one section of them was not yet satisfied with the extent of the ferment they had already produced, and was certainly not prepared to call it a day. Many of them were sore at the army's failure to put them into power and its efforts to restrain them. Many of them were suspicious of the army commanders and accused them of being "power holders."

Particularly after the incident at Wuhan,[1] there was an attempt by them to stir the cultural revolution in the army and to start a struggle against the "handful of capitalist-roaders" in the army command at various places. There are frequent references in the Chinese press and wall newspapers to this attempted assault on the army leadership by the extreme left. This alarmed the Maoist headquarters, for any large-scale disturbance in the army would have serious consequences for the unity of the country and the ability of the leadership to control the situation. It was one thing to remove individual commanders at the initiative of the Centre for proven (or suspected) disobedience of Mao, but quite another to make the army the target of the cultural revolution and to let the Red Guards agitate and throw the army into confusion. Mao knew that the army had not really stood foursquare behind the revolutionary rebels and, in many cases, it was difficult to say who was left and who was right, but he could not risk the dangers of chaos in the army. The soldiers would be aroused if they were indiscriminately attacked.

This, plus the general confusion and infighting, obliged Mao to issue a series of instructions and to undertake an inspection tour of North, Central-South, and East China. He went, among other places, to Cheng-chow, Wuhan, Ch'angsha, Nanch'ang and Shanghai. The instructions were issued during this tour in September. Reportedly, Mao said that the situation was most tense in June, July and August at Fukien, Chekiang, Kiangsi, Hunan, Hupeh and Honan. He described the events in Foochow as a rebellion. There was a civil war going on, he said, and not a struggle by reasoning. He deprecated the use of tactics he had himself prescribed for winning power all over the world—sorrounding the cities from the rural areas. He was obviously referring to the attempts by different factions to call in the suburban peasantry for support.[2]

His first instruction was to leave the army alone and to preserve the "army's prestige." The Red Guards were not allowed either to struggle against the army or to incite the soldiers against the officers. The army had "unavoidably" made some mistakes but the chief danger was that "some people want to beat down the PLA." He

[1]See the last chapter.
[2]*Cheng-fa Hung-ch'i*, Canton, Nos. 3 & 4, 17 October 1967.

criticized the slogan of seizing the "handful in the army" and said that the majority of the armed departments were good.[3] He remarked upon the wave of "extreme leftism" (which, of course, he had himself let loose, but which had now taken a frightening aspect), but cautioned against arrests and use of force, and, instead, advocated the mobilization of the masses to block the extreme leftists.

Reversing his earlier tactics, Mao now switched over to the policy of using the workers to control the Red Guard students. "There is no fundamental clash of interests among the working class. Under the dictatorship of the proletariat, there is no reason whatsoever for the working class to split into two big irreconcilable organizations," Mao was reported to have said in Honan and Shanghai. And he added that the working class must be put resolutely in the leading position and must not be led by the students.[4] He made it clear that, if there were two factions in a unit, he did not believe that one must be Left and the other Right.[5] The mere fact of a large membership of a particular organization did not by itself determine its place and role. The "core" was formed naturally and not just by those who selfishly strove for it.[6]

Mao's anxiety to curb the violence and factional struggle in the country and to bring the country rapidly under control was evident from these instructions. He was also constrained to limit the attack on the cadres to prevent total disruption, and, therefore, to declare that the majority of the cadres were good and should be retained. Moreover, having successfully knocked off the top leaders who were the target of his campaign, he could afford to keep the terrorized remaining ones, especially the rank and file, in the confident belief that they could not turn against him. It was reported that during his tour, Mao expressed dissatisfaction over the fact that so many cadres had been toppled. He did not even take a

---

[3] *Wen-ko T'ung-hsun*,   No. 1, 9 October 1967;   *Survey of China Mainland Press*, Hong Kong, No. 4060, 15 November 1967.

[4] Fn. 2; also *Kung-nung-ping Chan-pao*, Canton, No. 18, 14 November 1967.

[5] *Hung-chan Pao*, Canton, No. 10, 10 October 1967.

[6] Even the personnel travelling with Mao in the train from East China to Peking were reportedly divided into three factions, and Mao called them and lectured to them on the need to combat selfishness and to achieve unity. Fn. 4, *Kung-nung-ping Chan-pao*, 14 November 1967.

static view of the "rightists" of the present; most of them could be re-educated and changed.

It was conveyed to the Red Guards that Mao disapproved of the use of torture and other forcible measures like the "jet method," beating up people, hanging signboards on the opponents and making them wear dunce caps. The contradictions should be settled through reasoning and the application of Mao's formula of unity-criticism-unity.[7]   Lastly, Mao gave the terse slogan to the rebellious Red Guards: "Combat selfishness, Repudiate revisionism." The first part was directed against the developing discord among his pupils and the second part was an effort to preserve the essence of the cultural revolution.   Through this dual and dialectical approach, Mao hoped to save the revolution while retreating from its extreme manifestations.

HOW TO EAT YOUR CAKE AND HAVE IT

The clashes between the army and Red Guards and the Red Guard attack on the army were confirmed by a recorded speech of Chiang Ch'ing on 5 September which was played throughout the country. The gust of "evil wind blowing from the rightists was now matched by that stirred by the extreme left," she said. They had called for the seizure of "a handful" in the army; some army personnel were actually detained and weapons were seized on a nationwide scale. Even the war materials, earmarked for Vietnam, were seized. But, even though decrying such activities, Chiang Ch'ing could not perhaps hide her real sympathies and added— as half-hearted justification for the violence of the Red Guards— that if some people (obviously the rightists) insisted on having a violent struggle with her, she would surely defend herself and hit back—a remark which reportedly drew the loud shouting of "learn from Chiang Ch'ing and salute her" from the admiring Red Guard audience.[8] However, the burden of her speech was an appeal to the Red Guards against the use of force among themselves and against taking the army on.

This Red Guard swipe at the army could have been a crucial factor responsible for the reported displeasure of Lin Piao and for

[7]*Ibid.*

[8]*Survey of China Mainland Press*, No. 4069, 29 November 1967.

swinging him around the more moderate line and linking forces with Chou En-lai. Other considerations influencing him might have been the extent of disorder the Red Guards had managed to create and the dislocation of the urban economy and transport. But the attempt on the part of many Red Guard organizations to humble the army seemed to have infuriated him. The incidents involving the army and the Red Guards were frequently mentioned in the literature of the period and one ultra-leftist organization which particularly invited the wrath of the High Command was referred to as the "May 16" organization. This was declared to be a "counter-revolutionary secret organization" which sought to sow seeds of dissension in the Maoist headquarters, used "dirty tactics against comrades of the Central Committee," attacked Chou En-lai and criticized army leadership.[9]

The army had to be protected, while at the same time action taken against some particularly "stubborn" individual commanders. Chou En-lai, in a speech, on 17 September, before representatives of Red Guards from universities and colleges in Peking, conceded that there could be some wicked people in the army—and he mentioned Wang I-lun of Inner Mongolia, Ch'en Tsao-tao and Chung Han-hua of Wuhan and Chao Yung-fu of Tsinghai—but he warned them against any move against the army which was their Great Wall protecting the frontiers and "a pillar of the great proletarian cultural revolution."[10] The attempt to "drag out a handful in the army" reached its "height of frenzy," Chou said in August, and therefore, Peking was compelled to issue the order of 5 September, strictly forbidding the seizure of arms and interference by the Red Guards in the affairs of the army.[11]

Chou revealed that "some 10 people from Kansu" even dared storm into Chungnanhai and were apprehended close by the Huaijen Hall where Mao's headquarters was located. If true, this was an incredible act of daring which infuriated Chiang Ch'ing, Chou En-lai and other leaders. While Chiang Ch'ing (and perhaps the members of the Cultural Revolution Committee too) did not

[9]Chou En-lai's speech at a reception of representatives of universities and colleges in Peking on 17 September, *Chu-ying Tung-fang-hung*, Canton, 1 October 1967.

[10]*Ibid.*

[11]See Chapter Five.

wish to dampen the enthusiasm of the Red Guards, available evidence lends credence to the view that Chou En-lai was trying hard to discipline the Red Guards and bring about some normalcy, and that the excessive disruption caused by the Red Guards forced Chiang Ch'ing, Ch'en Po-ta and others of their group to go along, however reluctantly, with the measures intended to restrain the Red Guards. Chou En-lai, in his 17 September speech, issued a blunt order to the Red Guards to get back into their schools and colleges within a month, otherwise they would be expelled from their institutes, and those who were working would be denied their pay packets if they failed to return to their jobs. The new decision of the Peking leadership was that the Red Guards, and others too, should concentrate their energies on promoting the struggle-criticism-transformation in their own units. They were not to agitate other units and establish links there.

The army also was advised not to establish ties with the local cultural revolution and the latest instructions were: the army should support the Left but not any particular faction. The army must exercise military control and, at the same time, discipline the factions through military training. These instructions were subsequently repeated by *Chieh-fang Chun-pao*, which said editorially that the army must support all revolutionary organizations but need not side with any particular faction. Instead, the army should help the factious "revolutionary rebels" overcome their divisions and unite.[12]

Besides attacking the "handful" in the army, the leftists had also trained their guns on Chou En-lai. Wall posters had gone up criticizing him for "protecting" right-wing revisionists like Ch'en Yi, Chang Yen and others. This was the second time within months that posters had been put up criticizing the Chinese Premier. According to some Red Guards accounts, there was a highly acrimonious session between Red Guard students critical of Chou and the Cultural Revolution Committee leaders like Ch'en Po-ta, Hsieh Fu-chih, Ch'i Pen-yu, and Yeh Chun (Lin Piao's wife). Some of these were the leaders who had aided and abetted the onslaughts of the Red Guards, and they were still reluctant to apply too many brakes on them, but, besides the chaos of factional fighting which obliged them to agree to the curbing of the Red Guards, a section

[12]*Chieh-fang Chun-pao*, editorial, as in *New China News Agency*, Peking, 27 January 1968.

of the Red Guards had transgressed all bounds of permissive political upturning. They were hunting for enemies all around. They were attacking the army; they were denouncing the Prime Minister; they were shooting their arrows in all directions.

Among those who were called to the meeting were leaders of the Red Guards Congress and representatives of organizations which had put up posters against the Chinese Premier. The new Peking Revolutionary Committee chief, Hsieh Fu-chih who replaced P'eng Chen and became the head of the Peking Municipal Revolutionary Committee, lamented the disunity among the Red Guards and chided them for putting up fresh posters against the Premier after having been admonished earlier and having agreed that it was a mistake. A rather surprising statement he made was that the University students "looked down upon" him and that he was therefore asking Ch'en Po-ta to do the talking with the students. Ch'en Po-ta denied that the Premier had tried to "protect" Ch'en Yi and tried to take the blame on himself, saying that it was he who protected Ch'en Yi. He was not competent to be a foreign minister, nor were the students, so the student criticism was not sensible. When the students belonging to the "616" organization persisted in defending their criticism of Chou En-lai, both Ch'i Pen-yu and Ch'en Po-ta asked them not to talk nonsense. Chou En-lai, they said, was the "chief staff officer" of Chairman Mao and Vice-Chairman Lin and enjoyed high prestige at home and abroad. "When did Chairman Mao and Vice-Chairman Lin order you to oppose the Premier," Ch'i Pen-yu asked the students and added, "in the violent storms Chairman Mao has an elaborate strategic plan. Whether you understand it or not, you must follow it."[13] (Liu Shao-ch'i was castigated for advocating blind obedience to the Party!)

That things are not always what they seem to be in China was once more highlighted by the downfall of a number of members of the Cultural Revolution Committee for their involvement in intrigues against Chou En-lai and high army officials who had the support of Lin Piao. The casualty list in the Cultural Revolution Committee has been very high. Of the 18 original members, only five remained at the end of 1968. More surprising was the ouster

[13] *Wen-ke T'ung-hsun*, Canton, 9 October 1967.

of Wang Li, Kuan Feng and, eventually, Ch'i Pen-yu who rose to sudden prominence and then equally suddenly returned to the limbo of obscurity. These writers wrote in an earlier chapter that new stars had arisen on the political firmament of China:[14] Chiang Ch'ing, Ch'en Po-ta, K'ang Sheng, Wang-Li, Hsieh Fu-chih, Chang Chun-ch'iao, Ch'i Pen-yu, Kuan Feng and Yao Wen-yuan—all entrusted with the work of promoting cultural revolution—(only Ch'en Po-ta and K'ang Sheng were nationally important figures before the cultural revolution). But even this constellation did not remain intact. Wang Li, Ch'i Pen-yu and Kuan Feng fell one by one. Wang Li was accused of encouraging attacks against Chou En-lai. and Ch'i Pen-yu and Kuan Feng were believed to have been covertly backing the ostensibly extreme left-wing organizations, like the "May 16," which had embarked upon a sustained campaign against the army leadership. The political mortality rate among those appointed or promoted to lead the cultural revolution has been extraordinarily high. This can only indicate the fierceness of the struggle at the top and the shifting nature of internal groupings and alliances.

The presence of Yeh Chun (Lin Piao's wife) at the meeting to criticize the critics of the Premier was significant. It lends credence to reports that Lin and Chou had come closer in response to the chaos of the cultural revolution, and that Lin was thoroughly annoyed by the attempt of "ultra-leftist" Red Guards, with the obvious back-stage support of some higher authorities, to discredit the army, and particularly to oust some of his proteges, like Chief of Staff Huang Yung-sheng.

POSITION OF THE ARMY

The army's role in the cultural revolution has neither been easy nor smooth. The current campaign of supporting the army and preserving its prestige, directed primarily against irate Red Guards should not blind us to the fact that the army, too, has taken a great deal of knocking in the cultural revolution. Even though Maoist propaganda has emphasized that the army was "personally" raised and nurtured by the great leader, and the leadership has not permitted

[14]See Chapter Four.

the cultural revolution to be stirred within and against the army, individual casualties within the high-ranking personnel have been quite high. Despite all the indoctrination and control over the army,[15] Mao has been obliged to purge the army ranks again and again. Some of these purges must also have been connected with the intricate and ruthless struggle at the top.

The first major purge came in 1959 when the Defence Minister Marshal P'eng Teh-huai was involved in a sharp and consequential battle with Mao over various issues ranging from relations with Moscow to the rationalization, modernization and politicization of the Chinese army. With him went a number of his proteges in the army. Similar problems bedevilled the army leadership in the subsequent period and the next major purge came with the cultural revolution. The Chief of Staff, Lo Jui-ch'ing, was disgraced and dismissed and so, too, were some of his close associates. For a while General Hsiao Hua appeared to perform Lo's functions, but he too soon became the target of sharp criticism by the Red Guards and was ousted. In his place came Yang Ch'eng-wu, but Yang fared no better and was dismissed in February 1968 for, it is generally believed, alleged involvement in a campaign against Mao's wife. He has been replaced by Huang Yung-sheng, a protege of Lin Piao. Other victims of the storm of the cultural revolution were Marshal Ho Lung, General T'an Chen-lin, and a number of political commissars, including Li Ching-ch'uan of Szechuan. Marshal Chu Teh has also been under eclipse, though not formally thrown out. Marshals Ch'en Yi and Nieh Jung-chen have had to face a heavy storm and have lost considerable political influence. General Wang En-mao of Sinkiang fame and General Chang Kuo-hua of Tibet were involved in a bitter feud with the Red Guards and, although not purged, they have suffered some decline in their political standing. Wang has been recalled from Sinkiang and Chang transferred to Szechuan.

In Wuhan the most dramatic instance of the defiance of the army involved the Local Commander Ch'en Tsai-tao and political Commissar Chung Han-hua. Besides, a number of army officers who had earlier been inducted in the administration, like Lt-General Wang Ping-chang, Minister in the Machine Building

[15]See Chapter One.

Ministry, Lt-General Yu Ch'iu-li, Minister for Petroleum, former Commander Lu Cheng-ts'ao, Railway Minister, and a number of others were also thrown out. It is inconceivable that all this turbulence at the top and the ouster of so many high army officers and leaders would have had no impact on the army ranks. The shake-up has been so drastic that it does not confirm the Maoist claim about the purity of the army as an instrument of revolution personally nurtured by Mao. The Maoist spokesmen have had to concede that individual army leaders had proved to be "rotten eggs," but have denied that the army as a unit needed a cultural revolution within its ranks or that it was anything but the repository of revolutionary purity. Yet in view of the large number of high-ranking officers accused of disloyalty to the thought of Mao Tse-tung, the claim sounds a little hollow. There was perhaps no alternative for the Maoist headquarters but to present the army in the best possible light and to prevent the more radical Red Guards from pulling it to pieces. The army ensured the ascendancy of Mao at the top. It also ensured a measure of stability necessary for maintaining the tempo of development. Equally, it kept guard on the frontiers to watch against any attempt from outside to take advantage of the internal confusion. There was nothing else to fall back upon. Mao had prepared for this eventuality although he had probably hoped he would not have to take recourse to the ultimate step.

All the same, the repercussions on the army ranks of the periodic purge of high-ranking officers cannot be overlooked or ignored. Many officers fought to ward off onslaughts by the Red Guards and many others to help themselves and advance in the place of their erstwhile colleagues or superiors. How much heart-burning this might have caused can only be guessed. How this will manifest itself after the Great Helmsman is not there, time alone will show. But, certainly, it cannot be as if nothing had happened; the impact will be a long-range one.

The army was called in at a difficult and tense period. On the one hand, the Red Guards' overturning the Establishment led to desperate resistance from those who were so far ruling the country and, thus, to sharp fighting between the Red Guards, workers, and a section of peasants. The Establishment could not be struck down without a ruthless, life-and-death struggle, resulting in disruption and disorganization on a large scale. On the other hand, the Red Guards fell to fighting amongst themselves with increasing ferocity and contributed to widespread disorder and disruption. The army had to re-establish a semblance of normalcy and to keep the wheels of the economy moving. On top of it, it fell to its lot to determine from the myriads of "revolutionary rebel" organizations which were truly Maoist and which were reactionary—a well-nigh impossible task as all of them claimed to be more loyal than the others.

Under the circumstances, the army often took the least troublesome course available to it—that was to put the house in order and the quarrelsome Red Guards in their place. We are not suggesting that the army necessarily suppressed the Red Guards everywhere. The situation was different from region to region and hasty generalizations should be avoided. In some places, Peking claimed subsequently, the army showed patience under great provocation and even submitted itself to indignities in order to avoid violence. Sometimes when the opposing factions of the Red Guards attacked and tried to take away weapons, the army men and officers did not retaliate but tried to reason with the opponents.

But, by and large, the army was inclined to give immediate attention to the task of economic revival and development, and was frequently exasperated by the internecine and indiscriminate warfare of the Red Guards. There was no question of army disloyalty to the person of Mao or of any challenge to Mao's authority, but generally the army took more seriously the slogan of promoting production than of grasping revolution and acted to prevent the Red Guards from dislocating the apparatus of production. At many places the army burnt its fingers badly in trying to sort out the troubles of the Red Guards and in mediating between them. Those who did not get its full support turned their fury on it and dragged the local army command into the centre of struggle ·and controversy. The army became embroiled with the Red Guards and there were many sharp clashes, occasionally violent.

The army showed increasing impatience for the infinite controversies of the Red Guards. Faced with the nearly impossible task of choosing between innumerable factions of Red Guards, who were splitting heads and dislocating life, the army generally sought to end the disruption, without taking sides wherever possible, or by suppressing the particularly querulous and violent elements wherever necessary. As factional fighting leapt up, threatening the basic fabric of stability in the country, the army's tasks and role also leapt up to a point where the administration of the country virtually became its responsibility. The army had to keep the railway lines running, the factories open, the enterprises busy, the communes in shape, the security policy under protection (from the attacks of the Red Guards!), guard all the state buildings and finally even run the schools and colleges. It had to create the new institutional power structure, play a leading role in bringing about "three-way" alliances and the creation of revolutionary committees to replace the old Party structure, and became the nucleus of these committees, the so-called new organs of revolutionary power. It virtually constituted the new power strucure of China. The local army commanders in the various provinces and military districts became the new "power-holders," and in the growing confusion that prevailed and the certainty of this confusion spreading and becoming more serious left little choice for Mao but to let the army commanders exercise all the authority and power needed to control the situation. It took the army considerably more than a year to normalize the situation relatively and to weather the storms of Red Guard factional conflicts. Slowly and painfully, the new order was built by the army. In the process, the army became the paramount political factor in the country.

CONFUSION CONTINUES

All through 1967 and early 1968, the factional struggles among the Red Guards mounted and multiplied. Red Guard violence was at its peak during 1967 but continued to flare up even subsequently. There was serious trouble even during the spring and summer of 1968. There is massive evidence coming from Peking about the magnitude and fury of this factional fighting. The fact is incontrovertible and does not need much elaboration. All the Chinese reports, including Red Guard wall posters, confirmed a developing and large-scale struggle among the rival Red Guard organizations which no longer comprised only students and young teachers but also included workers and government personnel and even suburban peasantry. Very often the various Red Guard or "revolutionary rebel" organizations banded themselves into two or three big, federating associations and carried on a pitiless struggle against one another through these omnibus organizations. Much of the newspaper reporting in the outside world during this period was rather misleading by describing their clashes as the conflict between Maoist and anti-Maoist forces. In most cases, it was a factional struggle among the rival organizations, each proclaiming vociferous loyalty to Mao and branding the activities of the other as a rightist conspiracy. The Red Guard accounts themselves provided details of instance after instance of their clashes and conflicts. Here only one or two such graphic instances need be noted.

Canton was a prolonged battle ground for competing, contending Red Guard organizations and the scene of many ghastly incidents between the "Red Flag" on the one hand and "East Wind" on the other. Narrating one such incident, the mouthpiece of the "Red Flag" claimed that on 22 May (1968) and again on 3 July the "rightists" (the "East Wind" in turn called the "Red Flag" a "counter-revolutionary" rightist organization) seized, occupied and controlled key positions "paralysing communications and attacking and assassinating the revolutionary rebel faction." They were creating "white terror," "whipping" up the evil wind of armed fighting," this faction complained. The slogan of the adversaries was: "exterminate the Red Flag bandits."[16] The other side laid the same charge at the doors of the "Red Flag" supporters but both confirmed that a situation of armed struggle was still developing.

In an earlier instance on 24 March, the editor of *Nan-fang Jih-pao* was visited by a number of people who pointed the spear-head against the "Red Flag" "revolutionary masses." This was allegedly followed by "public executions" of the "Red Flag" supporters.[17] The "Red Flag" spokesmen complained that their rivals had set up private courts and used various methods of torture and violent retribution against them.

The "Red Flag" was itself accused of various crimes by the opponents. In Canton the army had become involved early in the bitter struggle among the rival factions, and notwithstanding the

[16]*Chan Kuang-tung*, Canton, 10 July 1968.
[17]*Ibid.*

appeals and efforts of the Centre for unity and moderation, clashes between the army and army-supported "rebels" and a number of organizations arraigned against them continued throughout 1968. A tabloid published by the "Three Services United Committee" in its issue of 10 August 1968 accused an organization known as "Canton's T'an Censure United Committee" of "criminal conspiracy" against the army leadership. It may be recalled that "Canton's T'an" referred to Huang Yung-sheng, the present Chief of Staff and a close collaborator of Lin Piao. Their aim was to bring him down along with the rest of the Canton army leadership for their failure to support them.

The group was accused by the army command of giving the slogans of "kill all," "wash Canton in blood," "armed conflict is a new stage of the cultural revolution," etc. The army-sponsored tabloid said that last summer Canton was the scene of a series of incidents of armed conflicts and bloodshed. The "revolutionaries" were "brutally slaughtered" and the safety of lives of the people was seriously threatened. It asked: "who is actually pulling the strings behind the curtain of such a tremendous scale of armed struggle." The answer it supplied was: Wang Li, Kuan Feng and Ch'i Pen-yu[18]—all important members of the Cultural Revolution Committee of the Central Committee of the Chinese Communist Party. All the three went into the limbo of silence, one by one. The "Red Flag" Red Guards, while trying to dissociate themselves from the extreme manifestations of the campaign against Huang Yung-sheng, nevertheless, insisted that the struggle against him and the Canton army command was necessary to save Huang from sliding into the reactionary camp and to enable him to "return to Chairman Mao's revolutionary line," as well as to prevent the army from siding with the rightists. They claimed that Chou En-lai's intervention had led to their exoneration and a change in the army's "anti-left direction."[19]

On the other hand, the "East Wind" supporters among the Chungshan University (Sun Yat-sen University) accused the "Red Flag" members of "maliciously pointing their spearhead towards

[18]*San-chien Lien-wei Chan-pao*, Canton, 10 August 1968.
[19]*Kang Pa-i* (published by Mao Tse-tung Thought, 1 August 1968, Fighting Regiment and Canton Revolutionaries Rebel United General Headquarters), June 1968.

the proletarian headquarters headed by Chairman Mao and Vice-Chairman Lin, towards the great Chinese People's Liberation Army, towards the provincial and municipal Revolutionary Committees." They had "created incidents and armed conflicts and, moreover, cruelly beat up or murdered PLA warriors who tried to stop the armed conflicts. They even dared to openly seize fire-arms of the People's Liberation Army." They had, the "East Wind" supporters charged, "plotted strikes and disruption of transportation, water, electricity and market supply after the trade fair to bring the national economy to a state of paralysis and to undermine the red regime economically."[20]

And all this despite the fact that a joint (three-in-one) revolutionary committee for Kwangtung had finally been brought off by Peking (through the painful efforts of Chou En-lai) with the avowed aim of uniting the feuding organizations under the leadership of the army. Unofficial reports spoke of a frightfully cruel struggle and of people hanging by the lamp-posts, and Hong Kong witnessed the spectacle of scores of corpses floating from the mainland washed down the Pearl River. These instances were not isolated and Chinese literature of the period provides ample evidence of the widespread factional fighting and dislocation. Peking directed all its efforts towards containing this conflict by asserting the authority of the Maoist centre. The faction-ridden Red Guards, while paying lip service to the Maoist centre, attempted to dispute the view that there need be one centre in the local areas where they were locked in bitter power struggles. The problem has harassed the Maoist leadership for a long time.

Even as late as December 1968, this problem was a continuing and serious one at many places. An editorial of *Fuchien Jih-pao* (Fukien Daily) condemned those elements who were still clinging to the theory of "many centres," engaged in factionalism, and were making every effort to expand the influence and power of their own "mountain strongholds." It was not enough to formally proclaim their submission to the Maoist headquarters in Peking. The proof of the pudding lay in its eating, and that was their submission to the authority of the leadership of the revolutionary committees (largely controlled by the army), and acceptance of one

[20]*Chung-ta Chan-pao,* published by Chung-shan University Revolutionary Rebel Committee and Canton East Wind Students' Revolutionary Committee.

centre there. As an instance, the editorial pointed out, if an organization or school was split into two centres, it had "one centre too
many" and amounted to the existence of "many centres." There
were people, it complained, who physically participated in the
revolutionary committees but whose hearts were still with their
respective factions. They talked about "special circumstances" of
their areas and units and expressed themselves against "mechanical
applications" of the "commands and policies of the proletarian
headquarters." The editorial warned that what it actually meant
was that these people were saying: "you can say what you please,
I will do what I please. Although they profess obedience to the
Party, they are in fact putting individual interests first and Party
interests second."[21]

Significantly, the editorial revealed the struggle between the
army and some of the revolutionary rebel organizations which
was, in fact, not a phenomenon peculiar only to Fukien. It said
that not only were revolutionary organizations branded as conservative, but attempts were even made to "settle accounts with the
PLA." This conflict between the army and the Red Guards occurr-
ed at many places. When instructions were given to unite with
"95 per cent of the revolutionary masses," the editorial said, those
who applied the theory of many centres "emerged to make a loud
outcry of 'right deviationism,' pretending that they were the most
revolutionary." The editorial warned that the revolutionary
committees at all levels must be "highly alert against the interference of the reactionary theory of many centres" and check
"how the commands, instructions and policies were being implemented in their own units."[22]

Wen-hui Pao of Shanghai was even more explicit about the
problem of so-called "polycentrism," which actually was the
problem of warring Red Guards not accepting the local authority
but paying theoretical homage to the Maoist headquarters in Peking.
An editorial of 6 January 1969 stressed that there should be "only
one political organ" in a factory or school. It was "not permissible
to have two political organs." There should be "only one unified
leadership and no dual leadership." Otherwise the people would
become confused as to where their loyalty was expected to be

[21]Fukien Radio, Provincial Service, 27 December 1968.
[22]*Ibid.*

reposed. It clarified that by unified leadership was meant "putting Mao Tse-tung's thought in command."[23]

The editorial warned that those who were still trying to "set up more 'centres' in opposition to the new-born revolutionary committees will find out that the task is not so simple." It sought to disabuse the minds of those who took the attitude that "whatever the masses say is correct." No: "the process of concentrating the correct ideas of the masses is a process of unifying our thinking according to Mao Tse-tung's thought." It acknowledged that many revolutionary committees could not function effectively because of internal squabbles between members and section chiefs, condemned their "small group mentality" and "individualism" and advised them to overcome their factionalism and non-proletarian ideas through the purifier of Mao's thought.[24]

One effective measure that Peking employed to curb the Red Guards and control the situation was to send them in large numbers to the villages. The *hsia fang* movement was not new to China. The leaders took recourse to this expedient at many crucial moments in the last decade or so. In 1958, after the Hundred Flowers became poisonous weeds, a large-scale trek to the villages was embarked upon and these writers, who were in Peking at the time, watched this movement unfold with hundreds of thousands "volunteering" to unite with the peasants through joint agricultural labour. Apparently, most of them managed to slip back to the cities, and, perhaps, to their old places of work or study. Again in 1963-64, there was fresh insistence on manual labour as Mao gradually began to work his way towards securing an unquestioned grip over the Communist Party and the country.

This time, however, the emphasis was on permanent resettlement in the villages, rather than doing a mere stint of labour there. The youth was being sent in hundreds of thousands to make the countryside their home and the source of their livelihood. They were assured that all this was for the sake of revolution and that by permanently settling down in the villages they were bringing glory to the socialist cause and to themselves. That this argument did not necessarily convince every one was clear from the spate of

[23]"On Democratic and Unified Centralism," *Wen-hui Pao*, editorial, Shanghai Radio, City Service, 6 January 1969.
[24]*Ibid.*

commentaries and articles on the problem. Some, at least, of the Red Guards felt betrayed and cheated by this shift in policy. They had risen in revolt at the call of Mao and were now being unceremoniously shunted off as inconvenient elements. Many others were too loathe to depart from the cities and from the proximity to the power structure. That "comfort teams" were organized at a large number of places to go and cheer up the educated youth settled in rural areas strengthens the impression that many of these young men and women were not altogether happy and enthusiastic about their new homes and occupations.

Some of them preferred the factories to the fields. In an effort to avoid being sent to the villages they took the ingenious plea that since they were expected to learn from the working class—which was the leading class—they would like to be sent to the factories for uniting with the workers! An article supposedly written by a student member of the Shanghai Congress of Middle School Red Guards and a 1968 graduate of a Shanghai middle school, broadcast by Shanghai Radio, denounced this as a pretext to avoid going to the countryside where life was hard. The "Achilles' heel of intellectuals," it said, was becoming all too obvious and all kinds of excuses were being given to wriggle out from the task entrusted to them. Some said that "there is nothing but hardship in the countryside" and refused to go there. Others said that there was no "labour protection" and so they would not go there. If this situation was allowed to develop, the article warned, Red Guards would become only "a flash in the pan." To be a Red Guard did not mean that one had become an official. It merely indicated, the article stressed, that the revolution had made greater demands on them.[25]

The campaign for resettling the educated youth in the villages was pushed vigorously during 1968 and 1969. Another aspect of this resettlement was the despatch of hundreds of thousands of Chinese youth to the sensitive minority areas in order to strengthen Peking's grip on them by increasing the Han population in relation to that of the ethnic minorities. This policy had been adopted even as a consequence of the revolt in Tibet. But now with the escalation of the conflict with the Soviet Union, Peking decided

[25] *Ibid.*, 24 January 1968.

to populate the explosive border areas with members of the dominant Han nationality. Inner Mongolia Radio, for instance, reported on 24 March 1969: "tens of thousands of energetic young intellectuals from Peking, Shanghai, Tientsin and Chekiang are expected to arrive here very soon for resettlement.... On their arrival, people are expected to turn out in groups along the snow-covered roads to welcome the young intellectuals from afar." They would all settle down in an area known to be the most northerly part of China, which has now become an "anti-revisionist outpost.' "[26] A similar movement took place in Sinkiang —another highly sensitive border region.

REVOLUTIONARY COMMITTEES: RIGHT, LEFT, RIGHT

It has already been noted that Mao had sought a way out of the confusion and violence of the cultural revolution as well as to fill the need for a new, legitimate authority at all levels in place of the old Party structure which had been struck down, by the estab-lishment of a kind of a united front at the local and provincial levels of the army leaders, "revolutionary cadres" and "revolutionary rebels" and called them revolutionary committees. It has also been noted that outside Peking only five such committees had come into existence by the summer of 1967: Shanghai, Kwaichow, Shansi, Heilungkiang and Shantung. It was only as a gradual recovery of order and extended control of the army that all the provinces and special regions could be brought under the umbrella of the revolu-tionary committees. The process took nearly two years and the last provincial and regional committees were established in the autumn of 1968.

The character and composition of these revolutionary committees varied considerably and was often indicative of the state of the cultural revolution. Since there were anywhere between 100-250 members of these committees, and many of them were largely unknown figures hitherto, it is extremely difficult to be positive about their "class" composition, and it is easier to investigate the character of the leadership than of the ordinary members. But the levers of power were controlled by those who held top

[26]*Inner Mongolia Regional Service*, Huehot, 24 March 1969.

positions in the committees—the chairman, vice-chairman and department or section chiefs. Certain general conclusions can, therefore, be fairly well substantiated. The leadership for these committees generally came from the army; in the first phase political commissars were represented in the leading positions, but in the second phase the local and regional army commanders were conspicuous by their presence. There was a sprinkling of old Party leaders ("revolutionary cadres") and representatives of the new mass organizations ("revolutionary rebels") in the new hierarchy of leadership, but their proportion often depended upon the left or right swing in the cultural revolution.[27]

In Heilungkiang, Shanghai, and Kwaichow, the cultural revolution had its direct impact and the chairmen in the three committees were radical leftists, but still the army and the former Party officials occupied a majority of the top positions. The Shantung and Shansi committees were predominantly under military control. From the period the revolution was put in reverse gear in the autumn of 1967 to March 1968, about 10 new revolutionary committees came into existence in various provinces and regions. Only one of them—that established in Inner Mongolia in November 1967—had a radical orientation. With one exception, all of them were army-controlled and army-dominated, and in a number of them even the Party leaders accused of following the capitalist road were included among the leadership of the revolutionary committees.

The formation of revolutionary committees was intended to re-establish legitimate authority and create order out of chaos. But, not unexpectedly, their complexion could not be divorced from the politics of Peking. A more militant mood in Peking increased the leverage of the radicals, while a more sober attitude at the head-quarters provided greater opportunity for the army and the old-time Party leaders. The cultural revolution went through a series of distinct phases which can be aptly described as left, right, left, right. In 1966, till September, the beginning of the cultural revolution heralded a militant, radical line. Then came the September-November pause. In December, the movement again

---

[27]For an analysis of the background of the chairmen and vice-chairmen of the revolutionary committees, see Richard Baum, "China: Year of the Mangoes," *Asian Survey*, January 1969.

gathered force and burst into the "January revolution," followed by a second pause and a retreat in which, according to the Maoists, the old Party warriors tried to avenge their humiliation and resulted in what is constantly referred to in Peking's literature as the "adverse February current." Then came the flood-tide of Red Guard violence, assault on all authority and factional fighting which rose to its peak in the spring and summer of 1967, and abated during September-March as a result of serious measures taken by Peking and the increasingly heavy reliance on the army, and erupted again in the spring of 1968, finally to be curbed and brought under control in a painfully slow and gradual extension of authority and normalization during the following year.

The period between April-July 1968 was another period of confusion, of renewed Red Guard attack on political and army leaders, of factional fighting and of the leadership in Peking speaking in two voices—an indication of the continuing struggle between the more radical and the more pragmatically inclined leaders. Thus, both at the Centre and in the provinces, differing speeches were made and equally differing and confusing articles appeared. Some provinces stressed the struggle against the rightists, while others laboured on the theme of polycentrism directed mainly against the Red Guards. Factional fighting flared up and was particularly serious in Kwangtung, Kwangsi, Fukien, Chekiang, Hupeh, Hunan, Yunnan, Tibet and Szechuan. In Inner Mongolia, too, the conflict continued and only serious efforts of the army saved the situation from dangerously deteriorating.

Generally, there was no doubt of the left-wing shift in Peking during this period (the spring and summer of 1968) and authoritative articles now tended to convey the message that the left factions were all right; it was only the right-wing factionalism which was at the root of the trouble. Therefore, the army must support the left factions. Chiang Ch'ing said in a speech in the late hours of 30 March that "the main danger at present is rightist conservatism, rightist splittism and rightist capitulationism."[28] In one sentence, she had made three charges: the rightists were once again active and posed the chief danger, it was the rightists who were dividing the ranks of the revolutionaries and, therefore, responsible

[28]*Chu-ying Tung-fang-hung*, Canton, April 1968.

for the factionalism plaguing the revolutionary movement, and the objective of the rightists was to smother revolutionary fervour and dampen the spirit of the revolutionary rebels and thus bring about conservative restoration. This was the last effort to shield the Red Guards and to keep the momentum of the movement of the rebels.

The ides of March, as in the last year, saw the renewal of Red Guard war against authority and of factional fighting. It was a reflection of the swing of the pendulum in Peking, where suddenly the new Chief of Staff, Yang Ch'eng-wu lost his job and was put in the category of "counter-revolutionary rightists." Dismissed along with Yang were Yu Lu-chin, Commander of the Air Force, and Fu Ch'ung-pi, Peking Garrison Commander. Huang Yung-sheng became the new Chief of Staff and General Wu Fa-hsien his deputy. The precise reasons for the sudden shake-up are somewhat obscure but all the material that Peking has put out lends weight to the belief that Yang was suspected by the Cultural Revolution group in the Maoist headquarters of an attempt to subvert the authority of Mme. Mao.[29] Yang's dismissal had been preceded by the ouster of Kuan Feng and Ch'i Pen-yu, both active and important members of the Cultural Revolution Committee. Obviously, notwithstanding the denunciation of the factional fighting of the Red Guards, Peking itself did not seem to be immune to this "petty bourgeois" disease.

Whatever the inside story about the fall of Yang Ch'eng-wu, it was accompanied by a lot of patting on the back of Red Guards and apparent exhortation to the army that the leftist factions were all right and that it was only the rightist factions which were to be denounced.[30] The Red Guards were ready to pick up the signal and simultaneously batter the doors of army authority and what was left of the Party structure and to intensify the power struggle against their rival Red Guard organizations, that is, to step up their factional fighting. Faced with a fresh spell of violence and dislocation, Mao had to make another about-turn and reconcile himself to the appropriation of virtually all authority and power by the army and to let the Regional and Local Commanders run the

[29]For instance *Chekiang Daily* on "Class Rank Purification," Chekiang Radio, Provincial Service, 18 June 1968.

[30]See Fn. 28.

state machinery, the economy, the revolutionary committees and all other forms of political, economic and social organizations so as to effectively curb the renewed violence and the factional fighting and to restore normalcy in economic activity and stability in the political order.

The revolutionary committee of Szechuan set up on 31 May 1968 partially reflected the left wind blowing in Peking and the top honours were shared between the army and the "revolutionary rebels," but the controversial General Chang Kuo-hua, who had run into serious trouble with the Red Guards in Tibet, emerged as the Chairman of the Szechuan Committee. Three of the other five provincial revolutionary committees established in Hunan, Liaoning, Anhwei, Ninghsia and Shensi bore heavily the imprint of army supremacy. The one in Liaoning contained a mixture of army leaders and revolutionary cadres and "rebels": Ch'en Hsi-lien, Commander of the Shenyang military region as Chairman, Yang Ch'un-fu, First Secretary of the former Shenyang Municipal Party Committee as Vice-Chairman, and a model worker "revolutionary rebel," as the second Vice-Chairman. Both in Shensi and Liaoning the same balance was sought to be maintained between the army and the rebels. In Hunan the old Party secretary, Chang Po-hua, who had commanded provincial authority, came under heavy fire and was ousted.

Prior to the leftward swing as well as during this period, the top leaders were reported to have denounced efforts by unmentioned people (but dark hints of their occupying high positions were thrown) to collect "black materials" on Chiang Ch'ing (Mme. Mao),[31] that is, words and acts damaging to her. There were allegations of a conspiracy against her in which even men like Kuan Feng and Ch'i Pen-yu were involved. The leftward swing had, however, to be rapidly retraced as the country was threatened by renewed violence and disruption.

The five regional and provincial revolutionary committees established subsequently were "unrevolutionary" in the composition of their leadership, four of them headed by army commanders and one (Kwangsi) by a "capitalist roader," the former First Secretary of the now defunct Communist Party Provincial Com-

[31]See, for instance, *Survey of China Mainland Press*, Hong Kong, No. 4120, 16 February 1968, p. 3.

mittee. The last two of the five committees came into being in Sinkiang and Tibet—on 5 September—both headed by military commanders. Wang En-mao made his exit from the Sinkiang scene (reports said that he was recalled to Peking), but the moderate nature of the committee remained.

By the end of 1968, practically, all the regions and provinces had been covered by the revolutionary committees and the flood-tide of violence and factional fighting, having spent itself, was finally receding. The revolutionary committees constituted new organs of state power and helped the consolidation of authority. They became the symbols of ordered government, normalcy and discipline. In the final analysis they provided the army with the legitimacy to rule and to restore peace and orderly economic functioning of the country. To begin with, Mao seemed to nurture a vision of the Paris Commune type direct elections so as to make these committees really novel, revolutionary forms of organization, but, as in the case of many other visions, the cold reality of factional fighting and disruption compelled Mao to settle for nominated committees from the top. In some cases only the top was fixed while the general membership of the committees had yet to be announced. In the circumstances in which they were created, the committees necessarily became the chief instrument for the re-establishment of authority and order.

MANGOES FOR THE WORKERS

While the Red Guards quarrelled and broke heads and disrupted life, Mao was obviously reviewing his strategy. His earlier plan had manifestly misfired. The hope and the trust placed in the youthful Red Guards turned out to be misplaced, for they showed as much avidity for power, as the old Party bureaucrats. Reportedly, Mao complained bitterly to a group of Tsinghua University students that they had woefully let him down. The three-way alliance meant essentially army rule and a partial return of the Party cadres and was calculated to restore peace and order. Mao's "agonizing reappraisal" in the light of the hard realities led to another turn in the strategy of the cultural revolution. This was to put the workers back in the driver's seat and to bring them to the fore to apply the brakes on the Red Guards who were taking the

country to the verge of civil war. Along with the army, the workers
—and "poor and lower middle peasants"—were called upon to
assume the leadership and to guide the Red Guards along the true
path of proletarian politics. Whereas, previously, the Red Guard
lead was justified by Mao with the assertion that most cultural
revolutions in China had been led by the students (witness the
May 4th movement), now the metaphor was changed with the
equally emphatic declaration that the working class was the leading
class and must, therefore, exercise its natural prerogative of taking
over command.

On 27 July 1968, Mao issued a new directive with the call that
"the working class must exercise leadership in everything." Mao
instructed: "Our country has 700 million people and the working
class is the leading class. Its role in the great cultural revolution
and in all fields of work should be brought into full play. The
working class should also raise its political consciousness in
struggle."[32] The ideological justification was that the working
class must penetrate all aspects of the superstructure of the state.

The most immediate result of the new policy was the despatch
of contingents of workers to schools and colleges and universities
to resolve all the problems there in cooperation with army units
who had already been assigned to them. Mao made it clear that
it was his intention that this occupation of the citadels of academicians by the workers should be a permanent feature. Only then
could the students and intellectuals be disciplined. And in a
symbolic gesture Mao sent a gift basket of mangoes to workers
stationed at Tsinghua University which had been the scene of a
fresh bout of factional violence among the students. Mao had
thus indicated his approval of the most extreme measure so far
taken to control Red Guard violence. Mao-thought propaganda
teams comprising workers and "poor and lower middle peasants"
were similarly posted at all educational institutions and centres of
intellectual activity to unfold what was described as a high tide of
"struggle-criticism-transformation."

As was the general practice during the cultural revolution, it
was left to Yao Wen-yuan to elaborate the new policy and provide the explanation and the rationale. In an article in *Hung-ch'i*,

[32]*Jen-min Jih-pao, Chieh-fang Chun-pao*, joint editorial.

Yao conceded that under the circumstances of the masses struggling and fighting among themselves, it was "impossible for the students and intellectuals by themselves alone to fulfil the task of 'struggle-criticism-transformation' and a whole number of other tasks on the educational front; workers and People's Liberation Army fighters must take part, and it is essential to have strong leadership by the working class." This had become necessary because the students and intellectuals were practising the theory of "many centres" and thus defying the authority of Mao and disorganizing life and economic activity.[33]

Yao warned the students and intellectuals that any attempt to resist the workers would be severely put down. "Whoever looks upon the workers as a force alien to himself," Yao said, "is, if not muddle-headed, himself an element alien to the working class; and the working class has every reason to exercise dictatorship over him." Clarifying the objective, Yao asserted that the workers and the army must go to "those places where intellectuals are concentrated, schools or other units, to break down the complete domination by intellectuals, occupy the 'independent kingdoms,' big or small, and take over those places in which the advocates of the theory of many centres, that is, the theory of 'no centre' are entrenched."[34] There can be no doubt that it was the problem of "many centres" or, in other words, the "anarchism" of the students and intellectuals and their relentless hankering after power which brought about the switch to working class leadership and army control.

Clearly, it was no longer the phase when the army men vowed to learn from the "little generals" and the workers pledged to take the Red Guards as their models; the factious students who stubbornly fought for power and who had been aroused by the Maoists to demolish the establishment and spread the cultural revolution were now required to quit the field and submit themselves, as a penance for their mutual quarrels and struggles, to supervision by the workers and army men and to melt into the countryside in their hundreds of thousands and thus be lost in the anonymity of China's villages. This was the unkindest cut of all, the hardest pill to

[33]Yao Wen-yuan, "The Working Class must Exercise Leadership in Everything," *Hung-ch'i*, No. 2, August 1968.
[34]*Ibid.*

swallow, the cruellest mortification to suffer. Mao had told the Red Guards that the world was theirs and had called upon them to rise up and strike down all his "enemies." After they had done a thorough job of it, they were being put down, almost as if the world was being snatched back from them. Paradoxically—and yet perhaps not so surprisingly—the return to "working class leadership" was a shift away from the left, just as the earlier appeal to the youngsters to storm the strongholds of authority and power and of Mao's adversaries was a distinct swing to the extreme left. The revolt of the radical students was being put down unmistakably and it was patent that the revolution had run out of steam. The radical students lost their realm before they had a chance of consolidating it. With his felicitating the workers' contingent at Tsinghua with mangoes, Mao had put the seal of approval on the suppression of Red Guard extremism and violence.

THE OCTOBER PLENUM OF THE CENTRAL COMMITTEE

Time was now considered ripe by Mao to formally excommunicate Liu Shao-ch'i and prepare for a purged Party meet in order to provide formal sanction for the new order in China. The humpty-dumpty of the badly mauled and maimed Communist Party had to be put together again and the Party myth retained. The enlarged 12th Plenary session of the 8th Central Committee met for its valedictory session in Peking on 13 October and concluded the meet on 31 October. Among the participants were the remaining regular and alternate members who had not lost their positions in the cultural revolution plus members of the Central Cultural Revolution Committee, "principal responsible comrades" of revolutionary committees of the provinces, municipalities and autonomous regions, and "principal responsible comrades" of the Chinese People's Liberation Army. The 12th Plenum was as packed with "irregulars" as the 11th Plenum, only the nature of the "irregulars" had changed and now there were many more army leaders present. Mao presided over the meeting and was reported to have made an "important" speech, and so did Lin Piao.[35] But, neither of the two speeches was made public.

[35] *New China News Agency*, Peking, 31 October 1968.

The communique issued on 31 October named Liu Shao-ch'i, so far referred to as "China's Khrushchov" as "the top person in authority taking the capitalist road," announced his expulsion from the Party and catalogued his crimes against Mao and the Party from his early days onwards. The denunciation of Liu followed the pattern already established and noted earlier. It can only be regarded as significant that the Committee mentioned only Liu for denunciation and expulsion but ignored the case of Teng Hsiao-p'ing who was often referred to in the past as "the other top person in authority taking the capitalist road." The plenary session also decided that the Ninth Party Congress of the Party be convened at an "appropriate time" and circulated a new draft constitution for discussion at lower levels. A new Party Congress was needed to reflect the changed realities of the Chinese scene and the new power structure.

The subsequent developments marked intensive preparations for the Ninth Party Congress which was in the air so long as to encourage the belief in the outside world that something serious had gone wrong. The chief problem remained that of establishing the authority of the revolutionary committees outside, and unity within the various factions represented on them. Reports of sporadic violence are still published in the Chinese press and articles continue to be written on the obligations of the "rebels" to submit to the authority of the revolutionary committees and to utilize the skills of the erstwhile Party cadres.

The Central Committee meeting was followed by a spate of meetings and articles in preparation for the Ninth Party Congress. Particularly, during December-February the revolutionary committees in the districts, provinces, and the regions of China were called into session with the ostensible purpose of "greeting" the forthcoming Ninth Party Congress. It is reasonable to assume that these meetings and conferences must have been primarily concerned with the selection of delegates and the finalization of the draft constitution.

That Mao had now thrown his weight on the side of moderation was apparent from a number of articles and speeches in the latter half of 1968. The joint editorial of *Jen-min Jih-pao*, *Hung-ch'i* and *Chieh-fang Chun-pao* on the occasion of the new year (1969) reflected the same trend. While announcing the "great, decisive victory" for the cultural revolution, it repeated the calls for narrowing the target of attack and helping more people through education. "The stress must be on the weight of evidence and on investigation and study." It underlined that, "it is strictly forbidden to extort confessions and accept such confessions." The article was equally critical of "factionalism" (of the Red Guards) and denounced it as the theory of "many centres." All that did not conform to Mao's thought and should be rejected and the People's Liberation Army should be supported and strengthened.[36]

THE NINTH PARTY CONGRESS AND AFTER

At long last the Ninth Party Congress met on 1 April 1969 at Peking. The new constellation of power was apparent from the galaxy which mounted the rostrum together with the Chairman in the following order: Mao, Lin Piao, Chou En-lai, Ch'en Po-ta, K'ang Sheng, Tung Pi-wu, Liu Po-ch'eng, Chu Teh, Ch'en Yun, Chiang Ch'ing, Chang Chun-ch'iao and Yao Wen-yuan.[37] Of these Tung Pi-wu, Chu Teh and Ch'en Yun were figure-heads and effective power at the centre resided with the remaining presidium. In this constellation the leftist cultural revolution group is dominant, but because of their special position, Lin Piao and Chou En-lai have considerable more authority than all the others put together. And, of course, all of them are subordinate to Mao who occupies an unchallenged position.

The Party Congress was attended by 1512 delegates who were "chosen unanimously by Party organizations at various levels and after extensively seeking the opinion of the broad masses." According to the first press communique of the secretariat of the Congress, among the delegates were a greater number than ever before of Party members from among individual workers of factories, mines, and other enterprises and from among "poor and lower middle peasants" and "delegates of women Party members on all fronts." There was also a large number of

[36]"Place Mao Tse-tung's Thought in Command in Everything," English text released by *New China News Agency*, 31 December 1968.

[37]Press Communique of the Secretariat of the Presidium of the Ninth National Congress of the Communist Party of China, *New China News Agency*, Peking, 1 April 1969.

"advanced elements" emerging from the cultural revolution. The new Congress was thus markedly different in character from the earlier ones.

The Congress adopted the revised Party constitution and the political report delivered by Lin Piao and heard an "important" but unpublished speech by Mao. It also elected a new Central Committee and a new Politbureau and the Standing Committee of the Politbureau. The members of the new high-level organs of the Party reflected the changed realities of the power equation in the country. The army was represented in strength at the highest levels. They were mostly practising army men and the background of many of them was obscure.

The Ninth Congress ended its deliberations after three weeks of secret discussions, but it raised more questions than it resolved and concealed more than it revealed. It was a Party Congress of its own kind. The delegates were not elected by all the Party members and only those were selected who were acceptable to the new power structure in China. The method of selection has not been made public but this much is patent that not the old Party branches but the new revolutionary committee, comprising the army officers, a section of the old bureaucracy and a part of the Red Guards, chose the members of the new Congress.

It was no surprise that the Congress confirmed the ascendancy of Mao Tse-tung and officially designated the Defence Minister Marshal Lin Piao as the successor of Mao. This again was unique that a Party's constitution should mention the Leader and his successor by name, as the new constitution of the Chinese Communist Party does. It was made amply clear that Mao was to be depicted as greater than even Marx and Lenin. Both the top leaders, Mao and Lin Piao seemed to have taken out partial insurance by including their wives in the prestigious and powerful Politbureau. The real rulers at the top were, however, in the new Standing Committee of the Politbureau: Mao, Lin Piao, Chou En-lai, Ch'en Po-ta, who has been Mao's ghost writer for many years, and K'ang Sheng, who was Mao's trusted lieutenant in the Party organization.

The last two were active promoters of the cultural revolution and were identified with a very left-wing approach. Lin Piao, despite his submission to Mao, represented an army which has generally stood for order and stability in the turmoil created by the Red Guards. Chou En-lai was the experienced politician—administrator whose efforts appeared to have been directed towards restraining the extremist postures and activities of the Red Guards. A delicate balance was thus maintained between the so-called moderate elements and the extreme leftists, with Mao as the arbiter, so that the pendulum would swing as the great helmsman throws his weight.

In the regular 21-member Politbureau, Lin Piao apart, Huang Yung-sheng, Yeh Chien-ying, Liu Po-ch'eng, Hsu Shih-yu, Ch'en Hsi-lien, Li Tso-p'eng, Wu Fa-hsien and Ch'iu Hui-tso were all from the armed forces. Among the four alternate members, at least one of them, Chi Teng-kuei, was a military man. The extent of the purge in the leadership can be gauged from the fact that only nine of the Politbureau members had continued from the old one, and three out of these nine, Chu Teh, Tung Pi-wu and Ch'en Yun were mere figure-heads (both Chu Teh and Ch'en Yun have been under a cloud). Besides those like Liu, Teng and P'eng, who were officially denounced, even Marshals Nieh Jung-chen, previously in charge of China's atomic research, and Ch'en Yi, the Foreign Minister, lost their places in the Politbureau.

The army's dominance in the new Central Committee was even more marked. Nearly a hundred of the 270-member new Central Committee (including alternate members) belong to the armed forces. Among them were eight Commanders, nine Deputy Commanders and 16 Political Commissars of military regions and districts, the Naval Commander and a member of the Naval Staff Office, two Deputy Commanders and one Deputy Political Commissar of the Air Force, and so on.

At the very top level of the leadership, a delicate balance seemed to have been maintained. This balance, we suspect, was the result of unresolved problems and unreconciled differences. In many ways the Ninth Congress was an inconclusive congress. It did not lay down any clear-cut line; the tasks ahead were too nebulously generalized. Marshal Lin Piao's political report[38] looked towards both right and left and failed to be precise or pointed. Few reports in Chinese Communist history have contained so many generali-

---

[38]Text released by *New China News Agency*, 17 April 1969.

zations which did not add up to any definite guidelines. The future remains somewhat uncertain and undefined.

Yet, within the outer shell of revolutionary slogan-mongering there was a kernel of moderate policies. Both internally and externally, Lin Piao's report gave the impression of avoiding adventurous policies. It appeared that Mao had—for the time being, at least—accepted the position of the moderates. The report used all the choice words about the fallen Head of State and previously designated successor to Mao, Liu Shao-ch'i, and about all the hidden "capitalist-roaders," but, in fact, the programme of action suggested was far from revolutionary. The Marshal exhorted the people, chiefly the faction-ridden Red Guards, to form alliances with the old-time cadres and the army men and to use reason rather than force in carrying out the struggle. It was strictly forbidden, he repeated, to extort confessions and to use force to convert people to one's point of view. The slogan he gave was: grasp revolution and promote production. A convenient slogan which could mean "grasp revolution" during the period of upheaval and "promote production" when greater normalcy was required, which obviously now seemed to be the order of the day.

NEW PERSPECTIVES IN CHINESE FOREIGN POLICY

The sections dealing with foreign relations in Lin Piao's report were equally ambivalent, ambiguous and equivocal. They confirmed the view that Moscow had become the chief preoccupation of the Chinese leaders. The U.S. imperialists were only "imperialists," but the Soviets had become "social imperialists" and "social fascists." There was only one paragraph on the misdeeds and misfortunes of Washington, but there were pages after pages in denunciation of Moscow.

Lin Piao's report embodied the new Maoist thesis that there were four major contradictions in the world today: the contradiction between the oppressed nations on the one hand and imperialism (USA) and social imperialism (USSR) on the other; between the proletariat and the bourgeoisie in the capitalist and revisionist countries; between imperialist countries; between the socialist countries on the one hand and imperialism and social imperialism on the other. Lin Piao's report left little doubt that in Mao's world view the principal adversary was the Soviet Union and that the United States occupied the second place in the rostrum of enemies.

Mao views all the conflicts and problems, both domestic and foreign within the framework of the chief contradiction. It is the principal contradiction which should determine the strategy and all other contradictions should be subordinated to the needs of meeting the principal contradiction. The secondary contradictions may be kept in cold storage; in some cases, even a few concessions may be given. But all the forces must be mobilized against the primary contradictions. In Mao's view, the principal contradiction now is that with the Soviet Union. This contradiction overrides all other contradictions and must assume priority in hammering out China's strategy.

Mao's first preference would have been to continue to work on the premise of the Vietnam war. This war seemed to be straight from the Maoist text-book with its united front, anti-imperialist and armed struggle, and reliance on internal strength. But since Hanoi and the National Liberation Front had to look to their own interests, they were not necessarily willing to go on fighting to prove Mao correct. A rethinking on strategy in Peking was, therefore, necessary. The reappraisal induced by the Paris Peace Talks on Vietnam was pushed by the equally significant developments in Eastern Europe. Soviet intervention in Czechoslovakia was a watershed in China's assessment. Peking had attempted to pursue a policy of drawing away as many countries of Eastern Europe as possible from Moscow's orbit. This fitted in well with China's historical diplomacy around its northern frontiers of seeking allies in the enemy's camp in order to divide that camp and to isolate and control the chief enemy. Albania had been wooed away and Rumania was being courted despite serious ideological differences. Peking remained on the look-out for other such stragglers.

By its action in Czechoslovakia, the Soviet Union had made it clear that it would stand no nonsense and would no more allow any other country in Eastern Europe to be detached from its sphere. Peking's policy was, therefore, stalled, leading to a worsening of relations. Secondly, the Soviet action in Czechoslovakia brought home to Peking the new danger and possibility of actual physical conflict on the border. The Soviet Union was no longer a mere political adversary but also a national enemy with whom China had a long border. The subsequent violent clashes at the Sino-Soviet border have added a new dimension to the conflict. The Sino-Soviet confrontation has become a territorial, political, national and emotional conflict. The conflict has been converted into an emotional and potentially more dangerous problem.

It has also come in handy as a national issue for arousing the emotions of the people and rallying them around the Peking leaders. An anti-Soviet wave swept the country. Millions of people were involved in meetings and demonstrations to denounce the "new Tsars" and to resolve to be ready to fight the new enemy. Everywhere the call was given for war preparedness and the immediate threat to the independence and territorial integrity of the country was stressed.

The conflict with the Soviet Union is dwarfing China's other conflicts and problems which could not fail to leave its mark on Chinese policies elsewhere.

There is no immediate prospect of a Sino-US detente or deal. Both sides are governed by compulsions which rule out such a relationship. But the internal situation in the United States is producing new compulsions within the country for a re-evaluation of the policy towards Asia generally, and China particularly. Opinion is rapidly swinging there towards a movement forward in defreezing relations with China. Both sides are also governed by compulsions which necessitate an effort at reducing the scale of hostilities and an expanding dialogue over the years. For the United States, the relationship with the Soviet Union is of central importance and, therefore, there cannot be any ganging up with Peking against Moscow. The question of Formosa goes to the heart of the Sino-US problems and American opinion is not yet ready to write off Formosa. However, there are various possibilities in this regard (some of them mentioned by Senator Edward Kennedy in his recent, widely reported speech) which could conceivably break the stalemate. From the Chinese side, Peking has projected the image of a great revolutionary centre and has tried to mobilize support on that basis. It cannot allow its image to be dimmed too obviously.

Moreover China is dissatisfied with the present power structure of the world and would like to see it shake and crumble. It wants to end the two hegemonies, and at the very least to advance a third one. The new power structure must provide a place for China at the top, and until that happens, China is likely to carry on its campaign against both the US and the USSR.

However, the age of Sino-US confrontation is over and the age of Sino-Soviet confrontation has begun. For the Chinese also, the immeasurably important fact of a receding American threat and a growing conflict with the Soviets is not something which could be shrugged aside. There was now no question of any American strike against China. A de-escalation of the level of the conflict with China and a slight opening on that front would enable Washington to cut some of its increasingly unpopular commitments in Asia and would provide a useful counter pressure against Moscow. Until recently Washington had to face and worry about the Sino-Soviet alliance. A US-Soviet deal disturbs Peking and the spectre of a Sino-US dialogue haunts Moscow. By merely keeping alive the possibility of a dialogue with Washington, the Chinese could keep the Kremlin guessing. Peking can very well continue to denounce both of them while at the same time carrying on a conversation.

Lin Piao, in his political report, called for preparedness against a nuclear war. But behind this display of bravado one could detect a more sober note which was reflected in the repetition of the statement originally made by Mao: "We will not attack unless attacked. If we are attacked, we will certainly counter-attack." China's foreign policy promises to use two separate and parallel wave lengths to beam its message. For the international revolutionary movement, Peking would continue to insist on the acceptance of Mao's personal leadership and only those revolutionary movements abroad will be accepted as genuine which duly acknowledge Mao as the mentor and the guide. But Peking's encouragement and support to revolutionary movements in other countries will be given very selectively and the revolutionary class analysis will be applied restrictively and will normally be confined to those countries and areas where it can be done with the least damage to Peking's position and influence.

China stands poised to pursue a dualistic approach in foreign policy. There will be a selective advocacy of revolution in countries and at places where China is otherwise involved in important political or national conflicts, such as Burma, India, Thailand, etc. But the revolution will be put on ice wherever the prudence of national interests so demands. The struggle of the oppressed people of India invites the proletarian duty of China for assistance but that of Pakistan is to be ignored. There shall be more about revolution in some Southeast Asian countries than in many European and African countries or even in those Asian countries with whom Peking is politically friendly. Peking seems ready to make a gradual effort to readjust and improve relations on the state level with a large number of other countries. This new effort may be particularly directed towards European countries and, selectively, towards a number of African and Asian countries.

This dualist approach is evident from Lin Piao's declaration, on the one hand, about China's proletarian duty to help revolutionary struggles in other countries, and his insistence, on the other hand, that China was always ready to establish normal relations with other countries on the basis of peaceful coexistence and mutual non-interference in each other's internal affairs. Clearly, China will apply the revolutionary strategy where it helps it and side-step it where it does not. The over-all foreign policy will be influenced by the confrontation that is taking place with the Soviet Union.

There is one contingency in which substantial changes could take place. If Mao passes away from the scene, there might be an effort by the Soviets or by the new leaders in Peking to scale down the tension and bring about some normalization of relations. One cannot rule out some improvement in relations in case of a change in helmsmanship at Peking. When Mao is gone, new possibilities could open up. Even so, it is inconceivable that China would again accept Moscow as the sole leader of the Communist bloc or return to the kind of relationship that existed during 1950-57. China will continue to function as an independent centre of power.

CONCLUSION

It is obviously not possible to understand or explain Chinese developments without recognizing the crucial role that Mao Tse-tung has played in shaping them and giving them a direction. Never before in history has a leader, an engineer of human mind, attempted to accomplish on such a vast scale and so thoroughly what Mao is attempting, and never before (even including Stalin) has a single individual enjoyed so much power and influence during his life-time as Mao does.

Mao is, in the tradition of the great heroes and rulers of China, is perhaps the greatest of them, the most effective of them, the most ruthless of them. His background, his mental and spiritual equipment, his knowledge, his whole framework of reference is all Chinese. The ideology that he came to subscribe to was also put in the Chinese mould. As he himself described it, Marxism for him was "the most powerful weapon for the liberation of China."

In the Chinese tradition, Mao believes in the role of heroes in the service of society, performing miracles of Herculean effort and labour, changing human conditions and human society. Of course, Mao does not think in terms of one individual but, again in the Chinese tradition, if there were a band of determined people, they could achieve a great deal. Therefore, he stirs the masses into motion believing that the more active elements among them will be galvanized into action. And an essential ingredient of Mao's thought is the belief that subjective will can transform objective reality. More and more Mao has come to believe in the primacy of the subjective over the objective. In the thirties and forties, Mao paid great regard to objective conditions in the formulation of policies, but in the evening of his life he is stressing more and more subjective determination to overcome and transform objective limitations. There is nothing that man cannot do, provided he has the will to do it.

Mao's commitment to modernization is both resolute and superficial. Mao's goal is the regeneration of the Chinese nation as a strong, hardy, unified, determined, disciplined nation, the envy of all, the fear of many, and for the attainment of this goal the instruments of modernization and industrialization are to be fully pressed into service. But he has no use for westernization as such. He has set out to do exactly what the Chinese authorities are proclaiming these days—to wash the brains of the modern Chinese generation of all that is ancient as well as foreign and to fill in its place the thought of Mao Tse-tung. This is an attempt at the transformation of men's ideas and ideology on a scale that has never been attempted before in history.

In Mao's world view there is, now, a four-way division, instead of the three categories previously mentioned. There is the world of China and its allies, the true socialists of the world. There has obviously been a great shrinkage of this socialist world, but Mao believes that this is a temporary phase and that his camp will grow in strength and numbers soon. Then there is the large revisionist camp headed by the Soviet Union which has betrayed the cause, which in other words means that it has betrayed China. The leadership of this world is in league with the imperialists against China, and revisionism is a half-way house between the slide-back from socialism to the revival of capitalism. The only attitude that could be adopted towards this camp was that of uncompromising struggle in the hope that the leadership would be discredited and replaced by those who would pay due homage to Peking's leadership. The imperialist camp now consists of only the United States and the Soviet Union. The physiognomy of the third world has also undergone a change and it now consists not only of Asian, African and Latin American countries but also such Western countries as France, West Germany and, potentially, Britain.

As an authoritative article put it, the struggle against revisionism could at a certain stage become the primary antagonistic contradiction. In plain language this means that Moscow was the chief enemy now and Washington the second enemy. In the interests of the war against the chief enemy, that against the second enemy could be muted. It is quite clear that Maoism has replaced Marxism-Leninism and become the dominant element in the world view of China. There is a decisive difference between Mao of the thirties and forties, and Mao of the post-fifties. Mao of the thirties and forties was not the same as the Mao of present times, although, inevitably, many strands of thought and action remain constant. Mao of the thirties was a great realist, a supreme strategist, a unique statesman and a shrewd politician. He had a firm grip over the Chinese situation and an uncanny knack of anticipating developments. Mao of the post-fifties is more and more divorced from realities, more and more irrational and vainglorious, subjective and isolated, intolerant and inflexible.

Most of his life, especially before he took over power, Mao fought against dogmatism and left sectarianism. At many crucial moments in the history of the Chinese Communist movement, since Mao began to assume its stewardship, he had to struggle against ultra-leftism. On the issue of making the peasantry the main force of the revolution, an issue in which Mao revised the entire Marxist theory and understanding, on the question of a national united front against Japanese aggression, which involved giving concessions not only to Chiang Kai-shek but on the class front also to landlords and the rich peasantry, Mao had to face the opposition of the leftists, and even the rectification movements that Mao launched in the Party, particularly in 1942, were directed against dogmatism and sectarianism. All through this period as Mao himself said, "left sectarianism was the main danger"[39] to the Communist movement and this dogmatism, he enjoined on the Party, "must be laid to rest completely and thoroughly."

As early as 1938, Mao said: "If the Chinese Communists who form a part of the great Chinese nation and are linked with it by flesh and blood, talk about Marxism apart from China's characteristics that will be only Marxism in the abstract; Marxism in the void. Hence, how to turn Marxism into something specifically Chinese, to imbue every manifestation of it with Chinese characteristics becomes a problem which the whole Party must understand and solve immediately." He enjoined upon Chinese Communists to study China's historical legacy and sum it up critically from the Marxist point of view. "Our nation has a history of several thousand years, a history which has its own characteristics and is full of treasures. But in these matters we are mere school-boys. The China of today has developed from the China in history; as we are believers in the Marxist approach to history, we must not cut off our whole historical past. We must make a summing up from Confucious down to Sun Yat-sen and inherit this precious legacy. This will help much in directing the great movement of today."[40]

Mao was contemptuous of those who thought and spoke in terms

[39]"On Policy," *Selected works of Mao Tes-tung*, Vol. IV, Lawerence and Wishart, London, 1954.
[40]"The Role of the Chinese Communist Party and The National War," *Selected Works*, Vol. IV.

of foreign history and remote developments in other countries. "There are some comrades," he said, "who feel pride, instead of shame, in their ignorance of our own history. They have got only scraps of knowledge about ancient Greece and other foreign countries which, with pitiful industry, they have picked up bit by bit from the rubbish heap of obsolete foreign books."[41]

In one series of brilliant essays and speeches, Mao lampooned the Party's "Eight-Legged Essay," the style of writing of Party propagandists which was pretentious, involved, empty and repetitious, full of big but meaningless phrases. He likened such writings to the "foot bandages of a slut, long as well as smelly." He said this kind of writing was like the setting up of a Chinese drug store: "go and take a look at any Chinese drug store; there you see a cabinet with innumerable drawers, each bearing the name of the drug: toncal, foxglove, rhubarb, saltpetre—indeed, everything that should be there. This method has been picked up by our comrades. In their articles and speeches, their books and reports, they first use the Chinese capitalized numerals, then the Chinese small numerals, then the characters of the ten heavenly stems, then the twelve hoary characters, and then A,B,C,D, a,b,c,d, the Arabic numerals and what not."[42] And he quoted an ancient couplet to describe such Communists:

The rushes on the wall—swollen in head,
weak in legs, and loose in roots;
The bamboo shoots among the rocks,
sharp in tongue, thick of skin, but empty in the belly.[43]

"If the whole party is poisoned by it," Mao warned, "the revolution would be endangered."

Mao found the two keys to the lock of power in China and despite heavy opposition from the leftists within the Party never swerved from this straight path. The first was the role that the peasantry must play in any revolution in China and he decided that the revolution must start from there. In vivid language he underlined

---

[41]"Reform Our Study," *Selected Works*, Vol. IV.
[42]"Oppose the Party's Eight Legged Essay," *Selected Works*, Vol. IV.
[43]Fn. 41.

the importance of the peasant in a country like China:

> The peasants—80 per cent of the whole population.
> The peasants—the source of China's industrial workers.
> The peasants—the mainstay of the market for China's industry.
> The peasants—the source of the Chinese army.
> The peasants—the main force fighting for a democratic order in China at the present stage. How could you ignore the peasantry.
> The Chinese democrats can achieve nothing if they fail to rely on the support of peasant masses numbering 360 million.[44]

The national united front was also a significant departure from doctrinal purity. Mao realized and told his followers to stand shoulder to shoulder with their countrymen in the patriotic duty of repelling foreign aggression and uniting the people. He responded to the urge of the Chinese nation for unity and determined struggle. For this he was willing to make compromises and to give concessions.[45] He said the class struggle had not ceased but should be adjusted so as to draw patriotic rich peasants into the united front. He advised the Communists not to look down upon non-party people but to share power with them: his instructions were that Communists should not occupy more than one-third of the governmental and other positions. "There are many capable people outside the Party," he said and the Party "should not leave them out of account." After all, the Communists constituted only a tiny minority of the population. How could they ignore the vast majority that was outside and think that only they were capable and knew everything. Mao said: "Suppose there was one Communist in a hundred Chinese, then among China's population of 450,000,000 there would be 4,500,000 Communists. Yet, even if our membership reached such a colossal figure, the Communists would still form only one per cent of the whole population, while 99 per cent of our countrymen would not be Communists. On what grounds, then, can we refuse to co-operate with non-Party people?"[46]

[44]"On Coalition Government," *Selected Works*, Vol. IV.
[45]Fn. 40.
[46]Fn. 41.

Mao's theory of the democratic bourgeois revolution and his call for the united front in China is well known. He said it would be "a sheer illusion to try to build socialism on the ruins of the colonial, semi-colonial and semi-feudal order, without a united new-democratic state, without the development of private capitalist and co-operative enterprises, without the development of a national, scientific and popular culture, that is a new democratic culture, or without the liberation and development of the individual initiative of hundreds of millions of people—in short, without pushing to the end the democratic revolution which is bourgeois in character, a democratic revolution of a new type led by the Communist Party."[47]

Even as late as 1942, when the fortunes of war were turning, Mao persisted in his policy and was willing to share power with the Kuomintang and make concessions to the antagonistic classes. No doubt, some of it can be dismissed as mere tactical manoeuvring, but it is pertinent to remember that during all this time there was persistent opposition from the leftists within the party who looked askance at these compromises and concessions and regarded them as nothing less than opportunism and capitulation to the class enemies. Mao was committed to gradual, full-fledged socialism but he was also a hard-headed realist.

Today at the end of his life Mao has apparently become a dogmatist and ultra-leftist, in fact perhaps an ultra-nationalist. In China, today, there is no room for any other wind except the wind of Mao Tse-tung's thought. It is the intention of Mao Tse-tung and his followers in power to drive out all other ideas and ideologies; the flag of Mao Tse-tung's thought is to be planted in the hearts and minds of the seven hundred million Chinese. There is no room for the sharing of power even among the Communists with those who do not give evidence of being psychopathic Maoists.

How has this come about? There will be many explanations for Mao's transformation* and history has yet to sit in full judgement on this unique man and the strange developments in his country. It is entirely possible that Mao in his late seventies is an extremely impatient and, therefore, an increasingly intolerant person. The visions that he saw in his young age are as remote as ever; the

[47]Fn. 44.
*See Chapter Three.

millennium is nowhere in sight. He now wants to accomplish at break-neck speed whatever he possibly can in the last few years of his life. China had made impressive gains in economic development during 1950-57 and the rate of growth was significant, if not spectacular. Yet it was not fast enough to give promise of closing the gap with the advanced countries of the world in the foreseeable future and to fulfil the other political, world-wide goals and ambitions of the Maoist leadership. Mao, therefore, decided to take the big leap. The big leap failed but Mao did not basically change his approach and was soon ready to take the offensive again.

Mao is also worried that his work may be undone by his successors and he is, therefore, prepared to do whatever is humanly feasible to forestall that eventuality. He saw what happened to Stalin and thinks he can prevent it from happening to him. More importantly, the summit of power enjoyed single-handedly, the isolated glory in which he has reigned for a long time, the seclusion of his person and the unchallenged authority that he has wielded has made Mao more and more divorced from reality, victim of his own subjectivism, losing his grip over things, out of touch with the objective world. For over a decade and a half, the Chinese people have almost worshipped at the altar of Maosim; they have given him unquestioned loyalty, authority and power. It would turn any mortal's head and Mao is neither super-human nor infallible.

The cultural revolution has taken a heavy toll. The Communist Party structure lies in ruins. Only a part of the top remains, the body has disappeared. A considerable dislocation of the economy, more particularly of industry, transport and communications, became evident in the last two years. There was a general breakdown of standards of discipline and of the earlier norms. Violence, pilferage, larceny, rape and other acts of lawlessness became frequent. Even the phenomenon of teddy boys appeared, much to the concern of the authorities. There have also been frequent complaints about laxity of discipline and absenteeism in factories and offices. The cultural revolution has not so far led to any significant changes in socio-economic organization. If the objective of the cultural revolution was to oust Liu Shao-ch'i and his associates, and that purpose has been achieved. But if Mao had planned to introduce deep and fundamental socio-economic institutional changes, then the verdict so far will be negative.

There is a great deal of ideological propaganda against the capitalist modes of thought and organization in industry and agriculture and in general economic activity, and Liu Shao-ch'i and his followers are duly taken to task for attempting a reversion from collective forms of production and for one-sided stress on material incentives. There were even some isolated cases reported in a section of the Chinese press of regrouping some production teams into the larger agricultural unit known as the production brigade, which led some observers to conclude that the big leap in agriculture and at least a partial restoration of the original features of the rural communes was back on the anvil. But there is no evidence yet of any significant large-scale reorganization on this pattern, nor of any major change in the remuneration system either in the factories or on the farms from what obtained in 1965. Barring minor modifications, the socio-economic organizational apparatus has not yet been subjected to any drastic shake-up. The educational field has witnessed some changes. Besides the fact that a posse of workers are in position in all the educational institutions to supervise and discipline the students and the intellectuals, the school and college terms have been shortened and formal class room instruction has been reduced, while a proportionate increase has taken place in the dosages of Mao's thought administered at these "citadels of intellectuals." Most of these changes are largely confined to arts and humanities; the sciences have not been tampered with to quite the same extent. And it is too early to evaluate either their permanency or their impact.

The cultural revolution has revealed deep fissures among the leadership. There was ferment even at the top. Mao found a large part of the leadership out of step with him and purged it after a stormy movement which has left the country exhausted and still sharply divided. Even within the remaining galaxy at the top there is no evidence of unified thinking. These differences are likely to get accentuated after the exit of Mao. It is extremely unlikely that any leadership after Mao would have the necessary strength, stamina, determination and sway over the people to carry on with all of Mao's policies. Of all the present leaders, Chou En-lai is the only one who is able to communicate with all the various groups in the country. On the other hand, the army dominates the scene in China and will continue to do so for a long time and Lin Piao, at the head of the army occupies a crucial place. If these two leaders manage to pull along and remain united, a measure of stability and continuity could be ensured; if they pull apart, the situation would be uncertain and unpredictable. In any case, when Mao is no longer at the helm, there will be important changes in China and the policies of the cultural revolution would perforce be discarded by his successors, even when they try to retain the more abiding features of Maoism.

INDEX